Teach English

Trainer's Handbook

CAMBRIDGE TEACHER TRAINING AND DEVELOPMENT

Series Editors: Ruth Gairns and Marion Williams

This series is designed for all those involved in language teacher training and development: teachers in training, trainers, directors of studies, advisers, teachers of in-service courses and seminars. Its aim is to provide a comprehensive, organised and authoritative resource for language teacher training and development.

Teach English – A training course for teachers
by Adrian Doff
Trainer's Handbook
Teacher's Workbook

Models and Metaphors in Language Teacher Training – Loop input and other strategies
by Tessa Woodward

Training Foreign Language Teachers – A reflective approach
by Michael J. Wallace

Literature and Language Teaching – A guide for teachers and trainers
by Gillian Lazar

Classroom Observation Tasks – A resource book for language teachers and trainers
by Ruth Wajnryb

Tasks for Language Teachers – A resource book for training and development
by Martin Parrott

English for the Teacher – A languages development course
by Mary Spratt
Book
Cassette

Teach English

A training course for teachers

Trainer's Handbook

Adrian Doff

CAMBRIDGE
UNIVERSITY PRESS

in association with
The British Council

Published by the Press Syndicate of the University of Cambridge
The Pitt Building, Trumpington Street, Cambridge CB2 1RP
40 West 20th Street, New York, NY 10011–4211, USA
10 Stamford Road, Oakleigh, Melbourne 3166, Australia

Text © The British Council 1988
Illustration © Cambridge University Press 1988

First published 1988
Eighth printing 1995

Printed in Great Britain
by Bell & Bain Ltd, Glasgow

Library of Congress catalogue card number: 87–25588

British Library cataloguing in publication data

Doff, Adrian

Teach English: a training course for
teachers.
1. English language – Study and teaching
– Foreign speakers
I. Title
428.2'4'07   PE1128.A2

ISBN 0 521 34864 1 Trainer's Handbook
ISBN 0 521 34863 3 Teacher's Workbook

SE

Contents

Acknowledgements

This course is based on a series of teacher training modules which were developed at the Centre for Developing English Language Teaching, Ain Shams University, Cairo, Egypt and used on in-service training courses for Egyptian teachers of English. The original training modules were produced as part of a KELT (Key English Language Teaching) project administered by the British Council on behalf of the Overseas Development Administration and assisted by the Egyptian Ministry of Education. A report of this project is to be found in *ELT Documents 125: Language Teacher Education* (Macmillan, 1987).

I should like to express special thanks to Dr Roger Bowers, who initiated the training modules project in Egypt and who has been a source of support and ideas at every stage of the development of this course. I would also like to acknowledge the very considerable contribution of Dr David Cross, with whom I worked closely on the earlier version of the material, and whose ideas feature strongly in the design and content of this final re-written version.

A course such as this draws on the experience of many different people, and I should like to thank the many teachers and teacher trainers whose ideas have contributed to this book in its final form and who it is impossible to acknowledge individually.

In particular, I am grateful to former colleagues at Ain Shams University, at the Egyptian Ministry of Education and at In-service Training Centres in Egypt, and also to volunteers from Voluntary Service Overseas for their help and advice in developing the material in its early stages.

For specific contributions to the material, I would like to thank Jon Roberts of the Centre for Applied Language Studies, University of Reading, and Stephen Gaies of the University of Northern Iowa.

I would also like to acknowledge my debt to the large number of general and specialist books on methodology, as well as EFL textbooks, which have helped me develop ideas for the course. I am particularly indebted to Martin Bates and Jonathan Higgins, whose course for Egypt 'Welcome to English' has suggested a range of ideas in methodology for large classes.

I am grateful to British Council and KELT teacher trainers working in a number of different countries, and particularly Donard Britten and Ray

Brown, whose very useful comments and suggestions helped to shape the final design of the course.

Finally, I would like to thank the editors, Annemarie Young, Barbara Thomas and Margherita Baker, for their patience and support during the final stages of producing this book.

The authors and publishers are grateful to the following for permission to reproduce copyright material. It has not been possible to contact the copyright holders of all the material used and such cases the publishers would welcome further information.

Longman Group Ltd for the lesson based on an extract from the *Nile Course for the Sudan* Book 3 by M. Bates on p. 45, and for the table based on an extract from *Welcome to English* Book 1 by M. Bates and J. Higgens on p. 95; R. Leakey and Hamish Hamilton Ltd for the extract from *Human Origins* on pp. 57–8; H. M. Abdoul-Fetouh et al and the Ministry of Education, Cairo, Egypt for the texts based on an extract from *Living English* Book 3 on p. 89; S. Steel and A & C Black (Publishers) Ltd for the text from *Earthquakes and Volcanoes* (Junior Reference series) on p. 173–4; T. and J. Watson and Wayland (Publishers) Ltd for the extracts from *What the World Eats – Midday Meal* on p. 180; A. G. Abdalla et al and the Ministry of Education, Cairo, Egypt for the dialogue based on an extract from *Living English* Book 2 on p. 233.

Photographs and illustrations:
Christina Gascoigne for the photograph from the New Internationalist Calendar (February) 1986 on p. 163; BBC Hulton Picture Library for the photograph on p. 172; P. Beasant and Usborne Publishing Ltd for the illustration with text from the *Young Scientist Book of Medicine* on p. 178.

Drawings by Jackie Barnett, Leslie Marshall and Alexa Rutherford.
Book design by Peter Ducker MSTD

Introduction

1 CONTENTS AND ORGANISATION

1.1 Who the course is for

Teach English is a teacher training course which develops practical skills in teaching English as a foreign language. It can be used:
- on in-service training courses for teachers working at secondary level in schools or language institutes;
- in pre-service training of secondary teachers, as a practical component of a methodology course and as preparation for teaching practice;
- as part of a 'refresher course' in practical methodology for more experienced teachers.

The course is especially designed to meet the needs of teachers who:
- teach in large, inflexible classes with few resources;
- follow a set syllabus and textbook, and have little control over course content or choice of material;
- are not native speakers of English;
- have little time available for lesson planning or preparation.

The course therefore concentrates on methods and techniques which do not require lengthy preparation of material, elaborate use of aids or equipment, or complex forms of classroom organisation.

1.2 Structure of the course

The course contains 24 units. Each unit focusses on a different area of methodology and provides material for about four hours' teacher training.

The course has a modular structure, so although the units appear in a numbered sequence, they are completely self-contained and can be used independently of each other. Units can be omitted or used in a different sequence without disrupting the course. There is some overlap between units, allowing for natural recycling as teachers move through the material.

The course is designed to be used actively by a trainer working with a group of up to 30 teachers, and has two components: a **Trainer's Handbook** (this volume) and a **Teacher's Workbook**.

The Trainer's Handbook

The Trainer's Handbook contains detailed instructions for each training session. It includes transcripts of demonstrations, points for discussion with suggested answers, suggestions for organising activities, and master copies of visual material. It also contains all the Teacher's Workbook activities, apart from the 'Lesson preparation' sections.

The Trainer's Handbook is in the form of a step-by-step instruction manual. This is so that the course can be used without extensive preparation, and is intended to give support to less experienced trainers. It is of course expected that trainers will add their own ideas and adapt the material to suit their own needs and circumstances.

The Teacher's Workbook

The Teacher's Workbook is intended for use by the teachers on the training course, and contains activities which make up the practical part of the training session. These activities take the form of discussion, practice and simple workshop tasks, and are designed to develop insights into teaching methods as well as give practice in teaching techniques.

Each unit in the Teacher's Workbook contains five or six activities. The final activity is 'Lesson preparation', in which teachers apply techniques from the unit to one of their own lessons. This is followed by a 'Self-evaluation sheet', which helps teachers to reflect on their own teaching after the training session.

The Teacher's Workbook also contains four 'Background texts', which deal with more theoretical aspects of methodology. These appear after every fifth unit, but can be read at any point in the course. They also appear in the Trainer's Handbook.

At the end of the Teacher's Workbook, there are brief summaries of each unit for reference.

2 USING THE COURSE

2.1 The training session

Teach English is designed to encourage an active style of teacher training, with teachers participating as fully as possible. For the course to be effective it should be used with groups of not more than 30 teachers.

If possible, every teacher on the course should have his or her own copy of the Teacher's Workbook. For some activities, teachers will also need copies of the textbook they are using or another textbook at an appropriate level (see 2.4 below). Any special materials or equipment that are required for the training session are indicated at the beginning of the unit in the Trainer's Handbook.

Using the course on a training session will involve three main kinds of activity: *demonstrations*, *discussions* and *pair and group activities*.

Demonstrations

When a new technique is introduced, it is usually demonstrated, so that teachers can see how it works. The demonstration is sometimes at the teachers' own language level, so that they can experience the technique from the learner's point of view; sometimes it is at the language level of their students, so that they can see what would happen in their own classes.

The Trainer's Handbook gives notes on how to conduct each demonstration, and sometimes gives a 'script' of the demonstration.

Discussions

The new ideas in each unit are usually presented not through straight lectures but in the form of discussions, in which the teachers participate and contribute their own ideas. This has the advantage of involving the teachers more and allowing them to bring their own experience to bear on the topic under discussion; it also helps the trainer to see how well they have understood the new ideas being presented.

The Trainer's Handbook gives notes on the main points to be brought out of each discussion; these are intended as suggestions and as ways of providing a focus for the discussion, not as 'correct answers'. For the discussion to be successful, it is important for the trainer not to impose his or her own ideas too rigidly and to accept different points of view.

Pair and group activities

Many of the activities in the Teacher's Workbook are designed to be done by teachers working together in pairs or small groups. This allows more teachers to be involved in the activity, and gives a chance for teachers to help each other and develop ideas together.

Most pair or group activities have three stages:

1. *Introduction* to the activity. The trainer introduces the activity and makes sure that teachers understand what to do.
2. The *activity* itself. During this stage, teachers are working independently in their pairs or groups. The trainer moves from group to group, listening and giving help where necessary.
3. A *round-up* stage. The trainer asks teachers from different pairs or groups what answers they gave, or, after a discussion activity, what

conclusions they came to. If the activity involved preparing an exercise or a teaching technique, the trainer may ask individual teachers to try out their ideas using the others as a class.

Detailed notes on how to organise each activity are given in the Trainer's Handbook.

2.2   Lesson preparation

The final activity in each unit is 'Lesson preparation', in which teachers plan part of a lesson incorporating ideas and techniques that have been introduced in the training session. This is intended to act as a link between the training session and classroom teaching, and to encourage teachers to try out new techniques in their own classes.

If there is time, the preparation can be done in the training session under the trainer's guidance, either as a discussion with all the teachers together or with teachers working in pairs or small groups. Alternatively, teachers can be asked to prepare the lesson in their own time after the training session. Detailed instructions for the 'Lesson preparation' following each unit are given in the Teacher's Workbook.

Ideally, teachers should try out the lesson they have prepared in one of their own classes soon after the training session. If this is not possible (for example, on an intensive training course during a holiday period), the preparation could lead to either of the following activities:

1. *Peer teaching practice:* After the training session, teachers prepare part of a lesson, following the instructions in the Teacher's Workbook. In the next training session, a few teachers demonstrate, with the other teachers acting as a class.
2. *Written lesson plan:* Instead of preparing an actual lesson, teachers write a lesson plan, showing exactly how they would apply the techniques in teaching one of their own classes. This can be given to the trainer for comments, and be used as a basis for discussion in the next training session.

2.3   Self-evaluation sheets

At the end of every unit in the Teacher's Workbook there is a 'Self-evaluation sheet', with questions relating to the 'trial lesson' the teacher has given. The purpose of these sheets is to develop teachers' own self-awareness, so that they can improve their own teaching independently of the training sessions. By asking questions about the students and what they have gained from the lesson, the 'Self-evaluation sheets' also encourage teachers to think of their lessons from the learners' point of view, and shift the focus of attention from teaching to learning.

The 'Self-evaluation sheets' can be used in a variety of ways, according to how the training is being organised:

- If the teachers are able to try out techniques with their own class, they can complete the sheet privately after their lesson. It can then be used as a basis for feedback and discussion in the following training session.
- If several teachers from the same school or the same area are attending the training course, the sheets can be used for informal discussion sessions organised by groups of teachers.
- If teachers are giving lessons as part of supervised teaching practice, the sheet can be completed both by the teacher and the supervisor observing the lesson, and then used for discussion and comment.
- If techniques are tried out in peer teaching practice, the sheet can be used as an observation sheet by other teachers. Half the teachers can act as a 'class', and the other half observe the lesson and complete the sheet.

A summary of different possible training patterns is shown in the table on page 6.

2.4 Using the textbook

At several points in the course, teachers are asked to refer to the textbook they are using with their own class; this assumes that the teachers attending the training course are all using the same textbook and that they all have copies of it available. If this is not the case, it will be necessary to provide copies of a suitable textbook, or to make copies of individual lessons or exercises for teachers to refer to.

If the training course is being attended by teachers from several different countries, sample lessons can be taken from well-known international textbooks, at whatever level is relevant to most teachers' needs.

2.5 Adapting the course

The examples, texts and situations used in *Teach English* are intended to be applicable to a wide range of different teaching circumstances, but may not precisely suit any single country or group of teachers. If all the teachers on the training course are teaching at the same level and using the same textbook, the material can be adapted in the following ways:

- Examples, vocabulary and situations can be replaced by equivalent ones from the teachers' own textbook (e.g. Unit 1 Activities 2 and 3).
- Where necessary, situations for practice can be adapted to make them locally relevant (e.g. Unit 13 Activity 3, Unit 14 Activity 1).
- Where texts are intended as examples for use in class, they can be substituted by equivalent texts from the teachers' own textbook (e.g. Unit 5 Activities 3 and 4, Unit 15 Activity 1).

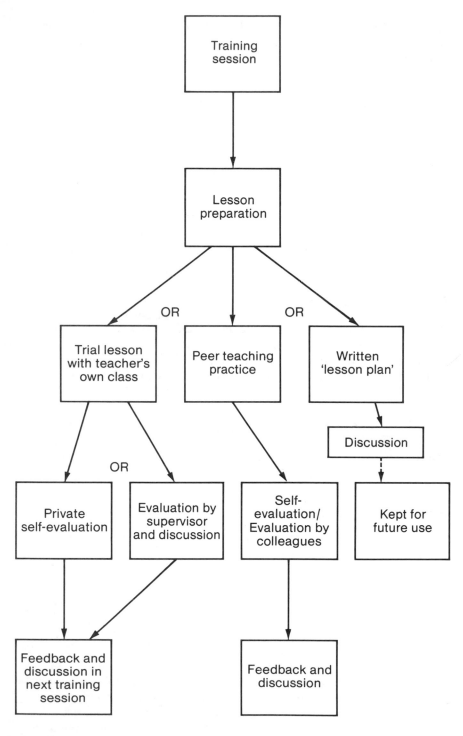

2.6 Further reading

Teach English is mainly concerned with practical classroom teaching. For trainers who wish to explore topics in greater depth, there is a 'Further reading' section at the end of each unit in the Trainer's Handbook, which lists relevant books on each subject. These lists are highly selective, and include only books which are widely available, which have direct applications to teaching and which are written in non-technical language. They include both specialist books on each subject, and also sections from general methodology books where they have something particularly useful to offer. They do not include articles from journals, as these are not readily obtainable in many countries.

3 THEORETICAL BACKGROUND

3.1 Syllabus

A fundamental division of teaching behaviour is often made into *preparation skills* ('before the lesson'), *teaching* and *class management skills* ('during the lesson'), and *evaluation skills* ('after the lesson'). These categories are reflected in the units of *Teach English* in the following ways:
- Most units are concerned primarily with teaching and/or class management skills, but develop relevant preparation or evaluation skills through particular activities (e.g. Unit 1: in Activity 6 teachers select active and passive vocabulary from a text; in Activity 2, teachers study inadequate examples and improve them).
- Preparation skills are the main focus of two of the units (Unit 8: Planning a lesson and Unit 23: Planning a week's teaching), and are developed through the 'Lesson preparation' at the end of each unit.
- Evaluation skills are the main focus of two of the units (Unit 22: Classroom tests and Unit 24: Self-evaluation), and are developed through the 'Self-evaluation sheets' following each unit.

The units concerned with teaching and class management skills cover the following broad skill areas:
1. *Language and skills development:* This area covers the basic procedures for presenting and practising language, and for organising speaking, listening, reading and writing activities.
2. *Use of aids and materials:* This area covers the teacher's use of the blackboard and other basic visual aids, the use of texts and of home-produced material on workcards.
3. *Classroom interaction:* This area covers the basic types of interaction between teacher and students and between students themselves.

The units of *Teach English* are organised as a series of separate but inter-related modules, each module focussing on one skill area. This allows for a natural overlapping between different skills which reflects the structure of actual teaching behaviour. For example, Unit 2: Asking questions focusses on basic question types and nomination strategies, but also includes a range of contexts in which teachers often need to ask questions: checking comprehension of new words and structures, organising the class, eliciting personal information from students, etc. The skill of 'asking questions' is also included in other units, where it appears as one of a number of different skills, e.g. Unit 1 (questions to consolidate vocabulary), Unit 5 (questions on a text), Unit 12 (question/answer work in pairs), Unit 14 (getting students to guess).

The main points of overlap between skills are indicated by cross-references at the beginning of each unit in the Trainer's Handbook.

3.2   Approaches to teacher training

Most people involved in teacher education are aware of the existence of two separate worlds. One is the world of native-speaker teachers and teacher trainers, who work in small, flexible classes with adequate resources and who are mainly responsible for developing new ideas in methodology. The other is the world of most other teachers, who work in large school classes to a set syllabus, and who attempt to apply the new methodology to their own teaching. It is the great differences between these two worlds that accounts for the failure of much teacher training; they are differences not only in resources and physical conditions, but also in underlying assumptions (e.g. about language, about learning, about the teacher's role) and in degree of freedom (e.g. freedom to experiment, to create material, to approach class relationships in a new way).

Teach English attempts to bridge the gap between these two worlds by presenting methodology in a form that is accessible to most teachers. The approach it adopts is based on the following underlying principles:
- The material aims to be *appropriate*; it is limited to ideas and techniques that teachers can apply to their own teaching.
- New ideas and techniques are presented *explicitly*. Even basic concepts in teaching and learning, such as 'presenting a structure', 'reading a text', or 'learning a rule' may be understood quite differently by different teachers, and simply describing techniques and procedures can lead to fundamental misunderstanding. Wherever possible, there-fore, new techniques are demonstrated and teachers are given a chance to experience them directly.
- Most teachers of English are not native speakers, and this limits their ability to adopt new teaching techniques. An important element in the

course is therefore *language improvement*. This is not treated separately, but integrated into the Teacher's Workbook activities: teachers are given practice in asking questions, writing examples, identifying structures, etc., and general oral fluency is developed through discussion and practice activities.

– The adoption of new teaching methods depends on teachers developing new insights and attitudes; so the course is concerned not only with practical training but also with *teacher education*. The teacher education is mainly carried out implicitly through the Teacher's Workbook activities; for example, teachers are asked to evaluate teaching techniques or choose between alternative teaching strategies.

– Teachers are not necessarily convinced by or interested in applied linguistic theory, but they usually do have well-developed insights into teaching and learning. So although new ideas presented in the course are often derived from applied linguistic theory and research, they are explained and justified in terms of common sense.

– The success of a training course depends on the extent to which teachers accept new ideas as 'their own'. This is more likely to happen if teachers are allowed to try out new techniques in the relative freedom and privacy of their own classes, rather than be forced to practise them immediately in front of their colleagues. For this reason, each unit of the course aims to lead teachers towards actual classroom practice, through a series of tasks and activities, but stops short of asking teachers to perform in the training session itself.

3.3 English teaching methodology

Over the last 20 years, ELT methodology has developed very rapidly and has been subject to changes and controversies that teachers often find bewildering. The methods and techniques included in *Teach English* are intended to represent a 'common core', drawing on what is of value both in traditional and in more recent approaches. Thus the course includes traditional techniques, such as substitution practice and presenting a structure through a situation, which are still in widespread use; it also includes more recent teaching ideas, such as eliciting, pre-reading activities, and information gap exercises, which have now become established and are part of the repertoire of most good teachers. The course does not include techniques which belong to 'fringe' approaches such as the Silent Way or Total Physical Response, since they cannot easily be integrated into normal patterns of teaching; nor does it include techniques which are only suited to particular kinds of classes because they require elaborate organisation (e.g. jigsaw listening).

An important recent development in methodology has been the shift of emphasis from the teacher to the learner, and this is reflected in this course. Throughout the course, teachers are asked to experience and evaluate techniques from the learner's point of view, and the 'Self-evaluation sheets' following each unit encourage teachers to judge their own lessons by what the students appear to have learnt from them. Thus, although its subject is teaching English, the course aims to make teachers more aware of their role as helpers in the learning process.

1 Presenting vocabulary

Aims of this unit
- To establish the importance of teaching the meaning of new vocabulary as well as the form, and of showing how words are used in context.
- To give teachers techniques for showing the meaning of new words.
- To show teachers how to reinforce new vocabulary by asking questions using the new items.

This unit is concerned with basic techniques for presenting new words, either before reading a text or dialogue, or as they arise in the course of a lesson. Other techniques for teaching vocabulary are developed in later units – Unit 5: Using a reading text (guessing unknown words), Unit 7: Using visual aids (using flashcards) and Unit 14: Eliciting (eliciting words from a picture).

INTRODUCTION

▶ Workbook Activity 1 ◀

1. Divide the teachers into pairs or small groups and ask them to discuss the questions in the Teacher's Workbook.

> Here are some techniques for teaching new words.
>
> Say the word clearly and write it on the board.
> Get the class to repeat the word in chorus.
> Translate the word into the students' own language.
> Ask students to translate the word.
> ✔Draw a picture to show what the word means.
> ✔ Give an English example to show how the word is used.
> ✔Ask questions using the new word.
>
> Which are the most useful techniques?
> Can you think of any other techniques you could use?

Briefly discuss with the teachers what answers they gave; but do not go into detail about any of the techniques at this point. The purpose of these questions is simply to start teachers thinking about their own teaching and about possible techniques for presenting vocabulary.

2. To focus on the value of different techniques, demonstrate two different ways of presenting a new word. The first involves direct translation followed by drilling; the second involves giving an example in English and asking the teachers to guess what the word means.

Demonstration one

Present the word 'rumble'.
i)   Write it on the board, give a direct translation of the word, and if necessary explain in the teachers' own language that it is the noise made by thunder – but do *not* give any examples.
ii) Get teachers to repeat the word a few times in chorus.

Demonstration two

Present the word 'grumble'.
i)   Write the word on the board, then give an example in English to show what it means, e.g.:
    Some people grumble about everything. For example, they grumble about the weather. If it's sunny, they say, 'Oh dear, it's much too hot today'; if it's cool, they say, 'Oh, it's too cold' – they're never satisfied.
ii) Check that teachers understand the word by asking them to say it in their own language.

Discuss the two presentations. Establish that the first presentation was obviously quicker, and also much easier for the teacher. The second presentation took a longer time, but it achieved more and was more interesting.
Try to bring out these points:
– Translating a new word is in itself a useful technique – it is often the simplest and clearest way of showing what a word means. But if we only give a direct translation, students cannot see how the word is *used* in an English sentence; to show this we need to give an *example*.
– Instead of *telling* the students what the word means, we can give examples and then ask *them* to give a translation. This checks that they have understood, and encourages them to listen to the word being used in English.
– Just getting students to repeat words is of limited value. It focusses attention on the *form* of the word only (how it is pronounced). It does not teach the *meaning* of the word, which is more important.

You will now consider in detail some basic techniques for showing the meaning of words.

SHOWING THE MEANING OF WORDS

Showing meaning visually

1. Write these words on the board:
     watch   window   elbow
   Ask teachers how they could most easily show the meaning of the words.
   Answer: By simply pointing at them and saying 'Look – this is a watch', etc.

   Point out that this is one way of showing the meaning of new words: by showing a *real object*. Discuss what kinds of words can be presented in this way.
   Possible answers:
   Anything that is already in the classroom: furniture, clothes, parts of the body. Also many objects that can be brought into the classroom: other items of clothing (hats, ties, handkerchiefs); food (oranges, rice); small objects from the home (soap, cups, keys), etc.
   If necessary, quickly demonstrate a presentation of the word 'watch':

   T: Look – this is a watch (*pointing to his or her watch*). A watch. A
      watch.
   Ss: A watch.
   T: (*gesture*) What is it?
      Ss: A watch.
      (*and so on*)

2. Write these words on the board:
     tree   tractor   cow
   Ask teachers how they could show the meaning of the words.
   Answer:
   By showing a *picture*. This can be done in two ways:
   – By drawing a picture on the board.
   – By showing a picture prepared before the lesson (a drawing or
     photograph).
   Discuss which of the words could easily and clearly be drawn on the board. Ask a teacher to come to the front and show how to draw each object.

3. Write these words on the board:
     sneeze   dig   stumble

Again ask teachers how they could show the meaning of the words.
Answer:
By *miming*, using *actions* and *facial expressions.*
Ask teachers to mime each of the three verbs. Then discuss what other
words could be taught using mime.
Possible answers:
Most action verbs (sit, stand, open, write); some adjectives (happy,
worried, ill).
If necessary, quickly demonstrate a presentation of the word 'sneeze':

T: Look – (*mime someone sneezing*) Atchoo! I've just sneezed.
   Sneeze. Sneeze. Can you say it?
Ss: Sneeze.
T: Again.
Ss: Sneeze.

4. Make these general points about presenting vocabulary visually (using
   real objects, pictures, or mime):
   – For suitable vocabulary, it is a very effective method: it is direct, it is
     interesting, and it makes an impression on the class.
   – Of course, not all words can be presented in this way. Vocabulary
     should only be presented visually if it can be done *quickly, easily,*
     and *clearly.*

Giving examples

1. Another way to show what words mean is by giving an *example*, using
   the word in a *context.* Demonstrate this by presenting the words
   'building' and 'lazy'.

Demonstration one

Houses are buildings. This school is also a building. In big cities
there are many large buildings – there are hotels, and offices, and
cinemas. They are all buildings of different kinds.

Demonstration two

Some people work hard. Other people don't work hard – they are
lazy. For example, I have a brother. He is very lazy. He gets up late,
and then he does nothing all day. I say to him, 'Don't be so lazy! Do
some work!'

Make these points:
– It is not necessary to give a complicated explanation; the meaning
  can be shown by simple sentences. This can be done by making

statements using the word (e.g. 'Houses are buildings. This school is also a building'), or by imagining an example (e.g. 'I have a brother. He is very lazy. He gets up late, and then he does nothing all day').

− A good example should clearly show the meaning of the word to someone who does *not* know it already. So it is not enough just to say 'My brother is lazy' − it doesn't show what 'lazy' means. We need to add, e.g. 'He gets up late, and then does nothing all day'.

− Examples are especially useful for showing the meaning of abstract words, e.g. love, happiness, imagine, quality, impossible.

▶ **Workbook Activity 2** ◀

2. Divide teachers into groups of four or five, and ask them to look at the examples in the Teacher's Workbook.

1. The examples beside the six words below are not enough to make the meaning of the words clear. *Add* one or two sentences to each one, so that the meaning of the word is shown clearly.
   a) *market* You can buy food at the market.
   b) *clothes* In the morning we put on our clothes.
   c) *noisy* Students are often very noisy.
   d) *look for* I'm looking for my pen.
   e) *visit* Last weekend I visited my uncle.
   f) *happiness* He was full of happiness.
   g) *impossible* Your plan is quite impossible.

2. What *other* techniques could you use (pictures, mime, etc.) to make the meaning of each word clearer?

In their groups, teachers should decide how to make each example clearer, by adding one or two sentences. At least one person in the group should write their examples down.

When most groups have finished, discuss the examples together. If you like, ask teachers to come to the front and demonstrate giving their examples.

Combining different techniques

▶ **Workbook Activity 3** ◀

1. Point out that often a *combination* of techniques can be used to show the meaning of a word. Demonstrate this by presenting the word 'smile', drawing a picture on the board first:

⟫→

T: Look – he's smiling. Now look at me. I'm smiling (*show by facial expression*). Smile. We smile when we are happy. Smile. (*gesture*)

Ss: Smile.

T: Good. What does it mean? (*students give translation*)

Discuss the different techniques you used in the demonstration, and why you used each one.
– Picture on board (interesting, students remember it).
– Facial expression (gives meaning clearly).
– Examples (show how 'smile' is used as a verb).
– Translation (to make sure everyone understands).
Point out that each technique is *very quick* (a few seconds), and they all reinforce each other.

2. Divide the teachers into groups and ask them to look at the words in the Teacher's Workbook.

> Look at these words. Decide exactly how you would present each one. If possible, think of a *variety* of techniques.
> laugh   absent   cheese   cold   apron   wall

In their groups, they should decide how they would present each word. Make sure that they discuss *in detail* what they would do: if they would give an example, they should decide exactly what example to give; if they would draw a picture, they should draw it on a piece of paper.

When most groups have finished, discuss each word in turn. If you like, ask teachers to come to the front and demonstrate the techniques they thought of.

USING A NEW WORD

► Workbook Activity 4 ◄

1. Ask the teachers to look at the picture in the Teacher's Workbook, which shows a teacher using a new word to ask a few simple questions round the class.

> A. The teacher has just presented the word 'market'. Now she is asking questions using the new word. What is the purpose of this?

Discuss the purpose of questions of this kind. Establish that:
– They help the teacher to be sure that students really understand the word.
– They give the students more examples of how the word is used, in a way that involves the class.
– They give a chance to practise other language (big, small, present simple tense, cook, etc.).

Point out that questions using a new word should be *simple* and require only *short* answers. If necessary, give a few more examples of your own, using other words.

2. Divide the teachers into pairs or groups, and ask them to look at the words in part B of the Workbook Activity.

> B. Think of two or three questions you could ask the class, using these words.
>
> to cook   lion   holiday   magazine   windy

They should imagine that they have just presented the words and should think of a few questions using each word.

3. If you like, ask teachers to 'try out' their questions, using the other teachers as a class.

VOCABULARY EXPANSION

[handwritten: use lexical sets when possible.]

► **Workbook Activity 5** ◄

1. When students come across a new word, they are likely to be interested
   in learning other related words, and this presents a natural opportunity for vocabulary development. This is sometimes called 'vocabulary expansion'.

   Ask the teachers to look at the sets of words in the Teacher's
   Workbook, which suggest two possible ways of expanding vocabulary based on the word 'cook'.

   > 1. Look at these sets of words. How are the words in each box related to
   >   'cook'?
   >
   >   a)   cook   b)   cook
   >   ↓   ↓
   >
   > | bake fry | | stove stir |
   > | boil grill | | pot   spoon |

   Discuss the difference between the two sets:
   - The words in (a) are *synonyms*: they are words of the same type and
     have the same general meaning (all methods of cooking).
   - The words in (b) are related by *context*: they might all be used when
     talking about cooking, although they are not synonyms.

2. Discuss possible techniques for introducing sets of related words like
   those in the examples:
   - The teacher could talk about cooking, introducing the new words
     and writing them on the board; then use the new words in questions
     to involve the class, as in Workbook Activity 4.
   - The teacher could try to *elicit* the new words from the students and
     then write them on the board, e.g.:
     What about bread? How do we cook bread? What about eggs?
     [*Note:* Eliciting techniques are dealt with in detail in Unit 14.]

3. Divide the teachers into pairs and ask them to look at the words in the
   second part of the Workbook Activity.

   > 2. Imagine you are teaching the words below.
   >   Think of four or five other related words that you could teach at the
   >   same time.
   >   a) thief
   >   b) carpet

[handwritten diagram: thief — shoplifter; thief — burglar; pick-pocket]

18

  c) customs officer
  d) marry

Ask teachers to think of other words that could be introduced as part of a vocabulary expansion activity. The words can either be synonyms or be related by context.
Possible words:
a) thief, burglar, robber; steal, rob, burgle; theft, burglary, robbery; crime, criminal; catch, arrest; attack, break in(to).
b) carpet, rug, mat, doormat; weave, woven; beat.
c) customs officer; go through customs; goods, declare, pay duty; smuggle, drugs, weapons.
d) marry, married, wedding; husband, wife, fiancé(e); get engaged, get married, separate, get divorced.

ACTIVE AND PASSIVE VOCABULARY

► Workbook Activity 6 ◄

1. Point out that we do not need to spend the same amount of time and care on presenting all new vocabulary; some vocabulary will be more important to students than others. In general, we can distinguish two types of vocabulary:
   – Words which students will need to understand and also use themselves. We call this *active vocabulary*. In teaching active vocabulary, it is usually worth spending time giving examples and asking questions, so that students can really see how the word is used.
   – Words which we want students to understand (e.g. when reading a text), but which they will not need to use themselves. We call this *passive vocabulary*. To save time, it is often best to present it quite quickly, with a simple example. If it appears as part of a text or dialogue, we can often leave students to guess the word from the context.
   Emphasise that students should understand far more words than they can produce – so we should not try to treat all new words as active vocabulary.

2. Divide the teachers into pairs or groups, and ask them to look at the text in the Teacher's Workbook and the new vocabulary below it.

In Britain, the weather is very varied; people never know what it will be like the next day.

The summer is warmer than the winter, but even in summer the average temperature is only 16°. Sometimes the sun shines, but at other times the sky is covered in cloud, and it often rains.

In winter it is sometimes very cold, especially in the north of the country. The temperature may fall below 0°, and then there is often snow and ice.

The best season of the year is probably late spring. At this time of year the weather is often sunny and quite warm; the countryside looks very green, and there are wild flowers everywhere.

(adapted from a text from *The Cambridge English Course* Book 1: M. Swan and C. Walter)

1. Imagine you want to present these new words from the text.

    weather   varied   average · temperature   cloud
    snow   ice   season   spring   sunny   countryside

    Which words would you present as *active* vocabulary, and which would you present as *passive* vocabulary? Write the words in *two lists*.

2. How would you *present* the words?

Ask teachers to write active and passive vocabulary in two lists.

3. When most groups have finished, discuss the words together. Encourage teachers to give their own views, and try to build up two 'agreed' lists on the board.

    A possible answer:

ACTIVE	PASSIVE
weather	varied
cloud	temperature
spring	average
sunny	season
(snow?)	countryside
(ice?)	(snow?)
	(ice?)

4. Discuss with the teachers how they might present:
    – the active vocabulary;
    – the passive vocabulary.

LESSON PREPARATION

▶ **Workbook Activity 7** ◀

Either organise the preparation during the training session, with teachers working together in pairs or groups, or let teachers prepare in their own time after the session.

FURTHER READING

R. Gairns and S. Redman (1986) *Working with Words*, Cambridge University Press. Discusses theoretical background behind vocabulary learning and gives practical ideas for teaching vocabulary.

J. Morgan and M. Rinvolucri (1986) *Vocabulary*, Oxford University Press. A resource book for teachers, containing practical activities for vocabulary learning.

M. J. Wallace (1982) *Teaching Vocabulary*, Heinemann Educational. A practical guide to vocabulary learning.

2 Asking questions

Aims of this unit
- To make teachers aware of basic question types and to show how they can be used for different purposes.
- To show teachers how to elicit short and long answers from students in a natural way.
- To make teachers aware of different possible strategies for asking questions.

This unit gives a general introduction to asking questions in class. The use of questions for particular activities is dealt with more fully in other units – Unit 1: Presenting vocabulary (questions to check comprehension of new words), Unit 5: Using a reading text (questions on a text), Unit 6: Practising structures (questions as part of language practice) and Unit 14: Eliciting (questions to encourage students to guess).

QUESTION TYPES

1. Begin by discussing *why* teachers ask questions in class. Encourage teachers to think of as many reasons as they can. For example:
   - *To check that students understand:* When we present new vocabulary or structures, we can check that students have understood by using the new language in a question. When we present a text, we can use questions to check that students have understood it.
   - *To give students practice:* If we want students to use a certain structure, one way to do this is to ask a question that requires a particular answer.
   - *To find out what students really think or know:* We can use questions to encourage students to talk about themselves and their experiences.

   In class, it is possible to ask many different kinds of question, and to ask questions in many different ways. In this unit, you will show how different kinds of question are appropriate to different purposes.

   ► **Workbook Activity 1** ◄

2. Ask teachers to look at the three groups of questions in the Teacher's Workbook, and discuss each group in turn.

> What is the difference between these three types of question?
> How might you reply to each question?
>
> a) Do you drink tea?
>   Can you swim?
>   Did he go to university?
>   Are they coming to the party?
>
> b) Do you prefer tea or coffee?
>   Are they brothers or just friends?
>   Will you walk or go by bus?
>   Did she study in Britain or in the United States?
>
> c) What do you usually drink?
>   Where did she study?
>   How long have they known each other?
>   When are you leaving?

Yes/No questions

Look at the first group of questions. Establish that:
– They are Yes/No questions.
– The reply can be 'Yes' or 'No', alone or with short forms: 'Yes, I do', 'No, I can't', etc.
Make sure that teachers understand how to form Yes/No questions. The auxiliary verb comes first; present simple questions use 'do/does', past simple questions use 'did'.

If necessary, give teachers practice by asking a few Yes/No questions to which they can give true answers, e.g.:
Have you been on a training course before?
Do you like living in . . . ?
Do you smoke?
Can you speak French?
Ask teachers to think of other Yes/No questions, which they could use in class.

Discuss when Yes/No questions can be used in class. Establish that they are especially useful for checking *comprehension*. They are often the easiest questions to answer – they do not require students to produce new language.

'Or' questions

Look at the second group of questions. Establish that:
– They are 'Or' questions (they are also sometimes called 'alternative questions').

– The reply is usually a word or phrase from the question itself, e.g.
'Friends' or 'They're friends'; 'Britain' or 'In Britain'.

Make sure teachers know how to form 'Or' questions. They are
formed in exactly the same way as Yes/No questions, but contain two
final elements – 'tea or coffee', 'brothers or friends'.

If necessary give teachers practice by asking a few 'Or' questions,
e.g.:

Is it hot or cold in here?

Are you married or single?

Do you teach at a primary or a secondary school?

Ask teachers to think of other 'Or' questions, which they could use in
class.

WH- questions

Look at the third group of questions. Establish that:
– They are WH- questions (also called 'information questions').
– With most WH- questions, it is natural to give a *short* answer. So the
natural answer to 'Where did she study?' is 'In Britain', *not* 'She
studied in Britain'. (A few WH- questions require long answers –
these are dealt with later in this unit.)

Make sure teachers know how to form WH- questions. They are
formed in the same way as Yes/No questions, but they begin with a
'WH- word' – 'When', 'Where', 'Why', etc. 'How', 'How long', and
'How much/many' are included as WH- words.

If necessary, give teachers practice by asking a few WH- questions
and getting them to give you short answers, e.g.:

Where do you come from?

How long have you been teaching?

How many students are there in your class?

Who's your favourite film star?

Ask teachers to think of other WH- questions, which they could use in
class.

Point out that some WH- questions with 'Who' or 'What' have the
same structure as a normal sentence. These are called 'subject
questions', because they ask about the subject of the sentence.
Give a few examples, e.g.:

Something happened. . . What happened? (Not 'What did happen?')

Someone saw him. . . Who saw him?

Someone knows the answer. . . Who knows the answer?

Something fell over. . . What fell over?

QUESTIONS WITH SHORT ANSWERS

Checking questions

▶ **Workbook Activity 2** ◀

Sneext check Q'r

1. An important use of questions is to check that students understand a
   new word or phrase.

   Give a demonstration. Ask teachers to imagine that you have just
   presented 'made of wood/metal/glass/stone'. Ask a series of questions
   with short answers:

   T: Look (*pointing to table*) – is this made of wood?
   Ss: Yes.
   T: (*pointing to wall*) What about this? Is it made of wood?
   Ss: No, it isn't.
   T: What is it made of?
   Ss: Stone.
   (*and so on*)

   Discuss why the students only need to give short answers. There are
   two reasons: because it is more natural, and also because at this stage
   the teacher only wants to check that they understand. Later they can be
   asked to produce the new language themselves.

2. Divide the teachers into pairs, and ask them to look at the words and
   phrases in the Teacher's Workbook.

   > Imagine that you have just presented each of these words or phrases.
   >   wide/narrow   belong to   inside/outside   far from
   >   depend on
   > Write down one or two questions you could ask in class, to check that
   > students understand each item.

   Ask them to write down the questions to ask in class. They can write
   'Yes/No', 'Or' or 'WH-' questions.

3. When they have finished, ask teachers to read out their questions. If
   you like, ask a few teachers to come to the front and demonstrate.

Real classroom questions

► **Workbook Activity 3** ◄

1. Point out that many situations which naturally arise in the classroom give an opportunity to ask real questions of the three types practised in this unit. If the teacher asks such questions in English, it will help students to feel that language is *real*, not just something in a textbook.

> What questions could you ask in these situations?
> a) It's a hot day, and all the windows are closed.
> b) One of your students looks pale and tired.
> c) You set homework last lesson. Today you are going to check the answers with the class.
> d) Several students are absent today.
> e) When you come into class, you find a bag on your desk.
> f) When you come into class, you find a face drawn on the blackboard.

Discuss what questions could be asked for the first situation.
Possible answers:
a) Are you hot? Do you feel hot? Do you want the window open?

2. Divide the teachers into pairs, and ask them to think of suitable questions for the other situations.
    When most pairs have finished, discuss the answers together.
Possible answers:
b) Do you feel ill? Do you feel all right? Are you tired?
c) Have you all done the homework?
d) Who is absent today? Is (Marcella) here today?
e) Whose bag is this?
f) Who drew this? What's this supposed to be?
(For other classroom situations which give opportunities to use English, see Unit 19: Using English in class.)

ELICITING LONG ANSWERS

1. Write these questions on the board:
    What time do you get up?
    What do you have for breakfast?
Establish that the *natural* answers to these questions would be short ('At seven o'clock', 'Bread and cheese').
    However, in class we often want students to produce longer answers, so that they practise making complete sentences, e.g.:

I get up at seven o'clock, and then I have breakfast. I usually have bread and cheese and a glass of tea.

Discuss three possible ways of eliciting long answers:

i) We could ask a question and insist on a long answer:

    T: Answer with a complete sentence. What time do you get up?
    S: I get up at seven o'clock.

    This gets students to practise language effectively, but only by forcing them to answer in an unnatural way. As a result, the 'conversation' that takes place in the class becomes artificial, and unlike real English.

ii) We could ask a more general question which would naturally lead to a longer answer:

    T: What do you do in the morning?
    S: Well, I get up at seven o'clock, then I have breakfast.

    This is much less artificial, and allows the conversation in the classroom to be more like language spoken in real life.

    To show other examples, ask the teachers a few general questions:

    What did you do yesterday? Did anything interesting happen to you?
    Do you have any children? What are they doing at the moment?
    Why did you become an English teacher?
    Did you read the paper today? What's happening in . . .?

iii) Instead of asking a complete question, we could give a short 'prompt':

    T: Tell me about your day.
    S: Well, I get up early, at about seven o'clock, . . .
    T: What about breakfast?
    S: I have quite a small breakfast, usually just a piece of bread and some tea . . .

    This is often an easier and more effective way of getting students to produce language than asking a question.

    To show other examples, get teachers to talk about various topics by giving these prompts:

    Tell me about your family.
    Describe this room.
    Tell me about your home town. What about shops? What about entertainment?
    What kind of things do you like? What about books? How about music?

► **Workbook Activity 4** ◄

2. Ask the teachers to look at the text in the Teacher's Workbook.

Emphasise that this text is from a previous lesson, so the students should already be familar with the language in it. This is an occasion when we might want students to give long answers, using complete sentences.

A teacher is reviewing a text from an earlier lesson. Now he wants the students to reproduce it in their own words. What prompts or questions could he ask which would naturally lead students to answer with complete sentences from the text?

On their first day in the capital, Diana and Peter visited the Old Tower which stood on a hill near the city centre. There were stairs leading to the top, but Diana and Peter decided to take the lift. At the top there was a café and a balcony where visitors could stand and admire the view. It was magnificent – you could see the whole city, the river and the hills beyond. On their way back from the Tower, Diana and Peter went past the main square in the city centre. They stopped at a stall to have some orange juice, and sat and watched the traffic for a while. The square was very busy, with cars, buses, bicycles and pedestrians going in all directions. In the centre of the square there was a policeman controlling the traffic.

Look at the prompts and questions in the picture, and discuss what answers the students might give, e.g.:

They went to the Old Tower.
The stairs went to the top of the tower, but they didn't use them.
The tower was on a hill near the city centre.
There was a café, and you could stand on a balcony. You could see the whole city.

3. Divide the teachers into pairs, and ask them to write prompts or questions to elicit sentences about the rest of the text. When the teachers have finished, discuss what prompts and questions they wrote.

   Possible prompts/questions:
   Tell me about the view.
   Then what did they do?
   What did they do at the main square?
   Describe the square.
   What about the policeman?

4. If you like, ask one or two teachers to come to the front and demonstrate. The other teachers should act as a class, and answer without looking at the text.

QUESTIONING STRATEGIES

▶ Workbook Activity 5 ◀

1. As well as knowing what questions to ask, teachers also need to know how to organise question and answer work in class. There are many different ways of asking questions: teachers can ask each student in turn round the class; they can let any student call out the answer; they can choose a student to answer; they can get the class to answer in chorus, and so on. These are called *questioning strategies* (or 'nomination strategies').

   Ask teachers to look at the pictures in the Teacher's Workbook, and establish what questioning strategies they show:

   A) The teacher asks questions and simply lets students *call out* answers. If students call out different answers at the same time, the teacher chooses one student to give the answer again.

   B) The teacher asks a question, then *pauses* to give the whole class a chance to think of the answer. Then the teacher chooses one student to answer. Students are not allowed to call out the answer or to raise their hand.

   C) The teacher first *chooses* a student (by pointing or saying the student's name), and then asks the student a question. If the student cannot answer it, the teacher passes it on to the next student.

   D) The teacher asks a question and lets students *raise their hand* if they think they know the answer. The teacher chooses one of the students with their hands raised to answer.

   ⟫⟶

Here are four different strategies for asking questions in class.

If you like, quickly demonstrate each strategy, so that teachers can experience them from the students' point of view. Use any questions you think are suitable – they could be vocabulary questions, general knowledge questions, or questions based on the textbook.

2. Divide the teachers into groups, and ask them to discuss the questions in the Teacher's Workbook.

> 1. Which of these strategies do you use in your own class? Which do you use most often?
> 2. What are the advantages and disadvantages of each strategy? Consider which strategies:
> – help the teacher to control the class;
> – help to keep the attention of the whole class;
> – give good students a chance to show their knowledge;
> – give weak or shy students a chance to answer;
> – give lazy students a chance *not* to answer.

3. When most groups have finished, discuss the questions together. Emphasise that there is no single 'best' strategy – it is important for teachers to be aware of *different* possible strategies and to be *flexible*. Try to bring out these points:
   – With a large class, strategy A can be effective for simple questions with Yes/No answers. Otherwise, it is likely to be too noisy and

uncontrolled. It would, of course, be suitable for a small class where there are no discipline problems (e.g. a group of adults).

- Strategy B keeps the class involved but still under control. It enables the teacher to give a chance to weaker students as well as more confident ones, although if the questions are too difficult it may make students feel threatened. In general, it is a good strategy for routine, fairly easy questions.
- Strategy C is highly controlled, but is not a good way of keeping the attention of the class, as all the students except the one answering the question can 'switch off'. In general, it is better to ask the question first and then choose who is to answer it.
- Strategy D encourages bright students and makes the class seem to be successful because students are volunteering answers. But if it is the *only* strategy used, it allows the class to be dominated by the best students while weaker and shy students tend to be excluded; it also makes it easy for students to avoid answering questions. In general, it is a good strategy to use for difficult questions that only some students will be able to answer.

LESSON PREPARATION

▶ Workbook Activity 6 ◀

Either organise the preparation during the training session, with teachers working in pairs or groups, or let teachers prepare in their own time after the session.

FURTHER READING

J. Heaton (1981) *Using English in the Classroom* (Chapter 4: Questions and questioning techniques), Longman. A simple guide to questioning techniques and the language used by teachers to ask questions.

G. Abbott and P. Wingard (1981) *The Teaching of English as an International Language* (Chapter 11: The teacher and the class), Collins. Contains a brief analysis of questioning strategies.

J. Willis (1981) *Teaching English through English*, Longman. Contains useful examples of questions to ask in real classroom situations.

3 Presenting structures

Aims of this unit
- To make sure that teachers know what structures are, and how they can be used to make a number of different sentences.
- To show teachers ways of showing the meaning of new structures as well as their form.
- To help teachers think of their own situations and examples to present new structures.

This unit is concerned with presentation techniques, and focusses on ways of introducing structures for the first time. It does not include techniques for practising structures: this is dealt with in Unit 6: Practising structures.

Other units which deal with presentation techniques are – Unit 1: Presenting vocabulary, Unit 4: Using the blackboard (presenting structures on the blackboard), and Unit 14: Eliciting (asking questions as part of the presentation).

STRUCTURES AND EXAMPLES

▶ Workbook Activity 1 ◀

1. Begin by establishing what is meant by a 'structure' and by 'examples of a structure'. Write this sentence on the board:
   I'd like to visit Paris.
   Ask teachers to identify the *structure* in the sentence, and underline it. Point out that this is one example of a structure. Ask teachers to give you other examples, and write a few of them on the board in the form of a table:

I'd like to	climb Mount Everest. earn more money. go home.

   Point out the importance of structures. We can use one structure to make many different sentences; so if students learn the main structures of English, it will help them greatly to speak and to write the language.

2. Ask teachers to look at the sentences in the Teacher's Workbook.

> Look at each sentence in turn. Think of two or three more examples of
> the structure in italics. Write the examples together in a table.
> a) *Shall I* open the window?
> b) He *seems to* be rich.
> c) *Is there any* tea?
> d) I *used to* live in the country.
> e) *She's writing* a letter.
> f) The room was *so* dark *that* I couldn't see anything.

Discuss the first two sentences together. Ask teachers to suggest other
examples of each structure, and write two or three on the board in the
form of a table, e.g.:

Shall I	open the window?
	bring you some water?
	lend you my pen?

He seems to	be rich.
	have many friends.
	work hard.

3. Divide the teachers into pairs. Ask them to look at the other sentences
   and write down two or three more examples of each. They should
   write them in the form of a table, like your examples on the board.
       When most pairs have finished, ask them to tell you some of the
   examples they thought of. Discuss which examples would be most
   suitable for teachers to use in their own classes.

SHOWING THE MEANING OF A STRUCTURE

When we present a structure, it is important to:
– show what the structure means and how it is used, by giving examples;
– show clearly how the structure is formed, so that students can use it to
  make sentences of their own.
In this section, you will focus on ways of showing the meaning of new
structures.

Showing meaning visually

1. The simplest and clearest way to present a structure is often to *show it*

directly, using things the students can see: objects, the classroom, yourself, the students themselves, pictures. Demonstrate this, showing a technique for presenting the structure 'too . . (adjective) . . to . . .':

T: (*point to the ceiling*) What's that?
Ss: The ceiling.
T: (*reach up and try to touch it*) Look – I'm trying to touch it. Can I touch it?
Ss: No.
T: No, I can't. Because it's too high. It's too high to touch. Too high. The ceiling's too high to touch. (*say this sentence again in the students' own language*)

2. Give a second demonstration, to show how you could present the same structure using a blackboard drawing.
   Draw this on the board:

T: Look at this. Is it light or heavy?
Ss: Heavy.
T: Yes, it's heavy. How heavy is it?
Ss: A hundred kilos.
T: That's right. It's very heavy. Could you lift it?
Ss: No.
T: No, of course you couldn't. It's too heavy. It's too heavy to lift.

Comment on your demonstration. Draw teachers' attention to the way you 'led in' to the presentation by focussing on a topic and asking questions about it.

If you like give a few other examples of the structure 'too . . . to . . .', and ask teachers to suggest ways to show their meaning (e.g. The wall is too high to climb, The words are too small to read).

Showing meaning through a situation

It is not always possible to show the meaning of a structure visually, using what is in the class. Another way of showing meaning is to think of a situation from outside the class, in which the structure could naturally be used. The situation can be real or imaginary.

1. Demonstrate how to use an imaginary situation to present a more advanced structure: 'There's no point in . . .-ing':

   T: Listen. Imagine you are with a friend. You're going to visit your uncle, who lives quite near. Your friend says, 'Let's go by bus'. What will you say? Yes or no?
   Ss: No.
   T: Why?
   Ss: Because he lives near.
   T: Yes, he lives nearby. So you might say, 'We can walk there in 15 minutes. There's no point in going by bus'. There's no point in doing it. No point. (*say this again in the students' own language*) There's no point in going by bus.

2. Continue your demonstration by giving other examples:

   T: Here's another example. You want to read a book. But I know it isn't a good book. I might say to you, 'Don't read that book. There's no point in reading it – it isn't at all interesting'. Another example: You have a bicycle, and you are going to clean it. But I know the weather is going to turn bad, so it would get dirty again. What could I say? There's . . . Yes?
   Ss: There's no point in cleaning the bicycle.
   T: Very good.

3. Again comment on your demonstration. Make these points:
   - By giving several different examples, the teacher helps the class to build up a clear idea of what the structure means and how it is used.
   - After giving a few examples, the teacher can just give the situation and try to get the students to give the example. This checks how well the students have understood, and also helps to involve the class more.

Discussion: Ways of showing meaning

▶ Workbook Activity 2 ◀

1. Read through the captions in the Teacher's Workbook.

   This is how different teachers presented *comparison of adjectives* to
   their students. Which presentation do you think is:
   – the most interesting?
   – the easiest?
   – the most useful?

Teacher A:

> I talked about two buildings
> in the town. ('The post office
> is bigger than the bank.')

Teacher B:

> I drew lines on
> the board. ('Line A
> is longer than Line B.')

> **-ER THAN**
> **NOT AS . . . AS . . .**

Teacher C:

> I called a tall and a short
> student to the front and
> compared them. ('Anna is
> taller than Maria.')

Teacher D:

> I drew pictures of two men
> on the board and
> compared them. ('Hani is
> taller than Abdou.')

2. Discuss the four presentations. Encourage teachers to give their own
   opinions, and also to suggest any other ways of presenting the
   structure.
   Possible comments:
   Drawing lines on the board: very simple and clear, but not very
     interesting.
   Comparing two students: would certainly be interesting, but it could
     be very embarrassing for the two students concerned; drawing two
     imaginary people on the board would be safer and just as clear.
   Referring to local buildings: would be very clear, could be made more
     interesting by showing pictures.

3. Look again at the first two structures in Workbook Activity 1, and
   discuss with the teachers how they could present them. Get as many
   suggestions as you can.

Possible answers:
- Shall I . . .? can easily be presented directly, using things in the classroom, e.g. 'It's hot in here. Look – the window's closed. Shall I open the window?'
- He seems to . . . could be presented through a situation, e.g. 'A man lives next door to me. I don't know him well. But I think he's rich, because he has many expensive things. He seems to be rich.'

4. Divide the teachers into pairs. Ask them to think how to present the other structures in Workbook Activity 1, using any of the examples they wrote down earlier.

   When most pairs have finished, stop the activity and discuss the ideas together. If you like, ask some teachers to give short demonstrations to show what they would do.

SHOWING FORM AND MEANING

Focussing on form

As well as making it clear how a structure is used and what it means, it is also important to show clearly how it is formed. There are two basic ways of doing this:
- By giving a clear *model* and asking students to listen and repeat two or three times. Quickly demonstrate this, using the example 'It's too heavy to lift':

  T: Listen. It's too heavy to lift. It's too heavy to lift. (*gesture for repetition*)
  Ss: It's too heavy to lift.

  Emphasise that the aim of this is just to give students the 'feel' of the structure, and especially to make them familiar with the way it sounds. It should not be continued for too long – a few repetitions by the whole class, perhaps followed by one or two repetitions by individual students.
- By *writing* the structure clearly on the board. Demonstrate this by writing 'It's too heavy to lift' on the board. Say the words as you write them, and underline the 'fixed' part of the structure:

  It's <u>too</u> heavy <u>to</u> lift.

An alternative technique is to get the students to tell you what to write. Quickly show this: rub off the example, then get teachers to 'dictate' it to you and write it again. (Prompt them with questions: 'What's the first word? And then?'). This has the advantage of involving the class and focussing their attention on the structure.

Presenting a structure

▶ **Workbook Activity 3** ◀

In this activity you will look at a complete procedure for presenting a new structure.

1. Read through the explanation in the Teacher's Workbook and the teacher's notes for the lesson.

> A teacher presented the structure 'has been . . . -ing . . . for . . .' to her class. To make the meaning clear, she drew pictures on the board and gave this imaginary situation: 'A woman starts waiting for a bus at four o'clock. At five o'clock the bus comes. She's been waiting for an hour.'
>
> Here are the teacher's notes for the lesson, but they are not in their correct order. What order should they be in? Are all the stages necessary?

> Say 'She's been waiting for an hour' and ask the class to repeat it phrase by phrase.

> Explain how the structure is formed.

> Write the sentence on the board:
> She's been waiting for an hour.

> Give other situations and examples:
> Another person arrived at 4.30.
> He's been waiting for half an hour.
> etc.

> Ask the class to copy the sentence.

> Ask individual students to repeat the sentence.

Draw pictures to show the situation, and give the example 'She's been waiting for an hour'.

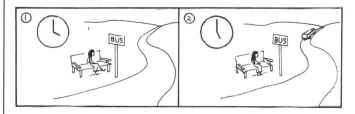

Discuss what order the stages should be in, and which of them are the most important. The most likely order would be:

i)   Draw the pictures and give the example.
ii) Give a model and ask the class to repeat.
iii) Ask individual students to repeat the sentence.
iv) Write the sentence on the board.
v)   Explain how the structure is formed.
vi) Ask the class to copy the sentence.
vii) Give other situations and examples.

[*Note:* Many variations are possible, e.g. the teacher could give several different examples at the beginning, or could write the structure on the board before asking the class to say it. Many of the stages could be left out. It would be important to give the situation and example (which could be done without pictures), and to give a clear model (although the class could just listen instead of repeating). Writing the sentence on the board would also be important, but it might not be necessary to explain the structure or ask students to copy it – this would of course depend on the type of class.]

2. If necessary, give a demonstration to show how the main stages might appear in practice.

Situation and example to show meaning

T: (*drawing picture*) Look, see this woman. What's she doing?
Ss: Waiting for a bus.
T: Yes. Look, it's four o'clock. She's just started waiting. (*drawing second picture*) What's the time now?
Ss: Five o'clock.
T: Yes – and look, the bus is coming. But the woman's been waiting for a long time. How long? Can you tell me?
Ss: One hour.
T: That's right. She's been waiting for an hour.

Model the structure

T: Listen. She's been waiting for an hour. Let's say it together. For an hour.
Ss: For an hour.
T: She's been waiting for an hour.
Ss: She's been waiting for an hour.

Model the example on the board

T: Now, let's write it. Who can tell me? (*write 'She's*) She's . . . What comes next?
Ss: Waiting.
T: Not yet – before that.
Ss: Been.
T: Good. (*write 'been'*) Now – what next?
Ss: Waiting.
T: That's right. (*write 'waiting'*) And then?
Ss: For an hour.
T: Good. (*write 'for an hour', and underline the structure*)

Other examples

T: (*draw another person, a man, and a clock*) Look – here's another person. He arrived at three o'clock. What can we say about him? He's been . . .?
Ss: He's been waiting for two hours.
 (*and so on*)

3. Finally, discuss the value of teachers giving their *own* presentation of a new structure, rather than just relying on the textbook. Make these points:
   – Often, examples and situations given in textbooks are not clear enough or sufficiently close to the students' interests. It is easy for teachers to find their own examples which will mean more to the class and be more interesting.
   – Teachers can use the situations and examples given in the textbook, but present them in their own way, before asking students to read them in their books. The class will be far more involved if they are watching and listening to the teacher, looking at the blackboard, and answering questions, than if they have their 'heads down' in the textbook.

Contrasting structures

1. Sometimes we need not only to present single structures, but to show the difference between two structures; this is especially important when there is a contrast between two structures in English which does not exist in the students' own language. There are two basic ways of doing this: by giving *examples* and by giving simple *explanations*.

   To illustrate this, talk about the structures 'How much?' and 'How many?':
   - We could give examples to show the difference between them: 'How much butter/flour/sugar? How many eggs/loaves of bread/plates?'
   - We could give an explanation: 'How many is used with words that have a singular and a plural form (an egg – eggs)'.

   Discuss the value of giving 'rules' and explanations to the class. Try to bring out these points:
   - Well-chosen examples are the clearest way to show how a structure is used. Rules and explanations can be useful by providing a kind of 'short cut' for the student, but they should be seen as an *aid* in learning, as something 'extra'. Only knowing rules will not help students to use language.
   - It may not always be necessary to explain differences between structures. Students can get a sense of the way structures are used by hearing or seeing examples, without ever 'knowing the rule'.
   - If we give explanations, it is usually best to give them in the students' own language, to increase their chances of understanding them (the language of the explanation will nearly always be more complex than the structure itself). Obviously, explanations should always be as clear and simple as possible.

   ▶ **Workbook Activity 4** ◀

2. Ask teachers to look at the three pairs of structures in the Teacher's Workbook and discuss the questions beneath them.

   a) I've got **some** bread. I haven't got **any** bread.
   b) I**'ve seen** that film. I **saw** that film last week.
   c) If they **build** a reservoir, there **will** be plenty of water.
      If they **built** a reservoir, there **would** be plenty of water.

   Discuss each pair of sentences in turn.
   - What is the difference between the sentences?
   - Can you think of other *examples* which would show the difference?
   - How could you *explain* the difference simply to your students, using their own language?

3. If there is time, ask teachers to suggest other structures which their students find confusing, and discuss ways of dealing with them.

LESSON PREPARATION

▶ **Workbook Activity 5** ◀

Either organise the preparation during the training session, with teachers working together in pairs or groups, or let teachers prepare in their own time after the session.

FURTHER READING

J. Harmer (1983) *The Practice of English Language Teaching* (Chapter 6), Longman. A detailed analysis of the stages involved in presenting new language, together with examples from recent textbooks.

M. Swan (1980) *Practical English Usage* and M. Swan (1984) *Basic English Usage*, Oxford University Press. Both books give simple explanations and examples of commonly confused vocabulary and structures. Useful reference books.

4 Using the blackboard

Aims of this unit
- To improve teachers' basic technique in using the blackboard.
- To show teachers ways of using the blackboard as an aid in presentation and practice.
- To show teachers how to do simple drawings on the blackboard.

This unit concentrates on basic uses of the blackboard: presenting new words and structures, writing tables for presentation and practice, and simple drawings of people, places and objects. It does *not* show how to use the blackboard to give models of handwriting, or for practice in reading or copying words. These topics are dealt with in Unit 9: Teaching basic reading and Unit 11: Teaching handwriting.

Some of the ideas and techniques included in this unit are also explored in other units, especially Unit 3: Presenting structures (writing examples on the board), Unit 7: Using visual aids (using drawings and tables) and Unit 14: Eliciting (using the blackboard to elicit language).

TECHNIQUES FOR USING THE BLACKBOARD

Introduction

Point out that the blackboard is one of the most useful of all visual aids – it is always available and can be used for various purposes without special preparation. Briefly discuss with the teachers some of the purposes for which the blackboard can be used (e.g. presenting new words, showing spelling, giving a model for handwriting, writing prompts for practice).

Our aim in using the blackboard should be to make things clearer to the class and help to focus their attention. So in order to use the blackboard effectively, it is important to develop good basic techniques of writing on the blackboard and organising the layout of what we write.

>>>→

Writing on the blackboard

▶ Workbook Activity 1 ◀

1. Begin by looking at the two pictures in the Teacher's Workbook and discussing the differences between them:
   - Teacher A is hiding the board, he is not involving the students in any way, and because he has his back to the class he cannot control what they are doing.
   - Teacher B is keeping 'eye contact' with the class as she writes, she is allowing the class to see what she is writing, and she is keeping their attention by saying the words as she writes them.

   Both these teachers are presenting language on the blackboard. Which teacher's technique is more effective? Why?

A.

B.

2. If necessary, give a demonstration yourself of how to write effectively on the board. Use your demonstration to establish these basic principles:
   - Write clearly. The writing should be large enough to read from the back of the class.
   - Write in a straight line. This is easy if teachers only write across a section of the board, not across the whole board.
   - Stand in a way that does not hide the board. Show teachers how to stand sideways, half facing the board and half facing the class, with their arm fully extended. In this way, the students can see what the teacher is writing, and the teacher can see the students.
   - Talk as you write. Teachers should say aloud what they are writing, phrase by phrase. To involve the class even more, they could sometimes ask students to suggest what to write (e.g. 'What's the next word?' 'How do I spell that?').

Organising the blackboard

▶ Workbook Activity 2 ◀

1. Ask teachers to look at the blackboard layout in the Teacher's Workbook. Explain how the lesson developed:
   - The lesson was about people selling goods at the market (shown by pictures in the textbook), and how much they had sold by certain times.
   - The teacher introduced the past perfect tense, and students practised sentences like 'By midday she had sold five mats'.
   - The teacher introduced key vocabulary for goods (e.g. mat, pot, basket), and added some other words which were not in the lesson (e.g. plate, bowl).
   - The teacher revised time expressions, and introduced the new item 'midday'.

   [*Note:* This lesson is taken from M. Bates: *Nile Course for the Sudan* Book 3.]

   Here is a teacher's blackboard at the end of a lesson. How could the layout have been organised more clearly?

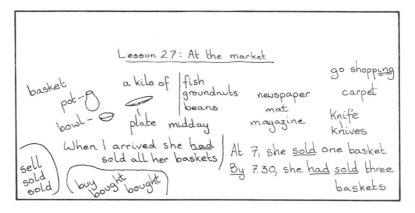

2. Either ask all the teachers to design an improved blackboard layout on a piece of paper, or discuss together what should be done and then build up a model version on the blackboard, getting suggestions from the teachers. Bring out these points:
   - The blackboard is too crowded. Some items could have been presented orally, or written on the board and then rubbed off again soon afterwards.
   - The most important item is the example showing the past perfect tense. It would be clearer if it were written in the centre of the board.

- Key vocabulary could be written down the side of the board, with similar items close together.

A possible layout (omitting some items) might be:

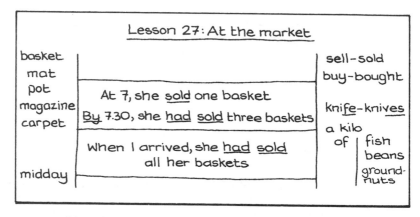

PRESENTING AND PRACTISING STRUCTURES

Blackboard examples

1. An important use of the blackboard is to show clearly how structures are formed, and to show differences between structures.
   To demonstrate this, write these sentences on the board:

   He played football.

   Did he play football?

   (Talk as you write, saying the words aloud and also commenting, 'Look – He – played – football. Now let's make a question. We use "did", so . . . did – he – play (not "played") – football?')

2. Discuss how to make the structures clearer.
   Possible answers:
   - By underlining the important features:

   He play<u>ed</u> football

   <u>Di</u>d he play football?

   - By using different coloured chalk (red, yellow and green stand out most clearly).

– Perhaps by drawing arrows or writing numbers to show the change in word order.

► **Workbook Activity 3** ◄

3. Divide teachers into pairs, and ask them to look at the Teacher's Workbook.

> Look at the examples below.
> – What grammar points do they show?
>   How would you present them on the blackboard?
>
> a) a book, a table, an egg, an orange.
> b) He plays football. Does he play football?
> c) shelf, shelves; wife, wives.
> d) I haven't seen her for a week. I haven't seen her since Saturday.
> e) She is reading. She's reading. He has arrived. He's arrived.
> f) He worked so hard that he became ill.

Ask teachers to write each set of examples out on a piece of paper, exactly as they would write them on the blackboard, using underlining, arrows, numbers, etc. to draw attention to important features.

4. Ask different teachers to come to the front in turn and present each set of examples on the blackboard. (As this is a simple task, use it to focus on basic techniques in using the blackboard. Remind teachers to write clearly and in a straight line; to stand so that they are not hiding what they write; to look at the class from time to time; and to talk as they write, saying the words and making any necessary comments.)

Structure tables

► **Workbook Activity 4** ◄

1. Explain that a good way of showing the different forms of a structure together is by means of a table (sometimes called a 'substitution table'). Ask teachers to look at the table in the Teacher's Workbook.

I'm You've He's She's We're They've	eating preparing	breakfast lunch dinner

⫸→

47

Look at this structure table, which shows forms of the present continuous tense.
1. How could you write the table on the blackboard but still keep the attention of the class?
2. How could you use the table for practice?
3. Design two more structure tables:
   – showing examples with 'How much?' and 'How many?';
   – showing examples of the present perfect tense with 'for' and 'since'.

Discuss the questions together.
Possible answers:
Keeping the attention of the class:
– A good way to involve the class would be to get students to suggest what to write in each column (e.g. by writing 'I'm' and then getting students to give the other forms). (If you like, demonstrate this, either using this table or another similar one.)
– Students could be asked to copy the table as the teacher writes it.
– If the table is too long or too complex to write quickly, it would be better to write it on the board before the lesson and cover it with cloth or paper until it is needed; or to draw it in advance on a large piece of card.
Using the table for practice:
There are many ways of using the table. For example:
– Students could read out sentences from it.
– Students could write sentences from the table in their books.
– The teacher could give situations, and ask students to make an appropriate sentence, e.g.:
   It's seven o'clock in the morning. What's Mrs Smith doing? (*She's eating breakfast.*)
   It's one o'clock. What are Mona and Lisa doing? (*They're preparing lunch.*)

2. Divide the teachers into pairs, and ask them to design two structure tables themselves, following the instructions in the Teacher's Workbook. They should write the two tables on a piece of paper, exactly as they would look on the blackboard. The tables should look something like this:

How much	bread milk	do we	need? want? have?
How many	eggs tomatoes		

				for	a week a year
I've He's She's They've	been	living here Learning English		since	April. Monday.

3. Ask two teachers to write their tables on the blackboard.

Prompts for practice

1. Show teachers how to use simple prompts on the blackboard as a basis
   for practice.
   Write this table on the board, line by line. As you write, talk and ask
   questions, to make it clear what the table is supposed to show, e.g.:
   Look, this is Eva's day. (*write first line*) OK – at half past six – what
   does she do? (*She wakes up and washes.*)
   (*and so on*)

EVA

6.30	get up, wash
7.00	breakfast
7.30	bus → work
12.00	lunch
3.00	home

Discuss what different kinds of practice the prompts could be used for.
Possible answers:
– Students make sentences from the table.
– Students ask and answer questions based on the table.
– Students make similar sentences about themselves.

▶ **Workbook Activity 5** ◀

2. Ask teachers to look at the examples in the Teacher's Workbook, and
   discuss what kind of practice each one might be used for.

49

Here are three examples of prompts written on the blackboard. What language could each of them be used to practise?

A.

	swim	speak French	dance
Karl	✓	✓	✓
Magda	x	✓	x
Anna	✓	x	✓
You	?	?	?

B.
How many?
doctors   rooms
nurses   blankets
patients   beds

C.
8 o'clock – got up – breakfast –
bus stop – bus – empty – surprised –
school – closed – remembered – holiday

Possible answers:

A. Oral practice, with various structures, e.g.:
   Can Karl swim? Yes, he can.
   Karl is quite good at swimming. He's very good at dancing.
   Does Karl enjoy dancing? Yes, he loves it.

B. Question/answer practice, perhaps about a local hospital, e.g.:
   How many doctors are there? There are six.
   Or as a basis for role play, e.g. setting up a new hospital for their town. Students decide how many doctors, nurses, etc. they need.

C. Outline of a story, for oral or written composition, e.g.:
   At eight o'clock on Monday morning, Hanka got up and had breakfast as usual . . .

If you like, give short demonstrations to show how each set of prompts could be used.

BLACKBOARD DRAWINGS

Introduction

Make these general points about blackboard drawings:

– Many teachers use the blackboard only for writing. But simple pictures drawn on the blackboard can help to increase the interest of a lesson, and are often a good way of showing meaning and conveying situations to the class.

– Blackboard drawings should be as simple as possible, showing only the most important details. It is not necessary to be a good artist to draw successfully on the blackboard – a lot of information can be conveyed by means of very simple line drawings and 'stick figures', which are easy to draw.

– It is important to draw quickly, so as to keep the interest of the class. It also helps for teachers to talk as they draw: in this way the class will be more involved, and will understand the picture on the board both from seeing it and from listening to the teacher.

Simple blackboard drawings

In this section, you will demonstrate how to draw faces, stick figures and other simple pictures. Draw examples of each type on the board, and encourage teachers to copy the drawings onto paper. Try to involve the teachers as much as possible: ask them to give their own ideas and examples, and discuss possible variations. Use the ideas below as a guide. [*Note:* Similar drawings are given in the 'Reference sheet' in the Teacher's Workbook on p. 16 and 17.]

Faces

Heads should be large enough to be seen from the back of the class. Show how you can indicate expression, especially by changing the shape of the mouth:

   happy   sad   laughing   crying

Discuss with the teachers how to show other expressions (e.g. surprise by raised eyebrows, anger by a frown):

Show how to indicate which way the speaker is facing by changing the nose (this is useful if you want to show two people having a conversation):

Show how to indicate sex or age by drawing hair:

Stick figures

Show how to draw basic male and female stick figures. The body should be about twice as long as the head; the arms are the same length as the body; the legs are slightly longer:

Show how to indicate actions by bending the legs and arms:

Ask teachers to suggest other actions, and discuss how they can be drawn (e.g. writing, kicking a ball, shaking hands).

Places

Show how to indicate buildings, towns, and directions by a combination of pictures and words:

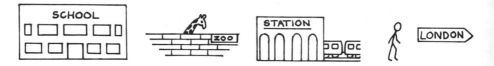

Discuss with the teachers how to draw other places (including well-known places in their own area).

Vehicles

Show how to draw vehicles and how to indicate movement:

Ask teachers to suggest other common forms of transport, and discuss how to draw them.

Using blackboard drawings

1. Demonstrate a technique for using blackboard drawings to build up a complete situation. This might be done to introduce a topic and new vocabulary, or as a preparation for reading a text or dialogue. Use the pictures and notes below as a guide. Talk as you draw, and involve the class by asking questions as much as possible.

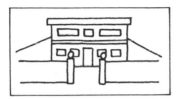

(*draw a school*)
What do you think this is? Yes – it's a school.

(*draw a boy*)
Look, there's a boy. He's running. Why is he running? (*students suggest possible reasons*)

Well, he's running because he's late for school. (*rub out the boy, and draw him again by the school*) There – he's arrived at school. What do you think will happen? (*students make suggestions*)

(*draw boy with head teacher*)
Well, look – where is he now? Who is he talking to? (*students answer*) Yes, the head teacher. What will he say? (*students make suggestions*)

▶ **Workbook Activity 6** ◀

2. Divide the teachers into groups. Working together, they should choose *one* of the pictures in the Teacher's Workbook, and decide what they think it represents. Then they should invent a simple story which they could show by a series of blackboard drawings; the drawing they have chosen should be one of the series (it could be the beginning, the middle or the end).

Ask them to practise drawing their series of pictures on a piece of paper. Go from group to group, and ask them to tell you their story.

Work in groups. What do these drawings show?

1. Choose *one* of the drawings. Think of a simple story based on it. Think of a series of blackboard drawings which you can use to tell the story (the picture you have chosen will be one of them).
2. Practise drawing the pictures and telling the story.

3. Ask one teacher from each group to come to the front in turn and 'tell' their story to the others. They should draw the pictures on the board, and try to involve the class by asking questions, as you did in your demonstration.

LESSON PREPARATION

▶ **Workbook Activity 7** ◀

Either organise the preparation during the training session, with teachers working together in pairs or groups, or let teachers prepare in their own time after the session.

FURTHER READING

P. Mugglestone (1981) *Planning and Using the Blackboard*, Heinemann.
   A practical guide to all aspects of using the blackboard.

The following are two guides to blackboard drawing techniques, with suggestions for practice exercises:
J. S. Crichton (1954) *Blackboard Drawing*, Nelson.
P. Shaw and T. de Vet (1980) *Using Blackboard Drawing*, Heinemann.

5   Using a reading text

Aims of this unit
- To make teachers more aware of what is involved in reading a text.
- To show teachers a range of techniques for using texts in class.

This unit is concerned with basic procedures for using texts in class: it considers ways of organising reading, and what can be done before and after reading. The ideas and techniques in this unit are further developed in Unit 15: Reading activities. This unit is not concerned with initial reading problems of students whose own language uses a different writing system; this is dealt with in Unit 9: Teaching basic reading.

READING A TEXT

1. How to use a reading text depends on the *purpose* for which we want to use it: Is it to develop reading comprehension skills? Is it a way of presenting new words and structures? Is it a basis for language practice? Ask teachers to consider the textbooks they use with their own classes, and discuss what the main purpose of the texts seems to be.

    ▶ **Workbook Activity 1** ◀

2. Point out that there are three possible ways of reading a text in class:
    - The students all read silently to themselves, at their own speed.
    - The teacher reads aloud, while the students follow in their books.
    - Students read aloud in turn.
    As a basis for discussion, demonstrate the first two ways, using the text in the Teacher's Workbook.

    [*Note:* This text is intended to work at the teachers' own level of reading comprehension, so that they can experience the two approaches to reading from the learner's point of view.]

    Demonstration one

    i)   To introduce the text, tell teachers they will read about how fossils are formed. If necessary, present the words 'fossil' and 'become fossilised'.

ii) Before teachers start reading, give this 'guiding question':
Only very few animal remains become fossils. Why?
(If you like, discuss the question briefly – then teachers can read the text to compare it with their own answer.)

iii) Ask teachers to look at the first part of the text in the Teacher's Workbook. Give them a few minutes to read it silently to themselves and find the answer to the guiding question. Then discuss the answer together.

1. Read the first part of the text silently.

How to get preserved as a fossil

Unfortunately the chances of any animal becoming a fossil are not very great, and the chances of a fossil then being discovered many thousands of years later are even less. It is not surprising that of all the millions of animals that have lived in the past, we actually have fossils of only a very few.

There are several ways in which animals and plants may become fossilised. First, it is essential that the remains are buried, as dead animals and plants are quickly destroyed if they remain exposed to the air. Plants rot, while scavengers, such as insects and hyenas, eat the flesh and bones of animals. Finally, the few remaining bones soon disintegrate in the hot sun and pouring rain. If buried in suitable conditions, however, animal and plant remains will be preserved. The same chemicals which change sand and silt into hard rock will also enter the animal and plant remains and make them hard too. When this happens we say that they have become fossilised. Usually only the bones of an animal and the toughest part of a plant are preserved.

Demonstration two

i) Give these guiding questions for the second part of the text:
How can soft parts of animals become fossilised?
What kind of fossils are often found in caves?

ii) Read the second part of the text yourself, and ask teachers to follow in their books. Then discuss the answers to the questions together.

2. Now follow while the trainer reads.

The soft body parts of an animal or the fine fibres of a leaf may occasionally become fossilised, but they must be buried quickly for this to happen. This may sometimes occur with river and lake sediments but is much more likely to happen with volcanic ash. One site near Lake Victoria, where my parents worked, contained many thousands of beautifully preserved insects, spiders, seeds, twigs, roots and leaves. A nearby volcano must have erupted very suddenly, burying everything in a layer of ash. The insects had no time to escape before they were smothered.

> Caves are another site where fossils are easily formed, and luckily our ancestors left many clues in caves which made convenient shelters and homes. Things that people brought in as food or tools were left on the cave floor, and they were buried by mud, sand and other debris washed in by rivers and rain.

(from *Human Origins*: R. Leakey)

3. Which technique:
   – makes it easier to understand the text?
   – is more helpful in developing reading ability?

3. After your demonstrations, compare the two ways of reading a text. Encourage teachers to give their own views and to say how they felt as 'learners' during the activity. Try to bring out these points:
   – *Understanding the text:* Teachers may intend to help students by reading the text aloud to them, but it can in fact make reading more difficult. In silent reading, students can all read at their own speed, and if they do not understand a sentence they can go back and read it again. If the teacher is reading the text aloud, this is impossible – everyone must follow at the speed set by the teacher.
   – *Developing reading ability:* When students read English in the future (e.g. for studying, reading instructions, reading magazines), they will need to do so silently and without help, so this is the skill they need to develop. We need to give them practice in *looking* at a text and trying to *understand* it, without always hearing it at the same time.
   – *Control of the class:* Teachers often prefer to read the text themselves because it seems to give them more control over the activity; but of course they cannot be sure that the students are actually following the text at all. In silent reading, nothing *seems* to be happening, but students are in fact concentrating on the text and thinking about meaning.

4. Briefly discuss the third way of reading a text: students *read aloud* in turn. Make these points:
   i) Reading aloud can be useful at the earliest stages of reading (recognising letters and words); it can help students to make the connection between sound and spelling.
   ii) For reading a text, it is not a very useful technique, because:
      – Only *one student* is active at a time; the others are either not listening at all, or are listening to a bad model.
      – Students' attention is focussed on *pronunciation*, not on understanding the text (and there are many other ways to practise pronunciation – see Unit 10).

- It is an *unnatural* activity – most people do not read aloud in real life.
- Because students usually read slowly, it takes up a lot of *time* in class.

iii) Reading aloud is very difficult – many people find it hard to read aloud in their own language. So if a teacher wants students to read aloud, it should be the final activity at the end of a reading lesson.

ACTIVITIES BEFORE READING

There are various things we can do *before* reading a text which will make it easier for students to understand the text and help them focus attention on it as they read. They include:
- presenting some of the new words which will appear in the text;
- giving a brief introduction to the text;
- giving one or two 'guiding' questions (orally or on the board) for students to think about as they read.

Presenting new vocabulary

1. We do not need to present all the new words in a text before the students read it; they can guess the meaning of many words from the context. An important part of reading is being able to guess the meaning of unknown words, and we can help students to develop their reading skills by giving them practice in this. Only the words which would make it very difficult to understand the text need to be presented beforehand (e.g. 'fossil' in Activity 1); other words can be dealt with after reading the text.

    Give an example to make this clear:
    The children were bleebing all over the playground.
Ask teachers to guess what the nonsense word 'bleebing' means. It should be possible to guess that:
    - it is a verb (from the form);
    - it involves movement (because of 'all over');
    - it is something children do, e.g. playing or running.

    ▶ **Workbook Activity 2** ◀

2. Divide the teachers into pairs and ask them to read the text in the Teacher's Workbook. Ask them to try to understand the story *in spite of* the words they don't understand.

1. Read the text and try to understand the *general meaning* of the story. (All the words in italics are nonsense words.)

A country girl was walking along the *snerd* with a *roggle* of milk on her head. She began saying to herself, 'The money for which I will sell this milk will make me enough money to increase my *trund* of eggs to three hundred. These eggs will produce the same number of chickens, and I will be able to sell the chickens for a large *wunk* of money. Before long, I will have enough money to live a rich and *fallentious* life. All the young men will want to marry me. But I will refuse them all with a *ribble* of the head – like this . . .'

And as she *ribbled* her head, the *roggle* fell to the ground and all the milk ran in a white stream along the *snerd*, carrying her plans with it.

2. Now look at the nonsense words again. Can you guess what they might mean?

When they have read the text, ask teachers to discuss the meaning of the nonsense words. Unless they know the words in English, they should try to give the meaning in their own language.

After a few minutes, go through the words together. (The actual words are: road; can; stock; sum; luxurious; shake; shook; can; road.)

3. Discuss what this tells us about reading a text. Bring out these points:
   - It is quite possible to understand a text without understanding every word, and it is possible to guess many unknown words from their context.
   - Asking students to try to guess the meaning of new words helps to focus attention on them, and makes them *want* to know what the words mean.

4. As a possible extension to this activity, ask teachers to look again at the text in Activity 1 and underline any words which are new to them. Ask them to guess what the words might mean.

Introducing the text

It is important to introduce the theme of the text before we ask students to read it. This serves two purposes:
- To *help* students in their reading, by giving them some idea what to expect.
- To increase their *interest* and so make them *want* to read the text.

One way to introduce the text is just to give a simple sentence (e.g. in Activity 1: 'We are going to read about fossils. The text tells us how animals and plants become fossils.'). This could be in English or in the students' own language. A more interesting way would be to have a short discussion, to start students thinking about the topic (e.g. in Activity 1: 'Do you know how fossils are formed? Where do they come from? Have you ever seen a fossil? What was it like?').

Emphasise that teachers should not say *too much* when introducing a text, or they will 'give away' what it has to say, and kill the students' interest instead of arousing it. If you like, give an example of a bad introduction which gives too much away: 'You are going to read a text about fossils. The text tells us that very few animals become fossils. When they die, most animals are eaten by insects or by other animals. To become a fossil, the animal must be buried soon after it dies.'

[*Note:* Pre-reading activities are dealt with in more detail in Unit 15: Reading activities.]

Guiding questions

Before the students read the text, the teacher can give one or two *guiding questions* (either orally or written on the board), for students to think about as they read. Remind teachers of the guiding questions you gave in Activity 1 ('Only very few animal remains become fossils. Why?' 'How can the soft parts of animals become fossilised?' 'What kind of fossils are often found in caves?'). Discuss the purpose of these questions:
– To give the students a *reason* to read, by giving them something to look for as they read the text.
– To lead (or 'guide') the students towards the *main points* of the text, so that after the first reading they should have a good general idea of what it is about.
Point out that, to achieve their purpose, guiding questions should be concerned with the general meaning or with the most important points of a text, and not focus on minor details; they should be fairly easy to answer and not too long.

If you like, give a few examples of good and bad guiding questions for the text in Activity 1, and discuss them:

Good: Very few animal remains become fossils. Why?
What kind of fossils are found in caves?
How do animals become fossils?

Bad: What is a fossil? (*we already know the answer*)
What are hyenas? (*focusses on a single difficult word*)
Where did the volcano erupt? (*a detail*)
Why did the site near Lake Victoria contain such well-preserved
fossils? (*question too long and difficult to understand*)

Preparing for silent reading

▶ **Workbook Activity 3** ◀

1. Divide the teachers into groups. Ask them to look at the text in the Teacher's Workbook and follow the instructions.
2. When all the groups have finished, discuss the answers together.

1. The new words are in italics in the text.
   Write them in two lists:
   – words which you would present before reading;
   – words which you could leave for students to guess, and deal with afterwards.

2. How would you introduce the text? Decide exactly what you would say.

3. Look at these possible guiding questions. Choose the *two* which you think would be best.
   a) Was the doctor rich?
   b) Was the doctor unhappy?
   c) What was the young man's problem?
   d) Where was the man's pain?
   e) What did the doctor advise?

A doctor who worked in a village was very *annoyed* because many people used to stop him in the street and ask his *advice*. In this way, he was never paid for his *services*, and he never *managed* to earn much money. He *made up his mind* to put an end to this. One day, he was stopped by a young man who said to him, 'Oh, doctor, I'm so glad to see you. I've got a *severe pain* in my left side'. The doctor *pretended* to be interested and said, 'Shut your eyes and *stick* your tongue out of your mouth'. Then he went away, leaving the man standing in the street with his tongue hanging out ... and a large *crowd* of people laughing at him.

CHECKING COMPREHENSION

1. Texts are usually used in English classes for two main purposes:
   – As a way of developing *reading comprehension* – by looking at the text and trying to understand its 'message' (what it has to say).
   – As a way of *learning new language* – by looking at the text and focussing on particular words and expressions.
   Often, these two aims are combined in a single lesson. First, students read the text and try to understand it. After they have understood its general meaning, the teacher goes through the text again, checking detailed comprehension and also focussing on important new vocabulary.

To demonstrate how this can be done, ask teachers to look at the text in Activity 1, and ask a series of comprehension questions, requiring short answers. Try to focus on the main points of the text, and explain any difficult words or expressions as they arise. (Possible answers are given in brackets.)

How old are most fossils? (*very old, thousands of years old*)
Do most animals become fossilised? (*no, very few*)
Do most fossils get discovered? (*no, very few*)
An animal or a plant dies. What's left? (*the remains*)
Will the remains become a fossil? (*not always*)
What has to happen? (*it has to be buried*)
And if it isn't buried, what happens? (*it's destroyed*)
What is it destroyed by? (*animals, insects, scavengers, the sun, rain, etc.*)
What do insects do? (*they eat the flesh of animals*)
What are hyenas? (*a kind of wild dog*)
What do they do? (*eat the flesh and bones*)
Can you guess what 'scavengers' are? What other animals are scavengers? (*rats, jackals, vultures, crows*)

After your demonstration, discuss the technique with the teachers. Encourage them to comment on it from the learners' point of view. Emphasise that the main purpose of asking comprehension questions should be to lead students to look closely at the main points of the text, and to help them understand it. To achieve this:

– It is best to ask a series of *short, simple questions* which help to 'break down' the meaning of the text and make it easier to understand.
– Students should only be required to give *short answers* (the aim is to check comprehension, not to get students to reproduce the text).
– Students should keep their *books open*, so that they can refer to the text to answer the questions.
– Even if the textbook contains good comprehension questions, it is often a good idea for the teacher to ask his or her own questions first; the teacher can be more flexible and modify questions if the students do not understand. The 'set' questions in the book could be answered afterwards in pairs, or the answers written in class or for homework (see Unit 15: Reading activities).

▶ Workbook Activity 4 ◀

2. Divide the teachers into pairs or groups. Ask them to look at the text in Activity 3.

Look at the text in Activity 3. ⟫→

Think of a series of short simple questions which you could use to
check comprehension and focus on important words and expressions.
Write them down.

3. When they have finished, ask teachers to read out their questions. If
   you like, ask one or two teachers to come to the front and demonstrate
   asking their questions, with the other teachers acting as a class.

[*Note:* Basic question types and questioning strategies are dealt with in
Unit 2: Asking questions. Unit 15: Reading activities further develops the
ideas in this section: it discusses different ways of handling comprehension questions in class and shows how to use reading tasks to check
comprehension of a text.]

FOLLOW-UP ACTIVITIES

▶ **Workbook Activity 5** ◀

If texts are fairly short and simple, and contain language which is useful
for students to *produce* as well as understand, they can be used as a basis
for language practice. This practice should of course only be done after
the students have understood the text completely.

1. Ask the teachers to look at the follow-up activities in Workbook
   Activity 5.

   Any of these activities could be done after reading the text in Activity 3.
   Which type of activity do you think is most useful?
   Which is least useful?

   ┌───┐
   │ *Discussion questions*   │
   │   │
   │ Do you think he was a good doctor?   │
   │ How do you think the young man felt?   │
   └───┘

   ┌───┐
   │ *Reproducing the text*   │
   │   │
   │ Tell part of the story from these prompts: │
   │ Doctor – village – annoyed.   │
   │ People – stop – street – advice.   │
   │ Never paid – never – money.   │
   └───┘

Role play

Act out the conversation between the doctor and the young man.

Gap-filling

Copy and fill the gaps:
One day, the doctor .... by a young man.
The doctor .... interested.
He left the man .... in the street with his
tongue .... out.

---

2. Point out that some of the activities (discussion questions, role play) use the *theme* of the text as a basis for free language practice; others (gap-filling, reproducing the text) give practice in the *language* contained in the text. Discuss with the teachers which types of activity would be the most useful in their own classes. Encourage them to suggest other follow-up activities that could be based on a reading text.

LESSON PREPARATION

▶ **Workbook Activity 6** ◀

Either organise the preparation during the training session, with teachers working in pairs or groups, or let teachers prepare in their own time after the session.

FURTHER READING

C. Nuttall (1982) *Teaching Reading Skills in a Foreign Language*, Heinemann. A comprehensive account of reading skills: discusses the theory behind reading, examines individual reading skills, and gives practical ideas for classroom teaching.

E. Williams (1984) *Reading in the Language Classroom*, Macmillan. A shorter practical guide to developing reading skills: discusses different approaches to reading and contains examples of texts and activities.

Background text: Reading

This text outlines important features of the reading process, which are relevant to the way reading is dealt with in class. It provides a background to the following units:
- Unit 5: Using a reading text
- Unit 9: Teaching basic reading
- Unit 15: Reading activities

The text can be read by teachers in their own time, and used as a basis for discussion in the training session.

This text summarises ideas which are explored in detail in the following books:

F. Smith (1978) *Reading*, Cambridge University Press.

C. Nuttall (1982) *Teaching Reading Skills in a Foreign Language*, Heinemann.

Before you read:

Here are some statements about reading. Do you think they are true or false?

1. Silent reading involves looking at a text and saying the words silently to yourself.
2. There are no major differences between how one reads in one's mother tongue and how one reads in a foreign language.
3. To understand a word, you have to read all the letters in it; to understand a sentence, you have to read all the words in it.
4. The teacher can help students to read a text by reading it aloud while they follow in their books.

Now read the text:

If we are to help students develop reading skills in a foreign language, it is important to understand what is involved in the reading process itself. If we have a clear idea of how 'good readers' read, either in their own or a foreign language, this will enable us to decide whether particular reading techniques are likely to help learners or not.

In considering the reading process, it is important to distinguish between two quite separate activities: *reading for meaning* (or 'silent reading') and *reading aloud*. Reading for meaning is the activity we normally engage in when we read books, newspapers, road signs, etc.; it is what you are doing as you read this text. It involves looking at sentences and understanding the message they convey, in other words 'making sense' of a written text. It does not normally involve saying the words we read, not even silently inside our heads; there are important reasons for this, which are outlined below.

Reading aloud is a completely different activity; its purpose is not just to understand a text but to convey the information to someone else. It is not an activity we engage in very often outside the classroom; common examples are reading out parts of a newspaper article to a friend, or reading a notice to other people who cannot see it. Obviously, reading aloud involves looking at a text, understanding it and also saying it. Because our attention is divided between reading and speaking, it is a much more difficult activity than reading silently; we often stumble and make mistakes when reading aloud in our own language, and reading aloud in a foreign language is even more difficult.

When we read for meaning, we do not need to read every letter or every word, nor even every word in each sentence. This is because, provided the text makes sense, we can guess much of what it says as we read it. To see how this happens at the level of individual words, try reading this sentence:

A m—— was walk———— d——n the s————t, c–r——ing a gr——n ————————.

Even though more than half the letters were missing, you could probably read the sentence without difficulty, and even guess the last word without the help of any letters. You may also have noticed that as soon as you guessed the second word, it helped you to guess the whole of the first part of the sentence. This example is an isolated sentence; if you are reading connected sentences in a text, each sentence helps you to guess what the next one will be, and so on through the whole text. Reading is an active process. When we read, we do not merely sit there as passive 'receivers' of the text; we also draw on our own knowledge of the world and of language to help us guess what the text will say next. It is only if we are reading a series of words that makes no sense at all, such as:

Man walking elephant the onto reading to help

that we have to slow down and read every single word, as we can no longer make guesses.

Normally when we read our eyes take in whole phrases at a time; they do not move from word to word in a straight line, but flick backwards and forwards over the text. You can easily test this for yourself. Try covering a text with a piece of paper and reading it literally word by word, moving the paper along from each word to the next. You will probably find that you soon lose track of the meaning, and you need to keep looking back to take in whole sentences. This highlights another important aspect of reading: it is not just that we do not need to read word by word, but rather that it is almost impossible to read and understand a text in this way. Attempting to read one word at a time slows down reading so much that we lose the sense of what we are reading.

There are of course differences between reading in our language, where comprehension does not usually pose a problem, and reading in a foreign language; and the differences are even greater if the foreign language uses a different writing system. But the characteristics of 'good reading' are the same in any language, and in developing reading skills we need to be sure we are not hindering our students but helping them to become good readers, efficient at extracting meaning from written texts.

Discussion

Look again at the statements at the beginning. Are your answers still the same?

6 Practising structures

Aims of this unit
- To show teachers how to move from presenting structures to practising them.
- To make teachers aware of the difference between mechanical and meaningful practice.
- To show teachers ways of organising controlled oral practice in class.
- To show teachers how to use real and imaginary situations for freer practice.

This unit is concerned with basic techniques for oral practice of structures, using the whole class. It does not include pairwork techniques or communicative activities (guessing games, information gap activities, problem solving): these areas are dealt with in Unit 12: Pairwork and groupwork and Unit 18: Communicative activities.

Practice activities are also dealt with in other units, especially Unit 13: Writing activities (written practice of structures), Unit 5: Using a reading text (practice based on a text), Unit 14: Eliciting (using a picture for discussion) and Unit 20: Role play (using imaginary situations for free oral practice).

FROM PRESENTATION TO PRACTICE

▶ **Workbook Activity 1** ◀

1. Ask teachers to look at the lesson plan in the Teacher's Workbook. Read through the notes for the presentation of 'Let's . . .' and quickly demonstrate it.

⟫→

Here is part of a teacher's lesson plan.

> Aim: To teach Ss to make suggestions using 'Let's . . .'.
>
> Presentation
> 1. Give a situation and example:
>   You're sitting at home with a friend. You can't decide
>   what to do. You suggest different things. For example,
>   you want to watch television – so you say 'Let's watch
>   television'.
> 2. Chorus repetition:
>   Let's watch television.
>   Write the sentence on the board.

?

2. Divide the teachers into pairs or groups. Ask them to look at the different ways of practising the structure, and to decide which ones are most useful.

What should the teacher do next? Consider these possibilities.

> *Repetition*
>
> T: Let's play football.
> Ss: Let's play football.
> T: Let's go swimming.
> Ss: Let's go swimming.
>   etc.

> *Substitution*
>
> T: You want to play football.
> Ss: Let's play football.
> T: You want to go swimming.
> Ss: Let's go swimming.

Single word prompts

T: cinema
Ss: Let's go to the cinema.
T: football
Ss: Let's play football.

Free substitution

Students make up their own
sentences, e.g.:
Let's go fishing.

Picture prompts

Discuss the techniques together. Get teachers to give their own ideas, and try to bring out these points:
- The easiest way to practise the structure would be to do a repetition drill: the teacher gives other examples and gets the class to repeat them. This might be useful as a first step only, just to make students familiar with the structure (although this has already been done in the presentation). It is a very *limited* form of practice – the students have to do almost nothing.
- It would be more useful to use one of the other techniques, which are all different kinds of substitution practice: the teacher gives *prompts*, and gets the students to give the examples. This would keep the class more active, and give students practice in forming the structure themselves. (Point out that the prompts can be a whole sentence, a phrase or word, or a picture.)
- The aim at this stage of the lesson is simply to give students practice in forming or 'manipulating' the structure. All the techniques shown are very controlled kinds of practice which would be done very quickly.

3. Discuss which techniques are easier for the students and which are more difficult. Ask teachers to put them in order of difficulty:
   i)   Repetition (students have to do nothing themselves).
   ii)   Substitution (students have to 'fit in' the structure).
   iii) Single word prompts (students have to add the verb).
   iv)   Picture prompts (students have to think of the whole sentence).
   v)   Free substitution (students have to invent a sentence).

All the techniques would not of course be used together, but a teacher might use a combination of them. Give a demonstration to show how this might be done.
(Teachers should imagine that you have just presented the structure.)

T: Now, can you make some more sentences? Listen. You want to watch television, so you say, 'Let's watch television'. Now – you want to listen to the radio. Let's . . .
S: Let's listen to the radio.
T: Good. Again.
S: Let's listen to the radio.
T: You want to go to the river.
S: Let's go to the river.
T: Good. (*Indicating another student*) Can you say it?
S: Let's go to the river.
    (*and so on*)

T: Now, I'll just say a word, and you say the sentence. OK? Television.
S: Let's watch television.
T: Radio.
S: Let's listen to the radio.
    (*and so on*)

T: Now – who can make another suggestion? Make your own sentence.
S: Let's go to the cinema.
T: Good. Another one.
S: Let's go for a walk.
    (*and so on*)

4. After your demonstration, discuss how to involve the whole class in the practice and give as many students as possible a chance to respond. With a large class (more than 30 students) there are two main ways of doing this:
   – By getting responses from individual students (to be sure that the response is correct) and then getting the whole class to repeat in chorus.
   – By getting two or three students to respond in turn to each prompt (by saying 'Again' or simply pointing). This is a good way of giving weaker students a chance to say something.
   With smaller classes there would be less need to do chorus drilling, and students could respond individually. Emphasise that chorus repetition is *not* an ideal way of involving the class – the more chorus repetition there is, the more mechanical the practice becomes.

CONTROLLED PRACTICE

Meaningful practice

1. Ask teachers to look again at the first two kinds of practice in Workbook Activity 1 – the repetition drill and the basic substitution drill. Emphasise that drills like these are useful only if done for a short time (a few minutes) as the first stage of practice, just to help students to 'get their tongue round' a new structure. This kind of practice is of limited value for three reasons:
   - It is completely *mechanical*. Students can easily do the practice with their minds 'switched off' – in other words thinking about something completely different while they are doing it. Because it is so easy to do, it is also easy to forget.
   - The teacher cannot be sure that the students *understand* what the words mean. It is quite possible to do drills like these without knowing what you are saying.
   (If you like, make this clear by demonstrating the same drills in a language the teachers do not know, or using nonsense words, e.g.:

   T: You want to muggle a wump.
   S: Let's muggle a wump.
   T: You want to figgle a wimp.
   S: Let's figgle a wimp, etc.

   Teachers should have no difficulty in giving the correct response, even though they have no idea what they are saying.)
   - All the students have to do is produce the correct *form*; they are getting practice in saying the new structure, but not in using the new structure to express *meaning*.
   It is obviously more useful to give students practice in which they have to think, in which they understand what they are saying, and in which they express meaning. This kind of practice is called *meaningful practice*.

   ▶ **Workbook Activity 2** ◀

2. This activity shows three pairs of exercises which highlight differences between mechanical and meaningful practice. Work through the exercises, demonstrating them quickly so that teachers can see how they work. After each pair of exercises, stop and compare them. Use the notes below as a guide.

⟫→

Do each pair of exercises. How are exercise (a) and exercise (b) different?

1a.

> Anne likes *tea* but she doesn't like *coffee*.
>
> a) folk music / pop music
> b) walking/swimming
> c) cats/dogs
> ... ...

1b.

> Say *true* sentences about yourself:
>   I like tea.
> *or* I don't like tea.
>
> What about: a) coffee?
>   b) pop music?
>   c) cats?
>   ...

Exercise 1a procedure: Teachers make sentences from the prompts, e.g. Anne likes folk music but she doesn't like pop music. If you like, give a few more prompts orally.

Exercise 1b procedure: Teachers make true sentences, using either 'I like' or 'I don't like'. Get responses from several different teachers about each topic. If you like, continue with other topics.

Comment: 1a is completely mechanical – it can be done without thinking or understanding, e.g. what pop music is. It is also quite meaningless, and so very uninteresting to do.

2a.

> You are a stranger. Ask about places in the town.
>
> a café:
> Is there a café near here?
>
> a) a grocer's shop
> b) a cinema
> c) a fruit stall
> ...

2b.

> You are a stranger. Ask about places in the town.
>
> You want to see a film:
> Is there a cinema near here?
>
> a) You want to buy some fruit.
> b) You want to post a letter.
> c) You want to spend the night here.
> ...

Exercise 2a procedure: Give the prompts orally – teachers respond with a question. If you like, continue with other shops or public buildings.

Exercise 2b procedure: Read out each situation; teachers give

responses. More than one response is possible, so encourage teachers
to think of different responses, e.g.:
a) Is there a fruit stall / a shop / a market near here?
b) Is there a post office / a post box near here?
c) Is there a hotel / a youth hostel near here?
Comment: 2a sounds natural and gives useful basic practice of the
structure. But it is mechanical – students could ask the questions
correctly without any idea what they were asking. In 2b, students must
understand the situations and must think about what to ask. So it is
more meaningful, but also more difficult than 2a as students have to
provide the names of places themselves.

3a.

> 'Where are you going?'
> 'I'm going to the
> station.'
>
> a) cinema
> b) zoo
> c) river
> . . .

3b.

> 'Where are you going?'
> 'I'm going to the
> station.'
> 'Why?'
> 'Because (I want to buy
> a train ticket).'
>
> a) cinema
> b) zoo
> c) river
> . . .

Exercise 3a procedure: Ask the question and give a different prompt
word each time, e.g.:
T: Where are you going? cinema
S: I'm going to the cinema.
Exercise 3b procedure: Ask the questions, teachers answer and give a
reason. They can give any reason they like that makes sense (e.g.
cinema: Because there's a good film on; Because I want to see a film;
Because I've got nothing else to do).
Comment: 3a is mechanical; the question is always the same and to
answer the student merely fits the prompt into the sentence. In 3b, the
exercise becomes meaningful because students have to add a reason,
so they must understand what they are saying. It is also of course a
freer exercise, so it could be done after 3a.

3. To summarise, point out that the exercises show three possible ways
    of making practice more meaningful:
    – By getting students to say *real* things about themselves.
    – By giving situations which *imply* the structure, but leave the
      students to decide exactly what to say.

– By letting them add something of their own.

As an extension to this activity, you could look at exercises in the teachers' own textbooks. If many of the exercises are mechanical, discuss how they could be made more meaningful.

Organising practice in class

▶ Workbook Activity 3 ◀

1. Divide the teachers into pairs or groups. Ask them to discuss the lesson in the Teacher's Workbook, and decide how it could be improved.

    Here is an exercise practising questions and answers with 'can'.

Can you . . . swim? drive a car? ride a horse?	Yes, I can.
speak English? stand on your head? sing? fly?	No, I can't.

    Here is a possible lesson plan:
    – Ask the students to close their books. Read out the questions and answers, and ask the students to repeat them.
    – Ask the questions, and the students reply 'Yes, I can' or 'No, I can't'.
    – Then the students open their books. Students read out questions in turn, and other students answer.

    Comment on the lesson plan. What improvements would you suggest?

2. When most groups have finished, discuss the lesson plan together. Make these suggestions yourself:
    – Getting the class to repeat all the questions and answers makes the practice very mechanical, and is unnecessary (it might be worth repeating just one example). Students would 'learn' the questions much better by *listening* and *responding* to them.
    – In the second stage of the practice, the teacher should insist that students give *true* answers, to make the activity meaningful.
    – Asking students to read the questions is again a very mechanical activity, and gives practice in reading aloud, not in asking questions

orally. Instead, the students could keep their books closed and try to *remember* the questions. (The teacher could prompt them if necessary, e.g. T: fly   S1: Can you fly?   S2: No, I can't.)

– At the end, the teacher could let students think of their own questions using 'Can you . . .?' to ask each other. This would make the activity much more interesting.

Suggest this possible lesson plan for the activity:

i)   Write example on the board. Students repeat it.

ii)   Ask questions. Students give real answers.

iii) Give prompts. Students ask each other questions.

iv) Students make up their own questions.

Discuss this plan, and encourage comments and suggestions from the teachers.

3. Give a demonstration to show how the practice might be done. Try to include any of the teachers' suggestions.

i)   Write on the board:
      Can you swim? Yes, I can.
                           No, I can't.
      Get students to repeat the question and answers.

ii)   T: Now, give me *true* answers. Can you swim?
      S1: Yes, I can.
      T: What about you? Can you swim?
      S2: No, I can't. (*and so on, with a few more students*)
      T: Now, listen. Can you drive a car? Can you drive a car?
      S3: No, I can't. (*and so on*)

iii) T: Now, can you remember the questions? Amir, ask Samir. Sing.
      S: Can you sing?
      S: Yes, I can. (*and so on*)

iv) T: Now, can you ask your own questions? Yes?
      S: Can you ride a bicycle?
      T: Good. Who can answer? Rashid?
      S. Yes, I can. (*and so on*)

After your demonstration, discuss the technique with the teachers. Point out that:

– During the third and fourth stages of the practice, the teacher says as little as possible, and lets the students take over the activity.

– To get students to ask questions it is best to give short prompts which do not 'give away' the question, e.g. 'Ask Samir. Car.' not 'Ask Samir if he can drive a car'.

– The technique you have shown can be used for any practice of questions and answers or for short dialogues. After this, the teacher could divide the whole class into pairs to ask and answer at the same time (see Unit 12: Pairwork and groupwork).

FREE ORAL PRACTICE

► Workbook Activity 4 ◄

1. Most of the exercises in this unit have been examples of *controlled* practice; students use a structure to make sentences or questions, but have only a limited choice about what to say. If possible, practice of this kind should be followed by a *freer* activity, which gives students the chance to use the structure to express their own ideas or to talk about their own experiences. Two kinds of topics are useful for free oral practice:
   - We can get students to talk about *real life* (themselves, their friends, things in the world).
   - We can ask students to *imagine* a situation which is not real.
   Ask the teachers to look at the topics in the Teacher's Workbook. They could all be used for free practice using the structure 'going to': in the first, students talk about real life; in the second, they imagine a situation; and in the third, they imagine events based on a picture.

   1. Talk about *one* of these topics.
      - What are you going to do at the weekend? What about your family and friends?
      - Choose one person in the class. Imagine it is his/her birthday soon. Everyone is going to give a present. Say what present you are going to give, and why.
      - Look at the picture of the farmers on page 66. Imagine what they are each going to do when they arrive home.

   2. Could you use this activity in your own class? How would you organise it?

2. Divide the teachers into either three or six groups, and give each group *one* of the topics to talk about. Ask one teacher in each group not to join in the activity, but to *observe* it. He or she should:
   - judge how *interesting* it is, by noticing how involved the teachers become;
   - judge how *productive* it is, by counting how many sentences teachers make using 'going to'.

3. When the groups have finished, ask each 'observer' to report on how successful they thought the activity was.

   Then discuss how teachers would organise each activity in their own classes. Get teachers to give their own ideas. They may think an activity is unsuitable for their students; if so, ask them to suggest similar activities that would be more suitable.

   Make these suggestions yourself:

   i)   Activities like these can be done with quite a low level class – students only have to make simple sentences with 'going to'. It would be important to *introduce* the activity very carefully, giving instructions in the students' own language and giving a few examples.

   ii) With a large class, it may be necessary to make the activity more *highly organised*, rather than done freely in groups. For example:
        – The teacher could ask students in turn to give sentences, and then get students to ask each other.
        – The teacher could give a few minutes preparation time – students work alone or in pairs and think of sentences they could say. Then the teacher asks students to give their sentences.

   iii) The aim of the activity is to get students to talk as much as possible. So the teacher should try to 'prompt' rather than ask full questions (e.g. 'What about you?', 'And you?', 'Lucie, ask Françoise'): the less the teacher says, the more chance students have to speak. If you like, demonstrate this, e.g.:

   T: Marie, what are you going to give?
   S: I'm going to give her a book – because she likes reading.
   T: Christina, what about you?
   S: I'm going to give her flowers.
   T: Why?
   S: Because it's spring.
   T: Lucie, ask Françoise.
   S: Françoise, what are you going to give?
   T: I'm going to give her some money – then she can buy a present for herself. (*and so on*)

LESSON PREPARATION

▶ Workbook Activity 5 ◀

Either organise the preparation during the training session, with teachers working together in pairs or groups, or let teachers prepare in their own time after the session.

FURTHER READING

D. Byrne (1986 2nd edition) *Teaching Oral English* (Chapters 5 and 6), Longman. Gives practical suggestions for controlled and freer practice.

J. Harmer (1983) *The Practice of English Language Teaching* (Chapter 7), Longman. Discusses techniques for practice and gives examples of exercises.

7 Using visual aids

Aims of this unit
- To make teachers familiar with a range of simple visual aids.
- To show teachers how to make their own visual aids.
- To show teachers how to use visual aids effectively.

This unit shows teachers how to incorporate visual aids into their normal classroom teaching; it concentrates on visual aids that are easy and cheap to make using readily available materials.

This unit gives a general introduction to making and using visual aids. Particular uses of visual aids are dealt with more fully in other units:
- using blackboard drawings, including 'stick figures', in Unit 4: Using the blackboard;
- using wordcards, in Unit 9: Teaching basic reading;
- using pictures for discussion, in Unit 14: Eliciting.

Preparation
Before the training session, you will need to make your own visual aids for use in demonstrations. They can be copied from the drawings on pages 85, 87, 89 and 90. You will need:
- A set of *five flashcards* for Activity 3. Copy these onto separate pieces of card.
- *Three charts* for Activity 4. Copy these onto large sheets of paper or card.

For showing how to display charts you will also need two nails, a piece of string long enough to go across the blackboard, and two or three clothes pegs.

In the session, teachers will practise making their own flashcards and charts. For these activities you will need to provide:
- A good supply of typing or duplicating paper.
- One black felt-tip pen for each group of teachers.

INTRODUCTION

1. Begin by establishing what is meant by 'visual aids' (pictures, objects, things for the students to look at), and talk about why they are important:

- Showing visuals focusses attention on meaning, and helps to make the language used in the class more real and alive.
- Having something to look at keeps the students' attention, and makes the class more interesting.
- Visuals can be used at any stage of the lesson – to help in presenting new language or introducing a topic, as part of language practice, and when reviewing language that has been presented earlier. Good visual aids are not just used once, but again and again, and can be shared by different teachers.

▶ **Workbook Activity 1** ◀

2. Ask teachers to look at the list of visual aids in the Teacher's Workbook. Give time for them to identify those they are familiar with. Then go through the list, saying a little more about each, and encouraging teachers to talk about their own experience of using the ones they know.

> 1. Which of these visual aids have you used in your own teaching?
> 2. How exactly have you used them?

a) Yourself	
b) The blackboard	
c) Real objects	
d) Flashcards	
e) Pictures and charts	
f) Others	

a) *The teachers themselves:* The teacher can use gestures, facial expressions, and actions to help show the meaning of words and to illustrate situations. (This is dealt with in Unit 1: Presenting vocabulary.)

b) *The blackboard:* The teacher or students can use it to draw pictures, diagrams, maps, etc. (This is dealt with in Unit 4: Using the blackboard.)

c) *Real objects* (sometimes called 'realia'): The teacher can use things in the classroom and bring things into the class – food, clothes, containers, household objects, etc.

d) *Flashcards:* cards with single pictures which can be held up by the teacher. They can be used for presenting and practising new words and structures, and for revision. (Quickly show the flashcards you will use for Activity 3.) The teacher can draw a picture on the flashcard, or stick on a picture from a magazine; flashcards can also be used to show words or numbers.

e) *Charts:* larger sheets of card or paper with writing, pictures or diagrams, used for more extended presentation or practice. They would usually be displayed on the wall or blackboard. (Quickly show one of the charts you will use for Activity 4.)

[This unit focusses on using *real objects, flashcards* and *charts*. Of course there are many other visual aids which are not dealt with here. Some of them require special preparation or equipment, e.g. flannelboard, magnetboard, slides, filmstrip, coloured rods. Talk about them only if teachers mention them themselves.]

USING REAL OBJECTS

► Workbook Activity 2 ◄

1. Real objects are in many ways the easiest kind of visual aid to use in class, as they need no special preparation or materials. Simple objects can be used not only for teaching vocabulary but also as prompts to practise structures and develop situations. To make this clear, give a few examples of how the packet of tea shown in Workbook Activity 2 might be used:
   - To teach the words 'tea' and 'packet' (contrasted with other containers, e.g. a bag of sugar, a tin of orange juice).
   - To develop a description of the process of making tea: 'First you open the packet, then you put some tea in the pot . . .' (The teacher could also bring a pot, a spoon, etc.)
   - As part of a shopping dialogue, asking about price: 'How much is a packet of tea?' '50 piastres', etc.
   - To develop an imaginative dialogue, practising 'lend', e.g.:
     S1: Could you lend me some tea?
     S2: Yes, of course. What do you want it for?
     S1: My relatives have come to visit me.

2. Ask the teachers to look at the picture in the Teacher's Workbook and discuss how the objects could be used.

≫→

Prepositions of place: in, on, beside, between, etc.

Present perfect tense (have just . . . . -ed)

Is there . . .? Are there . . .?

X is made of . . .

Expressions of colour, shape, size.

Imagine that you have these real objects available in your classroom. Which ones could you use to practise the language in the circles?

Possible answers:

Prepositions of place: The box and other objects, e.g. 'The pen is in the box', 'The apple is on the box'.

X is made of . . .: All the manufactured objects, e.g. 'The bag is made of leather', 'The telephone is made of plastic'.

Present perfect tense: Teacher holds up an object, students imagine what he or she has just done, e.g. Soap: 'You've just had a shower', Shoe box: 'You've just bought some shoes'.

Is there? Are there? A guessing game. Teacher puts objects in the box or the bag. Students guess: 'Is there an orange in the box?' etc.

Colour, shape, size: All the objects, e.g. 'The bicycle pump is long, thin and round. It's longer than the pen', etc.

3. As a possible extension to this activity, divide the teachers into pairs, and ask them to choose *one* object. They should think of as many activities as they can for which they could use the object.

USING FLASHCARDS

▶ **Workbook Activity 3** ◀

1. Ask the teachers to look at the sets of flashcards in the Teacher's Workbook, and hold up the ones you have made to show what they really look like. Discuss what language items could be practised using each set, and get as many suggestions from the teachers as you can.

Establish that they can be used not only to practise words ('What's this? It's a car'), but also as prompts for practising structures:

    Sentences: e.g. I haven't got a car.
                    I often go swimming.
    Questions: e.g. Do you like fishing?
                    Have you ever travelled by plane?
    Dialogues: e.g. – What did you do yesterday?
                    – I went swimming.

    A. Here are two sets of flashcards. What language could you practise using each set?

2. Demonstrate how the second set of flashcards could be used to practise the past tense. Ask teachers to imagine that the language has already been presented and now you are moving to the practice stage.
   i)   Write on the board:
         What did you do yesterday?
       Show the first card only, and drill these sentences:
         What did you do yesterday?
         I went swimming.
       First the class repeats the question and answer, then you ask and they answer.
   ii) Show the other cards in turn, and ask 'What did you do yesterday?' Choose *one* teacher to answer each time. Go through all the cards twice, showing them in random order.
   iii) Hold up different cards in turn without saying anything, and indicate pairs of teachers to ask and answer.

After your demonstration, discuss the value of using flashcards for this kind of practice. Point out that when you use a picture, students see what meaning to express but have to find the words themselves; this focusses their attention on meaning and prevents the activity from being completely mechanical.

3. Ask teachers to look at the dialogues in part B of the Teacher's Workbook Activity.

> B. Think of four other objects that could replace 'broom' or 'knife' in the dialogues below.

> Copy the pictures of the broom and the knife onto flashcards. Then make four more flashcards showing the other objects.

If necessary, show how different dialogues could be developed by replacing 'broom' and 'knife' with other words, e.g.:
A: Could you lend me a pair of scissors?
B: Yes, of course. What do you want them for?
A: I want to make some flashcards.

Divide the teachers into groups, and give each group six sheets of typing or duplicating paper and a felt-tip pen. Ask them to think of four other objects that could be used instead of 'broom' in the dialogue. They should then:
i) Copy the pictures of the broom and the knife onto two of the sheets of paper, drawing them much larger.
ii) Draw pictures of the other four objects on the remaining sheets.
Go from group to group, giving help where necessary. Check that their drawings are recognisable and that they are large and clear enough.

4. Ask one or two teachers to demonstrate using their flashcards to practise the dialogues. The rest of the teachers should act as a class.

5. Finally, talk about how to make good flashcards. Make these points:
   - They should be large enough – at least 20 × 14 cm. (half a piece of typing paper).
   - Pictures can be drawn, using a thick pen so that they are clear, or they can be cut from a magazine; pictures from magazines are often more interesting to look at, but it is difficult to find pictures which are the right size and which are simple enough.
   - If possible, flashcards should be made on pieces of white card – then they can be kept and used again.

USING CHARTS

Flashcards are useful for showing very simple pictures, usually of a single object or action. But often teachers want to display more complex visual information, e.g. a series of pictures telling a story, a table of different verb forms, or a diagram showing how a machine works. The most convenient way of showing such information is on a *chart* (sometimes called a 'wallchart' or a 'wall picture') – a large sheet of paper or card which the teacher can either hold up for the class to see or display on the wall or the blackboard.

Charts for language practice

1. Show Chart one as an example of a simple picture chart which can be used for practice at an elementary level.

Chart one

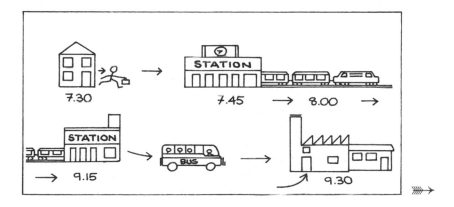

Discuss what verb tenses might be practised using this chart:
- *Present simple tense:* 'Every day Juan leaves home at half past seven . . .'
- *Past simple tense:* 'Yesterday, Juan left home at half past seven . . .'
- *Present simple questions and answers:* 'What time does the man leave home?' 'At half past seven.'
- *Present continuous tense:* 'What's the time now?' 'Half past seven.' 'What's the man doing?' 'He's leaving home and going to the station.'

2. Demonstrate how to use the chart to practise the present simple tense.
   i) Point to different parts of the chart, and ask questions:
       What does he do at half past seven? (*He leaves home.*)
       Then what happens? (*He walks to the station.*)
       etc.
   ii) Get teachers to go through the events again, using complete sentences. This time, prompt them by pointing to the pictures, but do not ask questions.

3. Discuss the advantages of showing these pictures on a chart, rather than drawing them on the blackboard. Establish that:
   - The teacher does not have to spend time in the lesson drawing on the blackboard.
   - As the chart is prepared in advance, it is possible to draw the pictures more carefully, and also to make them more attractive (e.g. by using colour).
   - The chart can be kept and used again with the same class (e.g. for review, or to practise a different tense), or used with other classes and by other teachers.

Using charts with a reading text

▶ **Workbook Activity 4** ◀

Charts can also be used with a reading text. The teacher can display some of the information from the text in the form of pictures, diagrams or tables, to make it clearer and more interesting.

1. Divide the teachers into pairs or groups. Ask them to look at reading text A in the Teacher's Workbook and discuss how the information in it could be displayed through pictures or diagrams on a chart. (They should of course imagine that there are no illustrations in the

textbook.) If you like, distribute sheets of paper and ask teachers to design a rough version of the chart.

> Can you think of pictures or diagrams which would make these texts clearer and more interesting?
> Design a *chart* to accompany each text.

A.

> One day, Paula and Richard decided to make a kite. First they went out and found two straight sticks of the same length. They brought them back home and tied them with a piece of string into the shape of a cross. Then they took some more string and used it to tie the four ends of the sticks together. Then, they spread some brightly coloured paper over the frame and glued it around the string. They stuck a tail made of paper to one of the corners, and tied a long string to the centre of the kite. On the next windy day, they took the kite to a hill near their house and flew it.

(based on a text from *Living English* Book 3: H. M. Abdoul-Fetouh et al.)

2. When most groups have finished, discuss their ideas together, and ask them to show any drawings they have made. Then show your own version (Chart two). Emphasise that it is only one possibility, and is not intended as a 'correct answer'.

Chart two

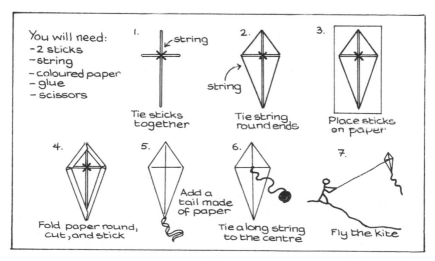

Discuss how the chart might be used:
- It could be shown before students read the text, as a way of presenting the main ideas and language.
- It could be on display while the students read, to help them understand the text.
- It could be used for practice after reading the text, or for review in a later lesson, e.g. the teacher could cover the words on the chart and ask students to explain how to make a kite.

3. Divide teachers into their groups again, and ask them to think of a suitable chart to accompany reading text B.

B.

> In order to stay healthy it is important to have a balanced diet – in other words, food that contains something from each of the three main groups of food. These groups are protein, carbohydrate, and fat.
>
> Proteins are very important for building our bodies; they help us to build new cells as old ones die. Meat and dairy products are major sources of protein, but not the only ones – we can also get protein from fish, eggs and beans.
>
> Carbohydrate and fat are important to enable us to store energy – they provide fuel for the body. Carbohydrates are found in sugar, and in cereals such as rice, maize and wheat. Fats are found in vegetable oil, in butter, and in nuts.
>
> Our body also needs minerals, such as iron and calcium, and vitamins. Fish, vegetables and milk contain most of the minerals we need. Vitamins are found in fresh vegetables and fruit.

(based on a text from *Living English* Book 3: H. M. Abdoul-Fetouh et al.)

4. Discuss possible ideas together, and again show your own version (Chart three).

Chart three

A Balanced Diet	
PROTEIN	meat, dairy products, fish, eggs, beans
CARBOHYDRATE	sugar, cereals
FAT	oil, butter, nuts
MINERALS	fish, vegetables, milk
VITAMINS	fresh vegetables, fruit

Discuss how the chart might be used:
- It could be used before students read the text, in order to check the class's knowledge (they should of course already know the facts in their own language). The teacher could cover the right-hand column, leaving only the names of the groups visible, and ask students to think of examples in each group.
- The teacher could give students a blank table (on pieces of paper) to complete as they read the text. Then he or she could show the chart afterwards as the correct answer.
- It could be used later for review – the teacher could cover the chart, uncovering it line by line as students give the information.

5. As a possible extension to the activity, ask teachers to look at the reading texts in their own textbook, and discuss what charts could be made to accompany them.

[*Note:* If the textbook used by the teachers is up-to-date and has good illustrations, there may be no need for teachers to make charts. However, it may still be worthwhile to copy some visual material from the book onto charts, so that the teacher can introduce the lesson in a more interesting way, or review earlier lessons, or simply to make a change of activity. If the textbook lacks good visual material, charts will be a very important way of making lessons more interesting.]

Displaying charts

Finally, talk about different ways of displaying charts in class and the advantages and disadvantages of each. Discuss these possibilities:
- The teacher can hold the chart up.
- Two students can come out to the front and hold the chart.
- The teacher can pin the chart to a wall or to the blackboard.
- The teacher can hang the chart from a piece of string tied across the blackboard. Show how this can be done, using two nails, string and clothes pegs:

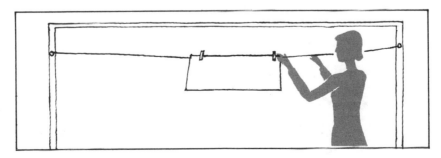

LESSON PREPARATION

► Workbook Activity 5 ◄

Either organise the preparation during the training session, with teachers working in pairs or groups, or let teachers prepare in their own time after the session. Make sure that teachers can obtain any materials necessary for their preparation (e.g. paper, card, pens).

FURTHER READING

A. Wright (1976) *Visual Materials for the Language Teacher*, Longman. A clear and detailed account of all kinds of visual aids, how to prepare them and how to use them.

J. McAlpin (1980) *The Magazine Picture Library*, Heinemann. Suggestions for collecting magazine pictures for use in class.

(For books on blackboard drawing, see Unit 4: Using the blackboard.)

A. Wright (1984) *A Thousand Pictures for Teachers to Copy*, Collins. A sourcebook of simple drawings and pictures.

8 Planning a lesson

Aims of this unit
- To make teachers aware of the aims and language content of the lessons they teach.
- To help teachers to distinguish the various stages of a lesson, and to see the relationship between them.
- To show teachers how to make a simple lesson plan.

This unit shows how individual techniques and activities fit into the lesson as a whole. It assumes that teachers are already familiar with basic techniques for presentation, practice and using texts. These are dealt with in Unit 1: Presenting vocabulary, Unit 3: Presenting structures, Unit 5: Using a reading text and Unit 6: Practising structures.

How this unit is used will depend on the kind of textbook that teachers are using, and especially on the teacher's notes accompanying the book. If the teacher's book gives clear and detailed notes on each lesson, then the focus of this unit should be on knowing what it contains and using it effectively. If the teacher's book is inadequate, or if there is no teacher's book available, this unit should be used to help teachers to plan their own lessons.

[*Note:* If possible, teachers should bring copies of their textbook and teacher's notes to the training session.]

USING THE TEACHER'S NOTES

▶ Workbook Activity 1 ◀

Establish that there are four main things that a teacher needs to know *before* going into the class to teach a lesson:
- The *aim* of the lesson.
- What new *language* the lesson contains.
- The main *stages* of the lesson (i.e. how it divides into different activities).
- What to *do* at each stage.
If there is a teacher's book, it may give information about some or all of these things. Ask teachers to look at the notes for one lesson in their

teacher's book (if possible, a lesson which they have taught recently) and discuss the questions in the Teacher's Workbook.

Does your textbook have teacher's notes?
If so, look at the notes for one lesson.

Do the notes clearly tell you:

	Yes	No
a) the aims of the lesson?		
b) what language is taught in the lesson?		
c) the main stages of the lesson?		
d) how to teach the lesson?		

Make these points:
- If the teacher's book does not give enough information, it is important for teachers to decide the answers to these questions themselves – in other words, to make their own plan for the lesson.
- If the teacher's book does give adequate information, teachers should still decide for themselves how best to teach the lesson. They should use the teacher's book as a *guide* and a source of good ideas, not as a set of instructions that must be followed precisely.

AIMS AND CONTENT OF THE LESSON

Aims of the lesson

▶ Workbook Activity 2 ◀

It is always important to see what the general aim of the lesson is. A lesson may focus on:
- A particular *topic* – so the aim of the lesson may be 'To learn the names of colours' or 'To practise language for buying clothes'.
- A particular *structure* – so the aim of the lesson may be 'To describe actions using the present continuous tense' or 'To practise "going to" for talking about future plans'.
- A *skill* – so the aim of the lesson may be 'To understand instructions for using a machine' or 'To express opinions freely in English about marriage'.

1. Ask teachers to look at the example of a lesson in the Teacher's Workbook and discuss what its aim seems to be.

A. Here is part of a first year lesson. Students ask and answer
   questions from the table, then ask other questions.

When do you When does your friend	get up? eat breakfast? wash your face? go to school? finish school? go to bed? sleep?	In the morning. In the afternoon. In the evening. At night.
When do you clean your teeth? meet your friends? play games? learn English?		

(adapted from *Welcome to English* Book 1: M. Bates and J. Higgens)

What seems to be the *aim* of the lesson?

2. Now ask teachers to look at part B of the Activity.

    B. Three different teachers are about to teach the lesson. Compare
       their comments.

    'What are you going to teach today?'

Teacher A:

We're doing Lesson 15.
It's question and answer practice
using a substitution table.

Teacher B:

We're going to practise
present simple questions with
'When . . .', and time expressions.

Teacher C:

We're going to practise asking
and answering questions using the
present simple, so that students learn
to talk about *everyday* activities and
when they do them.

Which teacher has the clearest idea of the *aim* of the lesson?

95

Discuss the three teachers' comments. Try to bring out these points:
- Teacher A is not thinking of the aim of the lesson at all – he seems to see it just as 'a lesson in the book' that has to be taught.
- Teacher B has thought about what *language* is being taught in the lesson.
- Teacher C has the clearest idea of the aim of the lesson. She is thinking not only what language she will teach, but also what the students will *learn to do* in the lesson.

3. Talk about a lesson which the teachers have taught recently themselves or a lesson in a suitable textbook. Ask them what they think the aim of this lesson was, and what they think the students learnt to do.

Language

It is important for the teacher to know exactly what language will be taught in the lesson. Most lessons introduce either new vocabulary or a new structure, or both. Make these points:
- *New vocabulary:* Not all new words in a lesson are equally important. As part of the preparation for the lesson, the teacher should decide which words need to be practised, and which only need to be briefly mentioned.
- *Structures:* If a new structure is introduced in the lesson, it will need to be presented carefully and practised. The teacher should also be aware of any structures which are practised in the lesson, but which were introduced in earlier lessons.

Refer again to the lesson in the textbook which you discussed in number 3 above. Ask the teachers:
- What new words were introduced?
  Which were the most important?
- What new structures were there?
  What other structures were practised?

Skills

The teacher needs to be aware of what *skills* will be developed in the lesson: speaking, listening, reading or writing. If possible, the lesson should include practice of more than one skill – this will increase the variety and interest of the lesson.

Refer again to the lesson in the textbook discussed in number 3 above. Ask the teachers:
- What skills were developed in it?
- Which skill was practised most?

STAGES OF THE LESSON

1. Explain that any lesson we teach naturally divides into different *stages* of activity: for example, at one stage in the lesson, the class may be listening to a dialogue; at another stage, the teacher may be explaining new words and writing them on the board; at another stage students may be doing some oral practice. It is much easier to plan the details of a lesson if we think in terms of separate stages rather than trying to think of the lesson as a whole.

   Try to elicit from the teachers some of the stages of a lesson. Focus on the main stages of activity, not on particular activities and techniques (e.g. asking questions on a text). Build up a list of stages on the board, and comment briefly on each one, e.g.:

   Presentation: The teacher presents new words or structures, gives examples, writes them on the board, etc.

   Practice: Students practise using words or structures in a controlled way, e.g. making sentences from prompts, asking and answering questions, giving sentences based on a picture. Practice can be *oral* or *written.*

   Production: Students use language they have learnt to express themselves more freely, e.g. to talk or write about their own lives and interests, to express opinions, to imagine themselves in different situations. Like practice, production can be *oral* or *written.*

   Reading: Students read a text and answer questions or do a simple 'task' (e.g. complete a table).

   Listening: The teacher reads a text or dialogue while students listen and answer questions, or the students listen to a cassette.

   Review: The teacher reviews language learnt in an earlier lesson, to refresh students' memories, or as a preparation for a new presentation.

2. Make these points:
   - A single lesson would not, of course, normally include all these stages.
   - The stages are in *no fixed order.* Usually teachers present new language, then do some practice, then get students to use language more freely. But a teacher might, for example, present a structure, practise it quickly, then present and practise something else before going on to a final production activity – each stage could occur several times in a single lesson.
   - The stages *overlap.* For example, reading a text might be part of the presentation or it might be a quite separate activity; answering questions on a text is part of reading but also gives students oral

practice. When we talk about 'stages' of a lesson, we are thinking of the *main focus* of the activity.

[*Note:* The stages listed here are only the most important ones; there are other activities that could form part of a lesson. If you like, give some examples, e.g. setting and marking homework, introducing the lesson (chatting to students, introducing a topic), giving a test.]

▶ Workbook Activity 3 ◀

3. Ask teachers to read the first description in Workbook Activity 3 and compare it with the list of lesson stages in the box. Ask them to mark the end of each stage with a line /.

   1. Two teachers describe lessons they gave. For the first one, match the description with the lesson stages in the box.

      'Well, first we talked a bit about deserts, and what it's like to travel across a desert. Then we read a text about an explorer who's crossed every desert in the world, and the students answered questions on it. In the text, there were several examples of the present perfect tense; I wrote some of these on the board, and I gave a few more examples orally. Then we did a grammar exercise in the textbook. After that, I asked students to make up their own questions using "Have you ever . . .?", to ask each other.'

1.	Introduction.
2.	Reading.
3.	Presentation.
4.	Practice.
5.	Production.

Now ask teachers to read the second description, and write the five stages in the box. The suggested answer is filled in below.

   2. Now write the stages of this teacher's lesson in the box.

      'First we reviewed words for clothes, which the students had learnt last week, and then I taught them adjectives to describe materials (woollen, cotton, leather, etc.), and wrote them on the board. Then we looked at some pictures of people in the textbook, and they made sentences about them ("She's wearing

1.	*Review*
2.	*Presentation*
3.	*Oral practice*
4.	*Written production*

a green cotton dress"). Then I asked them to write a few sentences about themselves, beginning "Last weekend I was wearing . . ." After that we read a text in the book about clothes people wear in different countries.'

> 5. Reading

4. Point out that the *students*, as well as the teacher, need to know the aim of the lesson as a whole and the purpose of each stage. So it is important for the teacher to *introduce* each stage of the lesson.

   Ask teachers to look at the description of the second lesson again. Discuss:
   - what the teacher could say to introduce the lesson, to make the aims clear to the class;
   - what the teacher could say to introduce each new stage of the lesson.

   Possible answers:

   Introducing the whole lesson: 'Today we're going to talk about clothes. We're going to say what clothes people are wearing. Then you're going to write about your own clothes. And if there's time, we'll read something about clothes as well.'

   Introducing each stage:
   1. Do you remember last week's lesson? We learnt some words for clothes. Can you remember them?
   2. Now, let's learn some new words. Here are some clothes. What are they made of? . . .
   3. Let's practise talking about clothes. Look at the picture on page 93.
   4. Now, I want you to write about yourselves, about your own clothes. What were you wearing last weekend? Do you remember?
   5. Now, we're going to read about other countries. First, look – here are three countries (writing on board). Where are they? . . .

WRITING A LESSON PLAN

▶ Workbook Activity 4 ◀

1. Ask teachers to look at the lesson plan in the Teacher's Workbook. Discuss which parts the teacher might have added himself, and encourage teachers to comment on them.

Here is the lesson plan the teacher made for the second lesson in Activity 3. The teacher's notes accompanying the textbook only gave the most basic information, so he added several ideas of his own. Which parts do you think he added himself? How do they improve the lesson?

LESSON 16

<u>Aim</u> To practise talking about clothes, materials + colours.
<u>New vocab</u>. Adjectives: woollen, leather, cotton, nylon, plastic.
<u>Structures</u> Present continuous: ... is wearing... (revision).

1. <u>Review</u> Show pictures of clothes. Ss give words: coat, hat, shirt, trousers, etc.

2. <u>Presentation</u> Show objects made of wool, leather, plastic, etc. Present new adjectives. Write them on the board.

3. <u>Practice</u> 1) p.93 Ss look at pictures and make sentences e.g. 'She's wearing a green cotton dress'.
   2) Pairwork. A: What's she wearing?
      B: She's wearing a green cotton dress.

4. <u>Writing</u> 1) Write on board : ⌐Last week-end I was wearing...'⌐
   Ss write sentences about themselves.
   2) Collect about 10 students' papers. Read them out. Others guess who wrote them!

5. <u>Reading</u> 1) Write on board: ⌐Peru   Ask: Where are they?
                                      Sudan   What's the climate like?
                                      Pakistan⌐   What do people wear there?
   2) Ss read text p. 94 silently, and find answers to guiding questions.
   3) Ask and answer questions p. 94.

---

2. Then discuss the value of writing a lesson plan of this kind. Emphasise that it should not be written just for the benefit of the inspector or head teacher; its main purpose should be to help the teacher. Try to bring out these points:

– Writing a lesson plan helps teachers to *prepare* the lesson; it helps them decide exactly what they will do and how they will do it.
– Teachers can look at the lesson plan again *after* the lesson, and use it to *evaluate* what happened. (Did they do what they planned to do? Was each stage successful?)
– They can keep the lesson plan and use it again next year.

Emphasise that there is no 'correct' way to write a lesson plan, although a good lesson plan should give a clear picture of what the teacher intends to do in the lesson. The plan in the Teacher's Workbook is intended as an example of how a lesson plan can include some of the features discussed in this unit, but not necessarily as the 'best' way to write a plan.

3. As a possible extension to this activity, ask teachers to look at the lesson in the textbook which you used for discussion earlier in this unit. Discuss the lesson together, and try to build up a 'collective' lesson plan on the board. As far as possible, let the ideas come from the teachers.

[*Note:* If the teacher's book already gives detailed instructions, encourage teachers to think of alternative ways of approaching the lesson and ideas of their own which they could add to the teacher's notes.]

LESSON PREPARATION

▶ **Workbook Activity 5** ◀

Either organise the preparation during the training session, with teachers working together in pairs or groups, or let teachers prepare in their own time after the session.

FURTHER READING

P. Hubbard et al. (1983) *A Training Course for TEFL* (Chapter 5: Planning and preparation), Oxford University Press. A detailed analysis of the language content of a lesson; designed to help teachers evaluate and supplement the textbook.

A. Matthews et al. (ed.) (1985) *At the Chalkface* (pp. 5–18), Edward Arnold. A practical account of the main stages of an oral lesson.

J. Harmer (1983) *The Practice of English Language Teaching* (Chapter 11: Planning), Longman. A general description of the principles behind lesson planning.

9 Teaching basic reading

Aims of this unit
- To make teachers more aware of what is involved in learning to read an unfamiliar script.
- To introduce teachers to simple techniques for developing reading skills at an elementary level.

This unit is concerned with reading at an elementary level and deals with the problems faced by students for whom the English writing system is unfamiliar, and who have difficulty recognising words in their written form. Reading skills at a more advanced level are dealt with in Unit 5: Using a reading text and Unit 15: Reading activities.

Preparation
For the demonstration of word recognition techniques following Activity 2 you will need to make two sets of wordcards.

LEARNING TO READ

▶ Workbook Activity 1 ◀

1. One of the problems of helping beginners to read is that it is very difficult to imagine oneself in the position of the learner. In the first activity in this unit, teachers practise reading English written in an invented script (called 'Newscript'); this puts them in a similar position to learners who are just beginning to read words which they already know in their spoken form. The purpose of this activity is to enable teachers to experience some of the problems faced by readers at an elementary level, and to give them insight into the reading process itself.

2. Ask teachers to look at the exercises in the Teacher's Workbook, and explain the purpose of the activity. Let teachers work through the first three exercises on their own. Stop after each exercise and check the answers together.

1. Here are some English words written in Newscript:

   school   2ɣλ|

   class   ⱶ|52

   student   2l,λscɣl

   teacher   l;ℙc↘

   Here are the words in a different order. Can you recognise them?

   2l,λscɣl

   2ɣλ|

   l;ℙc↘

   ⱶ|52

Now cover the page down to this line.

2. Match the Newscript with the English words.

2ɣλ|	student ....
ⱶ|52	teacher ....
l;ℙc↘	class ....
2l,λscɣl	school ....

   Write the Newscript words in the correct place.

Now cover the page down to this line.

3. Read this text.

   In our town, there are only two **2ɣλ|2** . This is not enough for so many people, so they are very crowded. In my **2ɣλ|** there are 1000 **2l,λscɣl2**, and only 25 **l;ℙc↘2** . There are 50 **2l,λscɣl2** in my **ⱶ|52** . In some **ⱶ|52 2** there are even more.

Now do Exercise 4. Follow this procedure:

i) Ask teachers to identify the words 'class', 'teacher' and 'students' in the text.

ii) Read the text aloud and ask teachers to listen and try to follow it:
In this class there are only 30 students. The students are sitting in rows and the teacher is writing on the blackboard.

iii) Ask teachers to read through the text quietly to themselves, trying to follow it word by word.

iv) Discuss the questions together.
Answers: '-ing' = ⊤ȣ; 'the' = ℓ; ȣ = b.

4. Find these words in the text below.
class   teacher   students

Now follow the text while the teacher reads. Then answer these questions.
– How are *-ing* and *the* written in Newscript?
– What is this letter? ȣ

3. After doing the exercises, discuss them with the teachers. Focus on these points:
– How much do teachers feel they have learnt to read Newscript?
– What seemed to be the most useful exercises? Which exercises were less useful?
– If they were really trying to learn Newscript, what would they want to do next?
Try to bring out these general points about reading:
– Reading involves looking at sentences and words, recognising them and understanding them – it is a process of making sense of written language. In the early stages, it may also help to say the words, but this is not an essential part of reading (it would be quite possible to do the exercises in the Teacher's Workbook without saying anything at all). So giving students sentences to look at and understand will give them more useful practice in reading than

asking them to repeat written sentences aloud over and over again or getting them to 'spell out' words.

- As Exercise 3 shows, reading sentences helps students to recognise words, because they can guess them from the context. So it is useful to give students practice in reading and understanding complete sentences even at the earliest stages.
- The main way in which students learn to read is by reading. In Exercise 4, simply by reading the text teachers probably learned to recognise new items they did not know before (e.g. 'are'); it was not necessary to actively teach these. The more practice students have in 'making sense' of written sentences, the better they are able to do it.

RECOGNISING WORDS

Look and say

▶ Workbook Activity 2 ◀

Note: For this activity you will need these wordcards:

a desk	a table	a window	a door

1. Point out that at the very earliest stages of learning to read it is useful to give students practice in recognising words. A simple way to do this is to write words or phrases on pieces of paper or card.

   Ask teachers to look at the technique shown in the Teacher's Workbook. Demonstrate it yourself, using the wordcards you have prepared.

Here is a technique for helping students to recognise words, using wordcards.

1. Hold up the first card ('a table'). Point to the card and say the words. Ask the class to repeat once.
   Do the same with the other cards.

2. Hold up the cards again, in a
    different order. This time, say
    nothing, and pause to give the
    whole class a chance to look at
    the word.

What is the advantage of using wordcards for this activity?

2. After your demonstration, discuss the value of using wordcards. Make
    these points:
    – Using wordcards makes the activity flexible: the teacher can show a
      word and then hide it, or show words in different sequences, or
      show combinations of words together.
    – Using wordcards makes more impact on the class: the teacher can
      make the words clearer and more attractive than they would be on
      the blackboard.
    – Wordcards take a very short time to prepare – they are the easiest
      visual aids to make; and they can be kept and used again.

Point out that this technique is called 'Look and say' because students
look at the word and then say what it is. But the important part of the
exercise is *looking* and *understanding*; saying the word is just a way of
checking that they can recognise the word. (For this reason, there is of
course no point in asking students to keep repeating the word – the
activity should focus on reading, not on speaking.)

Look and do

Give a second demonstration, to show how wordcards can be used to give
practice in reading whole sentences.
Note: For this demonstration you will need two sets of wordcards:

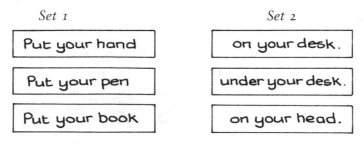

Set 1

Put your hand

Put your pen

Put your book

Set 2

on your desk.

under your desk.

on your head.

i) Hold up one card from set 1 and one card from set 2. Read the complete sentence, pointing to the words ('Look, it says "Put – your – hand – on – your – desk"'). Ask the class to do what it says. Show the other cards in the same way.

ii) Now hold the cards up again, in different combinations. This time *say nothing*. Give all the teachers a chance to read the cards silently and do what they say.

After your demonstration, discuss the technique. Point out that:

– This activity has the same aim as 'Look and say': students have to look at words (this time in sentences) and understand what they mean;

– Using wordcards makes it easy to change different parts of the sentence and so make many different combinations.

Note: Instead of holding the cards themselves, teachers can ask two or more students to come to the front of the class and hold them. This leaves the teacher's arm free to point to the words. Or they can be hung on a piece of string tied across the blackboard:

Simple reading tasks

► Workbook Activity 3 ◄

In the demonstrations, you showed two ways of checking that students have understood what they read: asking them to say words and asking them to perform actions. There are many other ways of checking understanding and giving students a reason to read: for example, we can ask them to match sentences with a picture, match halves of sentences together, or draw a picture. Activities of this kind are called reading *tasks*.

1. Divide the teachers into groups. Ask each group to look at *one* of the reading tasks in the Teacher's Workbook. They should make sure they understand how it works, and then make up a similar activity which

would be suitable for their own students, using different words or sentences. They should decide exactly how they would *organise* the activity in class. Suggest these possibilities:

- It could be written or typed on a worksheet, and copies given to students to do individually in class or for homework. This, of course, depends on the school providing paper and copying facilities (see Unit 21: Using worksheets).
- If it is not too long, it could be written on cards, and used in the same way as the 'Look and do' activity you demonstrated.
- It could be written on the blackboard. This is usually not a good idea unless it can be done beforehand, as it wastes valuable time in the lesson.

Which word is different from the others?

a) doctor   nurse   hospital   ambulance   tractor
b) student   lion   elephant   monkey   bear
c) orange   rice   lemon   mango   banana
d) sleep   walk   jump   kick   run

Choose the correct sentence.

    a) He's kicking a ball.
    b) He's catching a ball.
    c) He's throwing a ball.

Do these things.

a) Point to the window.
b) Give a book to your friend.
c) Raise your left hand.
d) Put your finger to your lips.
e) Put your hands on your head.
f) Stand up, and then sit down again.

Match the two halves of the sentences.

a) I ran to the station   because I was thirsty.
b) The postman knocked on my door because my leg hurt terribly.
c) The doctor gave me an injection because I was late.
d) I bought some lemonade   because there was a letter for me.

Choose *one* of these tasks. Design a similar activity, using words or
structures that would suit your class.

2. When all the groups have finished, ask one teacher from each group to
    show their activity to the others. They should describe how it works,
    and explain how they would organise it in class.

Making wordcards

Show teachers a simple way to make wordcards, using a folded piece of
paper:
i) Take a piece of typing or duplicating paper and fold it in half
    lengthways. A word can be written on each side of it.
ii) On each side, draw a thin 'guide line', then write the word or phrase as
    large and clearly as possible, using a thick felt-tip pen.

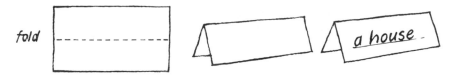

[*Note:* This is the quickest way to make wordcards. It is of course better
to use large pieces of card, which can then be kept and used many times.]

SOUNDS AND SPELLING

1. Make these points:
    – When we read our own language, we do not need to distinguish
      every single letter; if we did, we would only be able to read very
      slowly. If we can read fluently, we do not even read word by word –
      our eyes move rapidly across whole sentences.
    – However, when they begin to read an unfamiliar script, students
      may need to look at individual letters and try to 'match' the word
      with the way it sounds. Children learning to read their own
      language naturally try to read words sound by sound if they do not
      recognise them ('T – a – b – l – . . . Table!').
    – In English, this is quite difficult, because the relationship between
      sound and spelling is very complex. For example; *by, buy, fight, lie,*
      and *island* all have the same sound but different spellings: the letter
      'e' has a different sound in y*e*t, fath*e*r, b*e*, pal*e*.
    – We could not possibly *teach* all these relationships (even for the
      commonest words, there are more than 200 rules), and we do not
      need to; students can gradually become aware of them as they read.

But we can help students by drawing attention to sound/spelling relationships from time to time.

2. Demonstrate a simple technique for focussing students' attention on the sound of words and the way they are written. In your demonstration, you will focus on different spellings of the sound /aɪ/.
   i) Write these words on the board:
       fine   night   cry
       Ask teachers to give you other words which have the same sound. Add them to one of the columns according to how they are spelt, until you have several words in each column, e.g.:
       fine   night   cry
       line   light   fly
       five   sigh   my
       side   high
       ride
   ii) Point to different words, without saying them. Ask teachers to give a sentence using the word, e.g.:
       T: (*point to 'light'*)
       S: Please turn on the light.
   After your demonstration, discuss the technique. Point out that it could be used as a revision activity soon after students have started learning to read. Discuss what other common sound/spelling patterns could be used for the activity.

► Workbook Activity 4 ◄

3. Divide the teachers into groups, and ask them to look at the examples in the Teacher's Workbook. They should:
   − decide what sound/spelling pattern is shown in each one;
   − think of a few more examples of each pattern.

   Look at these examples. What does each one show about English sounds and spelling? Think of more examples of each type.

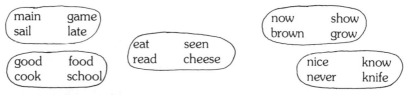

4. As a possible extension to this activity, ask teachers to choose one of the examples and use it to try out the technique you demonstrated. The other teachers should act as a class, and only suggest words that their students would know.

LESSON PREPARATION

▶ **Workbook Activity 5** ◀

Either organise the preparation during the training session, with teachers working together in pairs or groups, or let teachers prepare in their own time after the session.

FURTHER READING

F. Smith (1978) *Reading*, Cambridge University Press. An account of the reading process and what is involved in learning to read. It is mainly concerned with learning to read a first language.

E. Goodacre (1978) 'Methods of teaching reading' in L. Chapman and P. Cherniewska (eds) *Reading: From Process to Practice*, Routledge & Kegan Paul. A survey of methods used to teach children to read English as a first language.

C. Nuttall (1982) *Teaching Reading Skills in a Foreign Language*, Heinemann. Concerned with reading at a more advanced level, but gives a useful account of the process of reading a foreign language.

10 Teaching pronunciation

Aims of this unit
- To make teachers more aware of their students' pronunciation difficulties.
- To show a range of simple techniques for helping students to improve their pronunciation of individual sounds.
- To make teachers more aware of the importance of stress and intonation in spoken English, and to show ways of focussing on stress and intonation in class.

This unit assumes that teachers are familiar with the basic sound system of English (although not necessarily with features of stress and intonation), and that they can pronounce English adequately themselves.

Phonetic symbols (of the International Phonetic Alphabet) are used in the Trainer's Notes to this unit, but not in the Teacher's Workbook; so teachers can use the unit without being familiar with phonetic script. The model for pronunciation is 'received pronunciation', or standard educated English as spoken in southern Britain.

INTRODUCTION

▶ Workbook Activity 1 ◀

Ask the teachers to look at the table in the Teacher's Workbook. Make sure that they understand what is meant by each of the headings (consonant, vowel, etc.), and if necessary give a few examples to make them clear.

Think about your students' pronunciation. What are their main problems?

Consonants	Vowels	Stress	Intonation

Divide teachers into pairs or small groups. Ask them to try to identify the main pronunciation problems that their students have, and to note them down in the table under the appropriate heading. Then discuss them together; ask teachers to tell you the problems they identified, and build up a list on the board, focussing on the *most important* problems.

If teachers find it difficult to think of problems, you could help them by saying sentences with typical pronunciation errors, and ask teachers to identify the errors. Teachers will probably find it most difficult to identify problems of stress and intonation. There is no need to go into detail about these areas now, as you will deal with stress and intonation later in the unit.

Pronunciation problems will of course vary greatly from one country to another. Common problems that are likely to occur:
- Difficulty in pronouncing sounds which do not exist in the student's own language, e.g. for many students, the consonant /ð/ (in 'the') and the vowel /ɜː/ (in 'bird');
- Confusion of similar sounds, e.g. /iː/ and /ɪ/, or /b/ and /p/;
- Use of simple vowels instead of diphthongs, e.g. /iː/ instead of /ɪə/;
- Difficulty in pronouncing consonant clusters, e.g. /desks/, /fɪfθ/;
- Tendency to give all syllables equal stress, and a 'flat' intonation.

INDIVIDUAL SOUNDS

Focussing on a difficult sound

► Workbook Activity 2 ◄

1. Point out that there is normally no need to teach the sounds of English individually; students are able to 'pick up' the sound system of the language by listening to the teacher (or other voices on cassette) and by practising words and structures. However, there may be particular sounds or sound combinations which students find difficult (like those you discussed in Activity 1), or students may simply make mistakes in pronunciation without being aware of it. In such cases, it is useful to focus on the sound or group of sounds which is causing the difficulty.

2. Divide the teachers into pairs or groups. Ask them to look at the table in the Teacher's Workbook, which shows possible steps in teaching a difficult sound. They should decide which steps are most important, and mark their answers in the spaces provided.

A. Imagine that you want to focus on a sound which students find difficult. Which of these steps are most important? Which are not necessary?

Say the sound alone.	∼/
Say the sound in a word.	/
Contrast it with other sounds.	/
Write words on the board.	
Explain how to make the sound.	
Get students to repeat the sound in chorus.	
Get individual students to repeat the sound.	/

3. Discuss the table together. There is no single 'correct' answer, but try to establish these main points:
   - The basic steps are for the teacher to *say* the sound clearly in isolation (so that students can focus on it) and in one or two words; and for students to *repeat* the sound, in chorus and individually.
   - If students confuse two similar sounds, it is obviously useful to contrast them so that students can hear the difference clearly.
   - If students have difficulty in producing a particular sound (usually because it does not exist in their own language), it is often very useful to describe how it is pronounced, as long as this can be done in a way that students understand (using simple English or their own language).
   - Writing words on the board is not necessary, and could confuse the students – the focus should be on pronunciation, not on spelling.
   If necessary, give a quick demonstration, to show how the steps might fit together.

4. Divide the teachers into groups, and ask them to look at part B of Activity 2. Choose one person in each group to be 'teacher'. He or she should choose one of the 'problem' sounds from Activity 1 (e.g. /ð/ or /b/ and /p/), and teach it to the others. The others should act as a class, and make the kind of mistakes that their own students would make.
   When they have finished, another person in the group becomes the teacher, and they repeat the activity with a new sound.

B. Work in groups.
   Teacher A: Choose a sound. Teach it to the others in your group.
                  Help them with any difficulties.
   The others: Imagine you are students. Make the same mistakes as
                  your own students would.

5. After the activity, ask each group to tell you how successful the teaching was, and which techniques seemed to be most useful.

Practising sounds

▶ Workbook Activity 3 ◀

1. Ask teachers to look at the exercises in the Teacher's Workbook.

> *Minimal pairs*
>
> 1   2
> will   well
>
> Listen, and say the number: 1 or 2.

> *Missing words*
>
> Say a word to fill the gap.
> a) A boy and a ....
> b) First, second and ....
> c) A pigeon is a kind of ....
>
> Now listen to some more sentences, and say the missing words.

> *Making sentences*
>
> Make three sentences. In each sentence, use *one* word from group 1 and *one* word from group 2.
>
> | *Group 1* | | | *Group 2* | | |
> |---|---|---|---|---|---|
> | last | fast | calm | farm | part | rabbit |
> | dark | black | glad | party | jam | |
> | marvellous | bad | | car | hat | man |

Choose a sound that your students find difficult.
Make up an exercise like one of these to practise it.

Talk briefly about each exercise, and then demonstrate it.

Minimal pairs

Explain that minimal pairs are pairs of words which only differ in *one* feature, e.g. sing, song; park, bark; loose, lose; ship, sheep. They can be used to focus on differences in vowel or consonant sounds.

i) Say the words 'will' and 'well' in random order, and ask teachers to tell you the *number* of the word each time, e.g.:

    T: well Ss: two
    T: will Ss: one
    T: will Ss: one, etc.

ii) Say other words which have either the sound /ɪ/ or /e/. Teachers say which number fits the word, e.g.:

    T: bell Ss: two
    T: fill Ss: one
    T: win Ss: one, etc.

Missing words

The teacher says short sentences or phrases in which one word is missing. The students guess the word, which contains the sound that the teacher wishes to practise. (The sentences do not of course need to be written.) Give two demonstrations: one practising the simple vowel /ɜː/, the other practising the diphthong /eɪ/.

i) Ask teachers to complete the sentences in the exercise.

ii) Say these sentences, and ask teachers to give the missing word.
    Children love to .... games.
    Black and white together make ....
    After April comes ....

Making sentences

The teacher writes words on the board, and students say sentences using them. The words can either be used to practise one sound, or two similar sounds that are easily confused.

[*Note:* In the example in the Teacher's Workbook, the words are in two groups (adjectives and nouns); they are used to practise the vowels /ɑː/ and /æ/.]

i) Divide the teachers into pairs. Ask them to look at the two groups of words, and make three sentences. If necessary, give one or two examples first, e.g. She drives a black car.

ii) Ask one teacher from each pair to say *one* of their sentences. Pay attention to the pronunciation of the two vowels.

2. Divide the teachers into groups. Ask each group to choose a sound (or pair of sounds) that their students find difficult, and make up an exercise like one of those you demonstrated. Ask one teacher from each group to try out their exercise, using the other teachers as a class.

STRESS AND INTONATION

Stress

1. Check that teachers understand what a *syllable* is. If necessary, say a few short sentences, and ask teachers to count the syllables in each, e.g.:

    He/ came/ yes/ter/day. (5)
    He's/ ve/ry/ tired. (4)

    Point out that most words with two or more syllables have one *stressed* (or 'strong') syllable and two or more *unstressed* (or 'weak') syllables. Often the vowel in the unstressed syllables is pronounced as /ə/ or /ɪ/. We call these *reduced vowels*.

    Give some examples:
    - Asi*a*, *a*part: the 'a' is pronounced as /ə/.
    - betwe*e*n, want*e*d: the 'e' is pronounced as /ɪ/.
    - in 'able', 'table', the 'a' is pronounced /eɪ/; in 'vegetable', 'syllable', it is reduced to /ə/.
    - in 'day', the 'ay' is pronounced /eɪ/; in 'Monday', 'Tuesday', it is often reduced to /ɪ/.

2. Explain that in connected speech (when we say sentences rather than single words), many more vowels become reduced because complete words are unstressed. Give these examples:

    I ate bread and cheese. /aɪ et 'bred ənd 'tʃiːz/
    Look at us. /'lʊk ət 'ʌs/

    The vowels in many conjunctions and prepositions (and, but, at, for, of) are normally reduced unless the word is being specially stressed (e.g. 'John *and* Mary – both of them'). Reducing vowels in this way is a feature of normal spoken English – it is not 'uneducated' or 'substandard' usage. So it is a good idea for teachers to use reduced vowels in their own speech in the classroom, and encourage their students to do so.

3. Explain that English is a 'stress-timed' language. This means that the

length of time between stressed syllables is always about the same, and if there are several unstressed syllables they must be said more quickly. (This is why vowels tend to be reduced in unstressed syllables.) Give some examples to make this clear:
- He *wrote* a *let*ter.
- He *wrote* a long *let*ter.
- He *wrote* a very long *let*ter.

In each sentence, the unstressed syllables ('a', 'a long', 'a very long') took about the same amount of time to say: so 'a very long' had to be said more quickly.
- *Take John.*

Take it to *John.*

The two unstressed syllables ('it to') are said quickly to fill the space which would normally be left between two stressed syllables ('Take – John').

Emphasise that this 'stress-timing' is a very important feature of spoken English. If students become accustomed to hearing English spoken with a natural rhythm in class, they will find it easier to understand real English when they hear it spoken outside the class.

▶ **Workbook Activity 4** ◀

4. Ask teachers to look at the words and phrases in the Teacher's Workbook, and to mark the stressed syllables and the reduced vowels.

   1. Look at these words and phrases.
      - Which syllables are *stressed*? Mark them like this: disappointed
      - In the unstressed syllables, which vowels are *reduced*? Mark them like this: disappointed

   Suggested answer:

disappointed	a kilo of sugar
attractive	give me an orange
trousers	I'd like some coffee
suppose	he was late again
perfect	we can leave as soon as you are ready

   2. How could you show the stress pattern of a sentence in class:
      - using your voice?
      - using gestures?
      - using the blackboard?

5. Discuss ways of showing the stress pattern of a sentence in class. Get

the teachers to give their own ideas, and make these suggestions yourself:

Using your voice:
- Saying the sentence, exaggerating the difference between stressed and unstressed syllables.
- Representing each syllable with a sound, e.g. a kilo of sugar = de–DA–de–de–DA–de.

Using gestures:
- Using arms like a conductor of an orchestra, using a stronger gesture for the stressed syllables.
- Clapping (or tapping on a desk), clapping more loudly for the stressed syllables.

Using the blackboard:
- Writing dots and dashes: e.g. a kilo of sugar = .–..–.
- Underlining the stressed syllables: a kilo of sugar
- Writing the stressed syllable in heavier letters: a **kilo** of **sugar**. (This technique is often used in textbooks, and would be suitable for wallcharts.)

[*Note:* A list of common words containing weak forms is given in the Reference Sheet in the Teacher's Workbook.]

Intonation

1. Make sure that teachers understand what intonation is: it is the 'music' of a language – the way the voice goes up and down as we speak. Make these general points about intonation:
   - Intonation is very important in expressing meaning, and especially in showing our feelings (e.g. surprise, anger, disbelief, gratitude).
   - However, intonation patterns are quite complex, and it is better for students to acquire them naturally rather than try to learn them consciously.

   For teaching oral English at a fairly low level, teachers need to be aware of two basic intonation patterns:
   - *Rising tone:* used in asking Yes/No questions, and to express surprise, disbelief, etc. The voice rises sharply on the stressed syllable.

     Really?   Is he your friend?   Do you want some tea?

   - *Falling tone:* used for normal statements, commands, and for WH-questions. The voice rises slightly earlier in the sentence, and then falls on the key word being stressed.

     A ticket to London, please.   What's your name?

▶ **Workbook Activity 5** ◀

2. Ask teachers to look at the remarks in the Teacher's Workbook.

Look at these remarks. Which would normally have a *rising* intonation? Which would have a *falling* intonation?

A: I don't want anything to eat. ↘
B: No? ↗

A: Can I borrow some money? ↗
B: No! ↘

A: Who's that? ↘
B: It's George. ↘

A: Is that George? ↗
B: No, it isn't. ↘

How could you show intonation patterns in class?

Ask teachers to practise saying the remarks.

3. Discuss ways of showing intonation patterns in class. There are two main techniques:
   – By drawing arrows on the blackboard (as in the examples above).
   – By arm and hand movements, like the conductor of an orchestra.

Practising stress and intonation

1. The easiest way for students to practise stress and intonation is by repetition. If the focus is on pronunciation, traditional 'repetition drills', which are often boring for students to do, can be made interesting and challenging; students are not asked simply to repeat a sentence, but to repeat it using a particular stress and intonation pattern. For this to be effective, it is important for teachers to:
   – give a good model of the sentence themselves; saying it at normal speed, making a clear difference between stressed and unstressed syllables, and using natural intonation;
   – indicate the stress and intonation clearly, using gestures;
   – make sure that the students pay attention to stress and intonation when they repeat the sentence.
   One way to help students use natural intonation is to practise saying the sentence in *sections*, starting with the *end* of the sentence and

gradually working backwards to the beginning, e.g., *living* here / been *living* here / have you been *living* here / How *long* have you been *living* here? This technique is known as *back-chaining*.

[*Note:* The reason for starting at the end rather than the beginning is that it is the last stressed syllable that determines the intonation pattern of the whole sentence. So by repeating the end of the sentence, the correct intonation is preserved.]

2. Give a demonstration to show how back-chaining can be used as part of a repetition drill.
    i)   Say the whole sentence. Show the stress and intonation using gestures. Students listen.

    > T: Listen. How *long* have you been *living* here? How *long* have you been *living* here? de–DA–de–de–de–DA–de–de. How *long* have you been *living* here?

    ii) Students repeat, starting from the end.

    > T: *Living* here. *Living* here. Everybody.
    > Ss: *Living* here.
    > T: Been *living* here.
    > Ss: Been *living* here.
    > T: Have you been *living* here.
    > Ss: Have you been *living* here.
    > T: How *long* have you been *living* here?
    > Ss: How *long* have you been *living* here?

    iii) Groups of students repeat the whole sentence, then individual students.

    > T: (*gesture to indicate a group*)
    > G: How *long* have you been *living* here?
    >   (*and so on*)

▶ Workbook Activity 6 ◀

3. Divide the teachers into pairs. Ask them to look at the examples in the Teacher's Workbook, and:
    – decide what intonation pattern each sentence has, and mark it with an arrow;
    – decide which words are stressed, and underline them;
    – mark places where they could divide the sentence up for back-chaining.

    Emphasise that there is no single 'correct' way to divide a sentence up;

it could be practised in two or three or four sections, according to the length of the sentence and the ability of the class. Obviously, the breaks should be in natural places as far as possible.

> Imagine that you want your class to repeat the sentences below.
> – Practise saying the sentences.
> – Mark the stressed syllables.
> – Mark places where you could divide the sentences for 'back-chaining'. Mark rising or falling intonation.
> (The first one is done for you.)

Possible answers:

   a) How long/have you/been/living here? ↘

   b) Have you ever been|to London? ↗

   c) She's wearing|a green dress. ↘

   d) What are you|doing? ↘

   e) I haven't|seen her|for years. ↘

   f) Do you mind|if I open|the window? ↗

   g) You can|sit down|if you like. ↘

4. As a possible extension to this activity, ask teachers to come out in turn and practise using the sentences for pronunciation practice. The other teachers should act as a class.

LESSON PREPARATION

▶ **Workbook Activity 7** ◀

Either organise the preparation during the training session, with teachers working together in pairs or groups, or let teachers prepare in their own time after the session.

FURTHER READING

B. Haycraft (1971) *The Teaching of Pronunciation*, Longman. Covers all aspects of pronunciation teaching.

P. Hubbard et al. (1983) *A Training Course for TEFL* (Chapter 7: The teaching of pronunciation), Oxford University Press. Contains practical ideas for teaching stress and intonation, and for devising pronunciation exercises.

A. Gimson (1980 3rd edition) *An Introduction to the Pronunciation of English*,

Edward Arnold. A standard work of reference. It gives a comprehensive description of the sound system of English.

P. Roach (1983) *English Phonetics and Phonology*, Cambridge University Press. A complete basic course providing practice in pronunciation, discrimination and transcription with practical exercises on cassette.

Materials for pronunciation practice (including cassettes):

A. Baker (1982) *Tree or Three?* Cambridge University Press.

A. Baker (1981 2nd edition), *Ship or Sheep?* Cambridge University Press.

V. Cook (1968) *Active Intonation*, Longman.

C. Mortimer (1985) *Elements of Pronunciation*, Cambridge University Press.

Background text: Structures and functions

This text discusses what is involved in 'knowing a language', and outlines the relationship between structures and communicative functions. It provides a general background to all the units, especially those concerned with developing productive skills.

The text can be read by teachers in their own time, and used as a basis for discussion in the training session.

The ideas summarised in this text form part of the linguistic basis of the 'communicative approach' to language teaching. Detailed accounts of these ideas can be found in the following books:

C. Brumfit and K. Johnson (eds) (1979) *The Communicative Approach to Language Teaching*, Oxford University Press.

H. Widdowson (1978) *Teaching Language as Communication*, Oxford University Press.

The ultimate aim of all English teaching is for students to 'know English', or at least know enough English for whatever purpose they have in learning the language. In this text we shall consider what 'knowing English' entails – in other words, what are the aspects of the language that need to be learnt?

This question appears to be fairly straightforward. Clearly, students need to develop skills, e.g. speaking, listening, reading and writing; how much attention is paid to each skill will depend on the students' needs and interests.

Within the productive skills (speaking and writing), we can say that students need to learn words and phrases to *express* meanings in English; they also need to be able to produce basic structures correctly. In speaking, this will involve learning the sound system and stress and intonation patterns; in writing, it will involve learning features of the writing system, such as spelling and punctuation. Since we do not speak or write in isolated sentences, they will also need to learn ways of joining sentences together in connected speech or writing.

Within the receptive skills (listening and reading), we can say that students need to *understand* words and structures in their spoken and written forms, and also understand the connecting devices that link them together. (All of this says nothing, of course, about *how* students learn, and does not necessarily mean that all these items need to be individually taught.)

A student who has learnt all these things, then, would be able to understand connected speech and writing and produce correct sentences in English. But this does not quite amount to 'knowing English'; for language is not merely an abstract system which is used for making correct sentences; it is a way of communicating with other people. 'Knowing English', therefore, must mean knowing how to communicate in English. This involves not only producing language correctly, but using language for particular purposes; for example, being able to give advice in English, make predictions, describe people. We call these the *functions* (or 'communicative functions') of language.

Here are some examples of common English structures and the functions they express:

Structures	Functions
There's a hotel in the town centre.	Describing
I'm going to study engineering.	Expressing intention
I wish I'd left earlier.	Expressing regret
The population *is likely to* increase.	Making a prediction
You *can* go home now.	Giving permission

(Note that one communicative function can be expressed by a range of different structures, e.g. intention can be expressed by 'I'm going to', 'I'm planning to', 'I intend to', etc.)

If learners are able not only to produce and understand structures like those in the examples, but also use them to express the communicative functions they need, that is, to do things through language, we say that they have 'communicative competence' in the language.

How does this affect language learning and teaching? Obviously, students do not need to 'learn' functions, since they are universal to all languages; but they do need to learn how to express these functions in English. Recognising the importance of functions will give the lesson a different emphasis, and students will be more aware of *why* they are practising particular structures. For example, in a class where the teacher is aware of functions as well as structures, students will not learn 'there is/are' for its own sake or because it is a 'useful structure'. Rather, they will learn *how to describe places*, and in doing so will practise 'there is/are', as well as other necessary structures (e.g. place prepositions). Rather than doing a series of exercises which practise 'going to' for no obvious reason, students will practise using this structure for a recognisable communicative purpose: for example, to talk about their own intentions and plans.

This same difference of emphasis is shown in the comments of the three teachers in Unit 8 Activity 2. Teacher B is concerned with teaching a useful structure; teacher C is aware not only of the structure but also of the function the structure is used for. Of the two lessons, teacher C's is likely to have a much clearer purpose.

Discussion

1. Look at the exercises in these activities:

        – Unit 6 Activities 1 and 2
        – Unit 7 Activity 3B
        – Unit 13 Activity 1
        What functions are the structures used for?

2. Look at a lesson in your textbook or a suitable textbook. What are the main structures taught? What communicative function do the structures express?
3. Look at the Contents page in your textbook. Do the descriptions of each unit emphasise the structures taught or the functions?

11 Teaching handwriting

Aims of this unit
- To make teachers aware of the basic principles of teaching hand-writing.
- To give appropriate techniques for teaching individual letters and joining letters.
- To give techniques for practice in copying words and sentences.
- To help teachers develop strategies for dealing with handwriting problems.

This unit is concerned with teaching roman script to students whose own language uses a different writing system. The style of writing used as a model is 'simple cursive', i.e. with letters joined but retaining the same basic shapes as in printing. This style of writing is now used by most adults in Britain and is taught to British schoolchildren; it is also the style adopted in recent English language textbooks in most countries.

This unit is only concerned with writing skills at the most elementary level. Writing skills are also dealt with in Unit 13: Writing activities (sentence and paragraph writing), and Unit 21: Using worksheets (reading and writing activities based on worksheets).

Note: For Activity 6 ('Lesson preparation'), teachers will need to collect samples of their students' handwriting. If this is impossible, the examples of handwriting in Activity 5 can be used instead.

BASIC PRINCIPLES

Introduction

Begin by dealing with three general questions about teaching hand-writing:
- When to start teaching handwriting.
- What style of handwriting to teach.
- What order to introduce the letters in.

When to start?

Ask teachers to give their own ideas, and make these points yourself:
- There is no need to wait until students have mastered other skills before introducing writing; they can begin to learn individual letters from the very beginning. The earlier students begin learning to write, the more chance they will have to practise.
- If students learn to write early, this can help them to develop other skills: it can help with reading, and can help them to remember words.

What style to teach?

▶ **Workbook Activity 1** ◀

Discuss the three examples of handwriting in the Teacher's Workbook.

Thank you for your letter of 14th

thank you for your letter of 14th

Thank you for your letter of 14th

How are these three styles different? Which one do you think is:
- easiest to learn?
- most useful?

Establish that:
- The first style is *printing*. The letters are separate, and they look the same as in printed books.
- The second style is *simple cursive*. Most letters are joined, but they keep the same basic shape as in printing. Most children in Britain learn this style, and most adults use it.
- The third style is *full cursive*. All the letters are joined, and many have different shapes from printing. Many people in Britain still use this style, especially older people.

Discuss the advantages and disadvantages of each style. Make these points:
- Printing is the easiest to learn. However, students will need to write in cursive later, so it is probably more convenient to teach them cursive from the beginning.
- Simple cursive is easier to learn than full cursive. The basic shape of each letter is quite clear, and it is easy to see how to join the letters. In full cursive, the loops make it difficult to see the basic letter shape.
- In simple cursive, the letters look the same as those the students read, so reading and writing are more likely to help each other.

What order to introduce the letters?

Explain that it is not necessary to introduce letters in alphabetical order – the alphabet can easily be learned separately.

Ask teachers to look at the reference sheet in the Teacher's Workbook (page 56). This shows a possible order in which to teach the letters:
- Letters with similar shapes are taught together. This helps students see important differences between them (e.g. between 'n' and 'h').
- Vowels are introduced near the beginning. This is useful as they are common, and can be joined to other letters to make words.

(In practice, of course, the order of letters is often determined by the syllabus or the textbook. Spend time on this question only if teachers have freedom of choice in the matter.)

Features of roman script

Discuss ways in which roman script is different from the students' own writing system, and focus on features that will cause students difficulty. Get teachers to make suggestions, and build up a list of features on the board, e.g.:

    left to right direction
    writing 'on the line'
    shape and size of letters
    joining letters
    capital and small letters

As you build up the list, talk about each item and get teachers to suggest ways of helping students. For example:
- *Left to right direction:* Obviously, teachers should make this clear from the beginning and remind students constantly of it.
- *Writing 'on the line':* Teachers can make this clear by drawing lines on the blackboard. It is best to draw four lines: this makes it possible to show which letters go above and which go below:

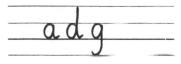

- *Shape and size of letters:* Students may find it difficult to form the basic shape of some letters. Before learning a new letter, they can practise making the basic shape: for example, before learning 'i', 'u', 'l' and 't' they could practise:

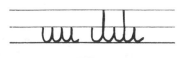

– *Joining letters:* This is dealt with in detail later in the unit.
– *Capital letters:* This becomes important later, when students begin to write sentences. But students can start practising capital letters by writing their own names and the names of towns, countries, months, etc.

TEACHING INDIVIDUAL LETTERS

Teaching a new letter

▶ **Workbook Activity 2** ◀

1. Divide the teachers into pairs or groups. Ask them to look at the table in the Teacher's Workbook, which shows possible steps in teaching a letter for the first time. They should decide which steps are important, and mark their answers in the space provided.

> Imagine you are teaching a new letter. Which of these steps are important? Which are not important?

Draw lines on the board.	
Write the letter clearly on the board.	
Describe how the letter is formed.	
Say the name of the letter.	
Give the sound of the letter.	
Students repeat the name of the letter.	
Students repeat the sound.	
Students draw the letter in the air.	
Students copy the letter in their books.	

2. Discuss the table together. There is no single 'correct' answer; the purpose of the activity is to make teachers think about different

possibilities. However, these points should naturally emerge from the discussion:
- The essential steps are writing the letter on lines on the board, and getting students to copy it several times. It is also very useful to describe the letter, to help students see how it is formed – this can be done in simple English or the students' own language.
- It is important to give the usual sound of the letter, so that students can connect sound with spelling. But there is no need to get students to repeat the sound: the aim is to practise writing, not pronunciation.
- Knowing the name of the letter is useful, for example when spelling words aloud, but is not really necessary for writing. Giving the name of the letter at this stage could be confusing, especially if the name is different from the sound (e.g. the vowels).
- Some teachers find it useful to get students to practise forming the letter in the air before they write it down; this helps students to 'feel' the shape of the letter. However, this can be difficult to control in a large class.

3. Give a quick demonstration, to show how the main steps fit together:
   i) Draw lines on the board, then write the letter 'n', large enough for everyone to see.

   Tell the class what sound it makes, and give some words it appears in (e.g. man, ten, no, new).
   ii) Show how to form the letter. Write it two or three times and describe the direction: 'Look – it starts here – then down, back up again, then round and down. See – it stands on the line'.
   iii) Teachers copy the letter in their books. Ask them to write it several times (separately) along the line, from left to right. Move around quickly, checking.

[*Note:* To make the demonstration more realistic, you could teach an invented letter, or one from a script that the teachers do not know.]

Practice

> ### ► **Workbook Activity 3** ◄
>
> Work in groups.
> Teacher A: Choose a letter. Teach it to the others in your group. Help
> them with any difficulties.
> The others: Imagine you are students. Practise writing the new letter.
> Make the same mistakes as your own students would.

1. Divide the teachers into groups. Choose one person in each group to be 'teacher'. They should choose a letter, and teach it to the others, using a piece of paper as a 'blackboard'. The others copy the letter, but make the kind of mistakes that their own students would make. The 'teacher' should check and help them to improve.

   When they have finished, another person in the group becomes the teacher, and they repeat the activity.

2. After the activity, ask each group to report briefly how successful the teaching was, and how the teacher corrected mistakes.

WRITING WORDS

Joining letters

1. When students have learnt a new letter, they can practise joining it to other letters they know already. Obviously, they should only practise combinations which *really exist* in words, and as soon as they know enough letters they should practise writing words and sentences.

   Write these letter combinations on the board:
   ta   ti   et   ot   yt   th   tg   nt   dt
   Discuss which combinations would be worth practising.
   Answer: ta, ti, et, ot, th, nt. All these exist in many common words (e.g. take, time, yet, note, this, went). The others are found only in one or two words (e.g. scythe, shotgun) and are not worth practising.

   If you like, give other letters, and ask teachers to suggest common combinations.

2. Letter joins can be taught in the same way as individual letters. It is very important to show clearly how we make joins from the *end* of one letter to the *beginning* of the next (not always the closest point). Give a quick demonstration. Ask teachers to imagine that you have just taught 'h' and the class already know 'c'.
   i)   Write 'c' and 'h' separately on the board:

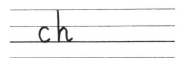

ii) Point to where 'c' ends and 'h' begins and draw a line joining them:

Then draw the joined letters several times, and describe the shape
('. . . round, then up to the top of the "h", then down . . .').
iii) Ask teachers to copy the joined letters several times. Go round the
class and check.

Copying words

1. Once students have learnt enough letters, they can start writing words
   and simple sentences. The simplest and most controlled form of
   practice is simple copying. Make these points about copying:
   – For students who have to learn English script, copying is a useful
     exercise; students do not have to produce words of their own, so the
     focus is entirely on handwriting.
   – Simply copying words or sentences from the board can be a very
     mechanical activity. Students can easily do it without really
     thinking, and it soon becomes very boring.

2. One way to make copying more challenging is to use a technique called
   'delayed copying'. The teacher writes a word on the board (or shows it
   on a card), and the students read it; then the teacher erases the word,
   and the students write it. In this way, students have to think what they
   are writing, and they have to think of the word as a whole, not just as a
   series of letters.
   Demonstrate the technique:
   i)   Write a word on the board. Ask teachers what it says. Spell the
        word. Teachers should not write anything yet.
   ii) Erase the word from the board. Teachers write it from memory.
        Go round quickly and check, making sure that teachers are joining
        the letters together. Repeat the procedure with other words.
   iii) As a check, ask individual teachers to come and write the words on
        the board.

Simple copying tasks

► **Workbook Activity 4** ◄

Another way to make copying more interesting is by including a simple *task* for the students to do. For example, we can ask students to match words together, match words with pictures, put words in the correct order, etc. This makes sure that students think about what they are copying and understand what the words mean; it also gives a reason for writing the words.

A.

Match the questions with the answers, then write them out.

What's the time?   Yes, I love them.
Do you like oranges?   At half past seven.
When do you get up?   No, I go by bus.
Do you walk to school ?   It's two o'clock.

B.

Copy the *true* sentences only.

This man is wearing a hat.
He's carrying a stick.
He's running.
He's smiling.

C.

Some of these are *farm animals*, others are *wild animals*. Write them in two lists.

	Farm animals	Wild animals

goat   tiger   horse
         buffalo
lion   bear   chicken
    cow   camel
	horse	lion

1. Divide teachers into groups. Ask each group to look at *one* of the three copying tasks in the Teacher's Workbook. They should make sure

they understand how it works, and then make up a similar activity which would be suitable for their own students, using different words or sentences. They should write the activity on a piece of paper.

2. When all the groups have finished, ask one person from each group to come out in turn and try out their activity on the others.
   Afterwards, discuss each activity, focussing on these points:
   – How well did it work?
   – How could it be organised in class?
   – What preparation would be needed?

HANDWRITING PROBLEMS

▶ **Workbook Activity 5** ◀

After students are able to write words and sentences in English, writing activities will be mainly concerned with expressing meaning and with sentence structure. Handwriting will of course be practised all the time, but incidentally – it will not be the main focus of writing practice. But even after they have 'learnt' to write in roman script, students will still have problems. So the teacher will need to focus on handwriting from time to time, perhaps to reteach a point of difficulty and organise a short practice activity on it.

1. Ask the teachers to look at the examples of students' handwriting in the Teacher's Workbook. Discuss the main handwriting problems that each student seems to have.

However, the tress are disappearing
By 1974, a quarter of the forest had already been cat down.

What handwriting problems do these students seem to have?

However, The Trees are disappearing. By 1974, a quarter of The Forest had already been cut down.

Choose one of the problems. Plan a short piece of teaching to focus on the problem.

2. Divide the teachers into pairs or groups. Ask them to choose one of the problems, and plan a short piece of teaching to deal with it. It should include:
   – a short presentation to focus attention on the problem area;
   – a short practice activity based on it.

If necessary, give an example to show teachers what to do, e.g.:
Problem: Students do not use capital letters for proper names.
Presentation: The teacher writes a list of words on the board, including some names of towns, people, etc., but all with small letters. Students decide which words should begin with a capital letter, and say why.
Practice: Teacher rubs the words from the board, and then dictates them; students write them down.

3. When most pairs have finished, stop the activity. Ask different teachers to describe the activity they planned.

[*Note:* Instead of using the examples in the Teacher's Workbook, the activity could be based on examples of handwriting from teachers' own classes. If this is done, the activity can take the place of 'Lesson Preparation'.]

LESSON PREPARATION

▶ **Workbook Activity 6** ◀

Either organise the preparation during the training session, with teachers working together in pairs or groups, or let teachers prepare in their own time after the session.

FURTHER READING

Very little has been written on teaching handwriting. A brief account can be found in:
D. Byrne (1979) *Teaching Writing Skills* (Appendix 2: Teaching the English script), Longman. (Chapter 4 of the same book gives ideas for elementary writing activities.)

12 Pairwork and groupwork

Aims of this unit
- To introduce teachers to pairwork and groupwork and to show the advantages of working in pairs and groups.
- To show teachers how to organise pair and groupwork effectively and how to deal with initial problems that may arise.
- To show how pair and groupwork can be used for various classroom activities.
- To give teachers confidence in using pair and groupwork themselves.

This unit is concerned with ways of *organising* activities in the class rather than with teaching techniques. Particular activities which can be done in pairs or groups are dealt with more fully in other units, especially Unit 15: Reading activities, Unit 18: Communicative activities, Unit 20: Role play and Unit 21: Using worksheets.

Preparation
For Workbook Activity 5 you could ask teachers to bring in examples of some of the activities listed: pattern practice, practising short dialogues, reading a text and answering questions, short writing exercises, discussions, grammar exercises. They should be able to find examples of these in textbooks.

PAIRWORK AND GROUPWORK

Introduction

Begin by making sure that teachers understand what pairwork and groupwork involve:
- In *pairwork*, the teacher divides the whole class into pairs. Every student works with his or her partner, and all the pairs work *at the same time* (it is sometimes called 'simultaneous pairwork'). Point out that this is *not* the same as 'public' or 'open' pairwork, with pairs of students speaking in turn in front of the class.
- In *groupwork*, the teacher divides the class into small groups to work together (usually four or five students in each group). As in pairwork, all the groups work at the same time.

Point out that pairwork and groupwork are not teaching 'methods', but ways of organising the class. They can be used for many different kinds of activity, and are naturally more suitable for some activities than for others.

Pair and group activities

▶ Workbook Activity 1 ◀

You will demonstrate three activities: the first two are examples of pairwork and the third is an example of groupwork. The purpose of these activities is to give teachers the experience of doing language practice in pairs and groups, as a basis for later discussion. They do not necessarily show exactly what teachers would do in their own classes.

1. Demonstrate Activity A. Explain that it is an example of pairwork used for controlled oral practice; it practises vocabulary and conditional structures.

> A. Work in pairs. Ask and answer the questions.
> What happens if . . .
> a) you eat unripe fruit?
> b) you eat too much food?
> c) you leave ice in the sun?
> d) you drive over broken glass?
> e) you drop a match into a can of petrol?
> f) you sit in the sun too long?
> g) you leave milk for a few days?
>
> Now think of two more questions like this.

  i) Ask the first two questions to the whole class, to show how the activity works. (More than one answer is possible: e.g. (a): You'll be sick / You'll get a stomach ache; (b): You'll be sick / You'll get fat.)
  ii) Divide teachers into pairs to ask and answer the other questions.
  iii) When most pairs have finished, go through the answers together.
  iv) Ask some pairs to tell you the questions they thought of themselves. Get other teachers to answer them.

2. Demonstrate Activity B. Explain that it is an example of a reading activity done in pairs. Students work together to try to understand the text.

B. Work in pairs.
1. Can you answer these
   questions?
   – What is acid rain?
   – How is it caused?
   – What damage does it do?
2. Read the text and find the
   answers.
3. Underline all the words in the
   text which you do not
   understand.
   With your partner, try to guess
   what they mean.

> Throughout Europe, and also in other areas of the world such as India, China and parts of America, forests are being destroyed. According to one prediction, 90% of Germany's forests will have vanished by the end of the century. This destruction is caused by air pollution. Power stations and cars are mainly responsible – they emit gases into the air which, after a series of chemical changes, turn into toxic acids. These acids fall as 'acid rain', raising the level of acidity in the soil, in lakes and in rivers to dangerous levels, and destroying not only trees but also fish and other wildlife. The industrialised world is slowly waking up to the fact that urgent action is needed to reduce air pollution, otherwise our environment will be damaged beyond repair.

i) Briefly explain what the teachers have to do. Then divide them into pairs to do the activity.
ii) When most pairs have finished, stop the activity. Discuss the questions together. Ask teachers to tell you any words whose meaning they could not guess, and discuss them together.

3. Demonstrate Activity C. Explain that it is an example of a discussion activity done in groups. This is a much freer activity, and aims to develop fluency in speaking.

C. Work in groups.

nurse	farm worker
doctor	taxi driver
teacher	engineer

1. Which of these people earns the most money in your country? Write them in a list, starting with the highest paid and ending with the lowest paid.
2. Who do you think should earn the most money? Who should earn more, and who should earn less?

i) Divide teachers into groups of four or five. Read through the instructions and make sure that each group understands what to do. If you like, choose one 'secretary' in each group to write the list – but emphasise that everyone in the group should agree on what to write.

ii) While the activity is going on, move from group to group, but do not interrupt more than is necessary.

iii) When some groups have finished their discussion, stop the activity. Ask one person from each group to report on what they decided.

Discussion: Advantages and problems

▶ **Workbook Activity 2** ◀

1. For certain types of activity, pairwork and groupwork have a number of advantages over working with the whole class together. Ask teachers to think what the main advantages are, and also what problems might be involved in pairwork and groupwork. As teachers make suggestions, summarise them on the blackboard in two lists; teachers can then copy the lists into the table provided in the Teacher's Workbook. Here is the Teacher's Workbook activity with some suggestions filled in.

What are the *advantages* of using pairwork and groupwork?
What *problems* might there be?

Advantages	Problems
More language practice.	Noise.
Students are more involved.	Students make mistakes.
Students feel secure.	Difficult to control.
Students help each other.	

How would you overcome the problems?

(Of course, your own list may look slightly different from this, but most teachers' suggestions will probably fit under these headings. If teachers already have some experience of pairwork or groupwork, you could first let them make their own lists of advantages and problems, using the table in the Teacher's Workbook, and then discuss them together.)

2. Discuss each heading in more detail, and refer to the activities which you demonstrated earlier. Encourage further suggestions and comments from the teachers, and try to bring out the points below.

Discuss the advantages first:

i) *More language practice:* Pairwork and groupwork give students far more chance to speak English. Refer to Activity 1A in your demonstration: working in pairs, each student makes seven sentences (either a question or an answer). If the exercise were done 'round the class', students would only say one sentence each, and in a large class many students would say nothing at all.

ii) *Students are more involved:* Working in pairs or groups encourages students to be more involved and to concentrate on the task. Refer to Activity 1C: if this discussion were conducted with the whole class together, it would probably be dominated by a few students and the others would lose interest.

iii) *Students feel secure:* Students feel less anxiety when they are working 'privately' than when they are 'on show' in front of the whole class. Pairwork and groupwork can help shy students who would never say anything in a whole-class activity.

iv) *Students help each other:* Pairwork and groupwork encourage students to share ideas and knowledge. In a reading activity (e.g. Activity 1B) students can help each other to explore the meaning of a text; in a discussion activity (e.g. Activity 1C) students can give each other new ideas.

Now talk about the problems, and discuss ways of overcoming them:

i) *Noise:* Obviously, pairwork and groupwork in a large class will be noisy, and this cannot be helped. But:
   - Usually the students themselves are not disturbed by the noise; it is more noticeable to the teacher standing at the side or to someone in the next room.
   - The noise created by pairwork and groupwork is usually 'good' noise – students using English, or engaged in a learning task.

ii) *Students make mistakes:* During a pair or group activity, the teacher cannot control all the language used, and should not try to do so. When doing controlled language practice in pairs or groups, the number of mistakes can be reduced:
   - By giving enough *preparation*. The activity can be done with the whole class first, and pairwork used for the final stage.
   - By *checking* afterwards. The teacher can ask some pairs or groups what they said, and then correct mistakes if necessary.

iii) *Difficult to control class:* The teacher has less control over what students are doing in pairwork and groupwork than in a normal class. To stop activities getting out of control, it is important to:
  - give *clear instructions* about when to start, what to do, and when to stop;
  - give *clearly defined tasks* which do not continue for too long;
  - set up a *routine*, so that students accept the idea of working in pairs or groups, and know exactly what to do.

ORGANISING PAIRWORK

Discussion

▶ Workbook Activity 3 ◀

1. Look at the exercise in the Teacher's Workbook and the pictures which show how the teacher organised the pairwork activity.

   Teacher X had an intermediate class. She presented 'like / don't like', and then she used this exercise for freer practice in pairs:

   Exercise 3 Likes and dislikes

   Pairwork. Ask what your friend likes and doesn't like.
   Ask about:
        food   sport   music   school subjects

   The pictures below show what she did before, during and after the activity.

Before: *During:*   *After:*

Do you think the activity was successful?
What do you think might have gone wrong?
What could she do to make it more successful?

2. Discuss why the activity was not successful, and what the teacher could do to make it more successful:
   - She could *prepare* for the pairwork by establishing what the questions and answers should be. She could also *demonstrate* the pairwork by asking questions round the class, or by getting one pair of students to ask and answer in front of the class. Then students would know exactly what to do.
   - She could be more active in starting the pairwork. Instead of just saying 'Work in pairs', she could show students who to work with, check that everyone had a partner, and check that everyone had started working in pairs. This would be very important if the class were not used to pairwork.
   - During the activity, she could move quickly round the class to check that students were talking and to see when they finished.
   - Instead of waiting for everyone to finish, she could stop the activity. Then there would be no chance for students to get bored and start talking about other things.
   - After the pairwork, she could ask some pairs what they said, or ask a few pairs to repeat their conversation in front of the class.

Demonstration

Give a demonstration to show how the activity could be conducted. Try to include any steps that teachers agreed would be useful. Pay particular attention to the way you *organise* the pairwork.

A possible procedure:
i) Introduce the exercise and show what questions and answers students can give:

> T: Now. You're going to talk about things you like and things you don't like. Look at the exercise. What questions can you ask? What about food?
> Ss: What food do you like?
> T: Good. What answer could you give?
> Ss: I like chocolate.
> I like eating fruit.
> I like rice.
> (*and so on*)

Write the basic question on the board:
> What   (food)   do you like?

ii) Ask a few questions round the class, to show the kind of conversation students might have:

> T: What kind of music do you like? Miguel?

S: I like pop music.
T: Pop music. Which singer do you like best?
(*and so on*)

If you like, ask two students to have similar conversations, while the others listen.

iii) Divide the class into pairs.

T: Now. You're going to work in pairs. (*Indicate pairs by pointing. If there are single students left without a partner, make groups of three.*) Ready? Ask and answer the questions. First one person asks all the questions, then change round. Start now.

iv) Students work in pairs. Move quickly round the class, checking that everyone is talking (but do not try to correct mistakes, as this will interrupt the activity).

v) When most pairs have finished, stop the activity. Ask a few students what their partner said:

T: Joanna, tell me about Lisa. What does she like?
S: She says she likes ice cream, pop music, and swimming. And she likes English, but not every lesson. She doesn't like writing.

Dividing the class

▶ **Workbook Activity 4** ◀

Pairwork and groupwork, like any other class activity, can quickly become a routine. Once students are used to it and have regular working partners, it can be organised quickly and easily (for example, simply by saying 'Now get into your groups', 'Do this in pairs'). The first few times that teachers try pair or groupwork are very important – they need to give more careful instructions and know exactly how they will divide the class.

1. Ask teachers to look at the diagram in the Teacher's Workbook.

> 1. Here are two rows of a class of 50 students. The desks are fixed, and the students sit on chairs. How could you divide the class into:
> – pairs?
> – small groups?
> What instructions would you give?

2. Draw a plan of your own class. Show how you would divide the class for a pairwork or a groupwork activity.

Discuss the best ways of forming pairs and groups in the class shown, and what instructions would be necessary.
Possible answers:
– *For pairwork:* Most students could work with the person next to them. Student 7 could turn round and work with Student 13, and Students 8, 9 and 10 work as three together. Or: Student 10 could move to work with Student 11, and the front row could be divided into two pairs and one three.
– *For groupwork:* Students could work in threes and fours along each row – this would be easy to organise but would make it difficult for students to work well as a group, as they would be in a straight line. Or: Students in the front row could turn round and form groups with those behind (either three groups of three and one of four, or two groups of four and one of five).

2. Ask teachers to decide whether they are more likely to use pairwork or groupwork in their class. Ask them to draw a plan of their classroom, showing clearly how they would divide the class, either into pairs or into groups.

[*Note:* If you like you could leave this stage to be done as part of the teachers' lesson preparation.]

ACTIVITIES IN CLASS

▶ Workbook Activity 5 ◀

1. Divide the teachers into groups, and ask them to look at the activities listed in the Teacher's Workbook. If they have brought examples of exercises, these can be used as a basis for the discussion. If you like, appoint one teacher in each group to lead the discussion.

⫸→

1. Which of these activities do you often do in your own class?
   pattern practice
   practising short dialogues
   reading a text and answering questions
   short writing exercises
   discussions
   grammar exercises

2. Discuss each activity.
   – Could you use pairwork or groupwork for part of the activity?
   – If so, exactly what would students do in pairs or groups?
   – What would you need to do before the pair/groupwork stage? Is there anything you would do *after* it?

2. When most groups have finished, talk about the most important activities together. Ask the leader from each group to summarise what they decided.

   If necessary, give these ideas yourself:

   – *Pattern practice:* This can be done in pairs in the same way as the 'likes/dislikes' activity you demonstrated. Any controlled oral practice can be done first with the whole class, and then in pairs.

   – *Practising short dialogues:* Acting out short dialogues can very easily be done in pairs, with little chance of students making mistakes. It can be done first with pairs of students in front of the class, and then with all the students working in pairs at the same time.

   – *Reading a text and answering questions:* Students can discuss questions in pairs or groups and then read the text; or they can read the text silently, and then ask and answer questions in pairs or groups. This is a good way of involving the whole class in answering questions.

   – *Short writing exercises:* Students can sit in groups and decide together what to write – one student acts as 'secretary'. This can be difficult to organise, but in a large class it has the advantage that students correct each others' mistakes and the teacher only has a few papers to mark at the end. Pairwork can be used for correcting written work (e.g. homework) – students sit in pairs and correct what their partner has written.

   – *Discussions:* With more advanced classes, discussions can be conducted in groups, as in Activity 1. It is important to define the discussion clearly, and to ask each group to report their conclusions afterwards.

   – *Grammar exercises:* Students can do grammar exercises orally in pairs; the teacher goes through the answers afterwards with the whole class, and students write the exercise for homework. This is more interesting and productive than students doing exercises alone, in silence.

LESSON PREPARATION

▶ **Workbook Activity 6** ◀

Either organise the preparation during the training session, with teachers working together in pairs or groups, or let teachers prepare in their own time after the session.

FURTHER READING

D. Byrne (1986 2nd edition) *Teaching Oral English* (Chapter 8.2), Longman. Discusses some of the factors involved in groupwork.

J. Willis (1981) *Teaching English Through English* (Chapter 9: Dividing the class up: pairs and groups), Longman. Includes discussion of pair and groupwork, and useful language for organising pair and group activities.

13   Writing activities

Aims of this unit
- To show teachers how writing skills can be developed through controlled activities in class.
- To show teachers how to prepare students for freer writing activities.

This unit is designed to help teachers who want to move beyond completely mechanical copying, but whose students are not yet ready to do completely free writing. It shows techniques for writing activities which focus students' attention on meaning and offer them some challenge, but which are sufficiently controlled to avoid serious errors.

This unit focusses on writing skills at elementary to intermediate level, and includes techniques for writing sentences and short paragraphs on general topics. It does not deal with writing at an advanced level (e.g. essay writing, summary writing) or for special purposes (e.g. scientific writing); these topics are beyond the scope of this course.

The activities in this unit can be done in class or for homework, and do not require special aids or materials apart from the blackboard. Reading and writing tasks which involve the use of worksheets are dealt with in Unit 21: Using worksheets. This unit is not concerned with introducing handwriting and letter formation to students who are unfamiliar with English script; this is dealt with in Unit 11: Teaching handwriting.

CONTROLLED WRITING

Introduction

1. First talk about the value of writing at the lower levels of learning English. Make these points:
   - If we think only of long-term needs, writing is probably the least important of the four skills for many students; they are more likely to need to listen to, read and speak English than to write it. Their need for writing is most likely to be for study purposes and also as an examination skill.
   - The main importance of writing at this level is that it helps students to *learn*. Writing new words and structures helps students to remember them; and as writing is done more slowly and carefully

than speaking, written practice helps to focus students' attention on what they are learning.

2. Now discuss what kinds of writing activity are most suitable at an elementary level. Get teachers to make their own suggestions and talk about activities they use themselves. Try to bring out these points:
   - If the students' own language uses a different writing system to English, the first task will be to master English handwriting. So the earliest activities will be copying letters, letter combinations, words, and simple sentences. (Activities of this kind are dealt with in Unit 11: Teaching handwriting.)
   - As soon as possible, we should encourage students to go beyond mechanical copying and give them exercises which require them to think and add something of their own; but exercises at this level should still be *controlled*, so that students do not make too many mistakes.

Moving beyond copying

1. Give a demonstration of a straightforward copying exercise, as a starting point for discussion. Write this sentence on the board, and ask the teachers to copy it:
   Sahiba goes to school by bus.
   Ask teachers to comment on the activity. Bring out these points:
   - The activity is completely *mechanical*. Students can copy the sentence even if they do not know what it means. Their attention is not focussed on the *meaning* of the sentence at all.
   - Because it is so mechanical, it is very *uninteresting*. The students are not required to think or use their imagination in any way.

2. Discuss ways of making the activity more meaningful and more interesting, while still keeping it fairly controlled. Get as many different ideas as you can. Here are some possible ways:
   - Leave out part of the sentence for the students to write themselves, e.g. 'Sahiba .... by bus' or 'Sahiba goes to school ....'. Either let students decide for themselves what to write in the gap, or say the whole sentence and ask them to write what they heard.
   - Say the sentence, but write only the outline on the board, e.g. 'Sahiba – school – bus'. Students write out the whole sentence.
   - Draw a picture to replace part of the sentence, e.g.:

Ask students to write the whole sentence in words.
- Write the sentence on the board, and ask students to write a similar *true* sentence about themselves.

Point out that in all these techniques, students have to *add* something of their own. The activities are still very controlled, with little chance of students making mistakes, but they have to *think* about what they are writing.

Controlled writing activities

▶ Workbook Activity 1 ◀

1. Ask teachers to look at the activities in the Teacher's Workbook, which are all examples of controlled writing activities. Point out that, as they are very short, they could easily be written on the blackboard. Quickly demonstrate them.

A.

> *Gap-filling* Listen to the teacher, then write out the complete sentences.
>
> Paper .... wood. It .... the Chinese in ....

    i) Read out these sentences: 'Paper is usually made from wood. It was invented by the Chinese in the first century AD.' Ask teachers to copy them, filling in the gaps in the Teacher's Workbook.

    ii) Ask teachers to read back the complete sentences, and write them on the board.

B.

> *Re-ordering words* Write the sentences correctly.
>
> We/six o'clock/and/tea/drink/get up/at.
> Then/the patients/wake/go/and/the wards/we/round.
> Sometimes/medicines/injections/them/we/or/give.

    i) Explain that the sentences describe the start of a nurse's working day. Ask teachers to write out the sentences correctly.

    ii) Ask teachers to read out the sentences, and write them on the board.

C.

> *Substitution* Write a true sentence like this about yourself.
>
> Samir enjoys playing football and reading adventure stories.

i) Ask teachers to write a similar sentence about themselves.
ii) Correct the sentences orally, e.g.:

    T: What do you enjoy doing, Juan?
    S: I enjoy sleeping.
    T: OK. (*write 'sleeping' on the board*) Who else enjoys sleeping?
    (*and so on, building up a list of words on the board*)

D.

> *Correct the facts* Re-write the sentences so that they match the picture.
>
> At the market, I saw an old woman sitting in a chair. She was selling eggs. It was raining.

i) Ask teachers to write the sentences, correcting the facts.
ii) Ask teachers to read out the correct sentences, and write them on the board.

[*Note:* This activity could be used with any picture in the textbook, and the 'untrue' sentences written on the board.]

2. Divide the teachers into groups. Ask each group to make up one activity similar to those in the Teacher's Workbook, which they could use with their own students. They should decide exactly how they would organise the activity in class.

3. Ask one teacher from each group to demonstrate their activity. The other teachers should act as a class, and make the same mistakes as their own students would.

Dictation

1. As a starting point for discussion, quickly demonstrate a short dictation, at a level of difficulty suited to the teachers. (Either use the text below or choose any other text of three or four lines.)
   i)   Read the text once through. Then dictate it phrase by phrase. Then read it through once again.

   > Important talks have been taking place today / between the Prime minister and Trade Union leaders. / They have agreed to co-operate to find ways of combating inflation / and reducing present levels of unemployment in the industrial sector.

   ii) Check the dictation orally, by asking teachers to read the text back to you sentence by sentence.

2. Discuss the activity, and try to establish the main advantages and disadvantages of dictation as a writing exercise.
   Advantages:
   - It is an intensive activity, which makes students concentrate.
   - The teacher can keep good control of the class, so it is a suitable technique for large classes.
   - It helps develop listening as well as writing.

   Disadvantages:
   - It takes up a lot of time in the class, especially if the dictation is corrected word by word afterwards.
   - It does not really develop writing skills – students do not have to express ideas in a written form, or find ways of constructing sentences. The main skill practised is spelling.
   - It is an unrealistic activity – listening is 'word by word' and at an unnaturally slow speed.
   - It can be done quite mechanically, without real comprehension.

3. An alternative to dictation, which develops both listening and writing skills and focusses on *meaning*, is for the students to listen to a text and then try to *reconstruct* it from prompts. Demonstrate the technique:
   i)   Write these prompts on the board:

   > Giovanni – fishing
   > friend's house – bus – river
   > tree – fishing
   > a few minutes – Giovanni – small fish

   ii) Read the text. Ask teachers to listen but *not* to write anything.

   > Giovanni decided to spend the day fishing. He went to his friend's house and they took a bus to the river. There, they sat

down under a tree and began fishing. After a few minutes, Giovanni caught a small fish.

iii) Ask the teachers to write a version of the text, using the prompts on the board. (It does not have to be exactly the same as the original; the first sentence could be, e.g. 'Giovanni decided to go fishing'.)

iv) Go through the exercise orally, asking different teachers to read out sentences.

After your demonstration, compare the technique with 'normal' dictation. Point out that students have to listen carefully to *understand* the text, and then have to think about *what* they are writing and *how* to construct the sentences.

If you like, ask teachers to find a short text in the textbook they are using (or any suitable one) which they could use for a similar activity, and to write a set of prompts based on it.

GUIDED WRITING

Problems of free writing

Ask teachers to imagine giving this writing task to a class of intermediate level students:

Write a paragraph, describing your town or village.

Discuss what problems might be involved in giving a completely free writing task such as this. Establish that:

- Many students would probably find it quite difficult, and make many mistakes. If so, they would find the task frustrating and probably not learn very much from it.
- Students would probably approach the task in different ways, and produce a wide variety of different paragraphs. So the only way to correct their work would be individually, book by book; this would be very time-consuming for the teacher.

As soon as they have mastered basic skills of sentence writing, students need to progress beyond very controlled writing exercises to freer paragraph writing. However, students will make this transition more easily and learn more if we can *guide* their writing. There are two main ways of doing this:

- By giving a *short text* as a model.
- By doing *oral preparation* for the writing.

Writing based on a text

1. Briefly explain how a text can be used as a model for writing, and give some examples:
   - Students read a short text, and perhaps study particular features of it (e.g. the way sentences are joined, the use of verb tenses, the use of the passive). They then write a paragraph which is similar, but involves some changes.
   - Examples of texts that could be used: Students read a paragraph about a student's day, then write about their own day; students read a description of a car, then write descriptions of other cars from notes; students read a description of a room, then write a description of another room shown in a picture.
     (*Note:* There may be examples of exercises like this in the textbook; if so, refer to them.)

▶ Workbook Activity 2 ◀

2. Ask teachers to read the text in the Teacher's Workbook. If you like, quickly go through the exercises orally, so that teachers can see how they work.

Jopley is a small town in the north of England. It is on the River Ouse, not far from Leeds. The town has a wide main street, with a stone church, the town hall and a cinema. There is a large supermarket in the town centre, and many smaller shops and cafés. Most people in Jopley work in the local factory, which produces farm machinery.

1. Write a similar paragraph about Bexham. Use these notes:
   Bexham – small village – south coast.
   Narrow street – two shops – church.
   Most people – farmers. Grow vegetables, wheat.

2. Now write about your own town or village.

Adapt this exercise so that it is about your own country.
Then discuss:
- What difficulty might your own students have in writing the paragraph?
- What preparation could you do to make the activity easier?

3. Divide the teachers into groups, and ask them to write a similar model text about a town in their own country (it can either be real or imaginary), and a series of notes for a writing exercise. When they have finished, ask each group to give their exercise to another group to try out.

4. Ask teachers to comment on the technique. Discuss what difficulties students might have in doing the exercises, and what preparation might be necessary. Make these points:
   - The model text might be too *limiting*, especially if the students' own town or village has quite different features. This may lead students either to follow the text too closely (and so write something which sounds unnatural) or to move away from it too much (and so make many mistakes). If all the students are writing about the same town, it would help to go through the exercise orally with the class first, and ask students to suggest what to include in the description.
   - The main problem with this kind of exercise is finding a *suitable text*. It is sometimes possible to adapt a text from the textbook – this can be written on the board before the lesson, or copied onto worksheets (see Unit 21: Using worksheets).

Oral preparation

1. Another way of guiding paragraph writing is to do oral preparation beforehand with the whole class; the students make suggestions, and the teacher builds up an outline or a list of key expressions on the board. The students then use this as a basis for their writing. This approach has several advantages:
   - It is *flexible:* it can be done in different ways according to the interests and ability of the class.
   - Ideas about what to write come from the *students themselves*; this makes the activity much more interesting and involves the class more.
   - It does not require specially-prepared texts or other material.

▶ Workbook Activity 3 ◀

2. Look at the picture in the Teacher's Workbook, and make sure that teachers understand what is happening: it is an Egyptian class, and the students are going to write a description of Cairo; to prepare for this, the teacher is asking questions about the city and writing notes on the board.

> 1. This teacher is building up notes on the board for a description of Cairo, in Egypt.   ⟫→

What were the teacher's first three questions?
What will he write next?

2. The teacher wants to elicit these other facts about Cairo, and write them on the board.

> *Important business centre*
> *– international hotels*
> *Tourists:*
> *– The Pyramids (2500 BC)*
> *– many famous mosques*
> *– market area (gold, copper, leather)*
> *Very crowded – traffic problems*
> *– new underground railway*

What questions could he ask?

Discuss what the first three questions might have been, and what the teacher will write next.
Possible questions:
 What is Cairo? How is it special? (*the capital of Egypt*)
 Where is it? In the south? (*in the north*)
 And it's on . . . which river? (*the Nile*)
He might write next:
 Very large city.
 Population: 10 million.

3. Divide the teachers into pairs. Ask them to write suitable questions that would elicit the information given in the box:
 Possible questions:
  What kind of city is it? What happens there?
  Where do people on business stay?

What about tourists? What can they do in Cairo? What can they see?
When were the Pyramids built?
What other buildings are there?
Where can tourists go to buy things? What are the best things to buy?
What are the streets like? What's the biggest problem?
What are they building now? Will this solve the problem?
When most pairs have finished, discuss the questions together.

4. As a possible extension to this activity, choose a writing topic from the textbook the teachers are using (or any suitable one), and ask teachers to plan an oral preparation stage. They should write:
    – a series of questions which they could use to elicit ideas and information from the class;
    – the notes that they might build up on the blackboard as students answer the questions.

[*Note:* Eliciting techniques are dealt with more fully in Unit 14: Eliciting.]

CORRECTING WRITTEN WORK

► Workbook Activity 4 ◄

1. Ask teachers to read the four correction techniques described in the Teacher's Workbook.

Here are four teachers' techniques for correcting written work.

Teacher A:

> I collect the books at the end of the lesson, and correct them during the lunch hour. Then I give the books back the next day.

Teacher B:

> I just go through the answers and get students to correct their own work. Sometimes I write sentences on the board

Teacher C:

> I ask the students to sit in pairs and correct each other's work, helping each other. Then we all go through the answers together.

Teacher D:

> I ask students to exchange books with the person next to them. Then I go through the answers and they correct each other's work.

Which of these techniques would succeed in your class?

2. Discuss the advantages and disadvantages of each technique, and how suitable they are for teachers' own classes. Get teachers to give their own ideas, and to comment especially on any of the techniques they have tried themselves. Try to bring out these points:
   - Correcting work orally in class is a good idea for a large class, as it greatly reduces the teacher's workload. As he or she corrects, the teacher can move around the class to check that students are correcting their own work.
   - Correcting work immediately in class (rather than returning it the next day) means that the teacher can draw students' attention to problems while they are still fresh in their minds.
   - Getting students to correct either their own or each other's work (before the teacher gives the correct answer) takes time in the lesson; but it gives students useful practice in reading through what they have written and noticing mistakes. It is also a good way of keeping the class involved.
   - Correcting in class works best with fairly controlled writing activities, where there are not too many possible answers.

[*Note:* This activity is only concerned with how to organise correction. Techniques for making written corrections (e.g. underlining mistakes) are dealt with in Unit 16: Correcting errors. Marking written work (i.e. giving a grade) is dealt with in Unit 22: Classroom tests.]

LESSON PREPARATION

▶ **Workbook Activity 5** ◀

Either organise the preparation during the training session, with teachers working together in pairs or groups, or let teachers prepare in their own time after the session.

FURTHER READING

D. Byrne (1979) *Teaching Writing Skills*, Longman. A practical guide to teaching writing at all levels, with examples of exercises. Chapters 4 and 5 deal with the earlier stages of writing.
R. White (1980) *Teaching Written English*, Heinemann. A practical guide to teaching writing, with the main emphasis on communicative writing. Contains examples of exercises and notes on procedure.
J. Harmer (1983) *The Practice of English Language Teaching* (Chapters 7 and 8), Longman. Gives examples of guided writing exercises and communicative writing activities.

14 Eliciting

Aims of this unit
- To show teachers the value of eliciting language from the students.
- To show teachers techniques for eliciting as part of their presentation of the lesson.
- To show how to encourage students to guess unknown words and structures, and to give more imaginative responses.

This unit builds on the basic questioning techniques introduced in Unit 2: Asking questions. It shows teachers how questions can be used as part of the teacher's presentation, as a means of involving the class more and getting students to contribute their own ideas and suggestions.

This unit also includes and further develops basic presentation techniques which were introduced in Unit 1: Presenting vocabulary, Unit 3: Presenting structures and Unit 4: Using the blackboard.

PRESENTING AND ELICITING

Introduction

1. In this unit you will be mainly concerned with techniques for the *presentation stage* of the lesson. Quickly discuss some of the things the teacher does at this stage (e.g. presents new words and structures, introduces the topic of the lesson, 'sets the scene' for a text or dialogue, gives examples orally, writes examples on the blackboard, etc.).

   In many classes, during the presentation stage, it is the *teacher* who talks, while the students listen. If the students speak at all, it is usually to repeat what the teacher says, or to answer a set question.

   Obviously, this part of the lesson will be dominated by the teacher – he or she is using English to introduce new material. However, it is possible to *involve* the students more in the presentation – by asking students for their ideas and suggestions, getting them to contribute what they know already, and encouraging them to guess new words. We call this *eliciting*.

2. To make the idea of eliciting clear, give two short demonstrations. In both demonstrations you will introduce vocabulary for parts of the

body: in the first, you will give a straightforward presentation; in the second, you will elicit the new words as part of your presentation.

Demonstration one

Present words for different parts of the arm and hand. Each time, say the new word, show what it means by pointing, ask the class to repeat it, and write it on the board.

T: (*pointing to wrist*) Look – this is my wrist. Wrist. Can you say it?
Ss: Wrist.
T: (*write it on the board*)
T: (*pointing*) Look – here are my fingers, and these are knuckles. Knuckles.
Ss: Knuckles.
T: (*write 'knuckles' on the board*)
   (*and so on, introducing other words, e.g. palm, pulse, fingertips*)

Demonstration two

Present words for different parts of the face. This time, try to *elicit* each word: point to the feature on your face, ask teachers what it is called, and then how to spell it. If no-one knows, give the word yourself.

T: (*pointing to eyebrows*) What are these? Anybody?
S: Eyebrows.
T: Yes. Eyebrows. Eyebrows. How do we write it? (*write the word on the board as students spell it*)
T: (*pointing to eyelids*) What about these? Look – I can open and close them. They are . . . eye . . .?
Ss: –
T: Well, we call them eyelids. Eyelids. (*write 'eyelids' on the board*) What about the hairs on your eyelids?
S: Lashes.
T: Yes, good. Eyelashes. Can you spell it? (*write the word as students spell it*)
   (*And so on, introducing other words, e.g. pupils (of eyes), nostrils, forehead, earlobes.*)

3. After your demonstrations, check that teachers understand the difference between the two techniques. Then discuss the value of eliciting. Try to bring out these points:
   – Eliciting involves the class by focussing students' attention and making them think. This happens even if students do not know the words being elicited; so elicitation can be used for presenting new

language as well as reviewing what was taught earlier.
- Eliciting encourages students to draw on what they already know or partly know. Because of this, it is a useful technique for mixed ability classes or classes of students from different learning backgrounds, where different students know different things.
- Eliciting gives teachers a chance to see what students know and what they do not know, and so adapt the presentation to the level of the class.
- Eliciting takes more time than straightforward presentation of new language. So most teachers would not try to elicit all the time, but rather use a mixture of eliciting and 'straight' presentation.

Eliciting from pictures

▶ **Workbook Activity 1** ◀

One of the easiest ways to elicit new vocabulary is by using pictures, either in the students' textbook or brought in specially. This activity focusses on what *questions* to ask to elicit language from a picture.

1. Ask teachers to look at picture A in the Teacher's Workbook, and to imagine that it accompanies a text about farming life in Africa. Before reading the text, the teacher decides to use the picture to 'set the scene' and to introduce key vocabulary.

A.

2. Divide teachers into pairs. Ask them to decide what questions the teacher should ask in order to elicit the answers given below the picture. If you like, ask them to write the questions down.

> A teacher uses this picture to elicit vocabulary. Below are the answers she wants the students to give. What questions should she ask?
>
> T: .... ?
> Ss: Farmers. They're returning from the fields.
> T: .... ?
> Ss: Donkeys. A buffalo.
> T: .... ?
> Ss: He's riding the donkey.
> T: .... ?
> Ss: It's evening. End of the day.
> T: .... ?
> Ss: Because the sun is low. It's setting.
> T: .... ?
> Ss: They're going home.

3. Discuss together the questions the teacher might ask.
   Possible questions:
   Who are these people? Where have they been? Where are they now?
   What animals can you see?
   What is the old man doing? Is he walking?
   What time of day is it?
   How do we know?
   Where are they going?
   Point out that, when eliciting, it is often best to ask fairly general questions that allow a variety of responses. This encourages more students to respond and leads them to say more (e.g. in answer to 'What time of day is it? How do we know?', students could say 'The sun is low', 'The sun is going down', 'The sun is setting', 'They are going home', 'They seem tired', 'There are long shadows', etc.).

4. Divide the teachers into pairs again, and ask them to look at picture B. They should decide what questions they could ask to elicit the words in the box below the picture. (These words would not of course be seen by the students.)

B.

You are using this picture to elicit the words in the box. What questions could you ask?
What other words could you elicit from the picture?

| rice |
| to plant |
| by hand |
| bend down |
| rows |

5. Ask teachers to tell you what questions they thought of.
   Possible questions:
   What are these people doing? (*They're planting rice.*)
   Are they using machines? (*No, they're planting it by hand.*)
   What exactly do they have to do? (*Stand in the water, bend down, push the plants into the mud.*)
   How are they planting the rice? Are they planting it just anywhere? (*No, they're planting it in rows.*)

6. Emphasise that, in using either of these pictures, it does not matter if students cannot answer the questions. If the teacher's questions show that no-one in the class knows the new word, the teacher will of course present it. The advantage of trying to elicit it first is that students' attention will now be focussed on the word and they should be listening with greater interest.
   If you like, demonstrate how this might happen by asking teachers to pretend that they do not know the new vocabulary. The elicitation might develop like this:

   Picture A: T: Who are these people?
                Ss: –

T: Well, they are farmers. (*write 'farmers' on the board*) What do farmers do? They work in . . .?

Ss: Country.

T: Yes. They work in the country. Often, they work in the fields. (*say 'fields' in students' own language*) (*etc.*)

Picture B: T: What are these people doing?

Ss: They're working in a field.

T: Yes. What work is this? What are they doing?

Ss: Rice. New rice.

T: Yes, this is new rice. So, they're . . .?

Ss: –

T: They're planting it. They're planting rice. Plant. (*write 'plant' on the board*) In the spring, farmers plant rice in the fields. (*etc.*)

7. As a possible extension to this activity, look at pictures in the textbooks the teachers are using. Discuss what vocabulary could be elicited from them, and what questions they could ask.

GETTING STUDENTS TO GUESS

There is no clear line separating what learners of a language 'know' and what they 'do not know'; there are many words and structures which they 'half-know', which they are not quite sure about but which they can guess. Because language follows rules, it is often possible to guess things which we have never actually been taught, and an important part of learning a language is developing this ability to make guesses. Eliciting is one way of encouraging students to guess and to work out rules for themselves.

1. Demonstrate this by giving a few examples of 'double noun' phrases used to describe occupations, and then elicit other examples which follow the same pattern.

   i) Write these examples on the board:

      He drives buses.   He's a bus driver.

      She sells books.   She's a book seller.

      Point out that we say '*bus* driver' and '*book* seller', not 'buses driver' or 'books seller'.

   ii) Now get teachers to guess what these people are called (answers in italics):

someone who drives lorries (*a lorry driver*)
someone who own ships (*a ship owner*)
someone who robs banks (*a bank robber*)
someone who hunts lions (*a lion hunter*)
someone who mends shoes (*a shoe mender*)
someone who loves dogs (*a dog lover*)
someone who reads the news on television
(*a television news reader*)

After your demonstration, make these points:
- Although teachers probably did not 'know' all the items, it was quite easy to guess them correctly.
- By *eliciting* the examples rather than simply presenting them, you helped teachers to see for themselves how the rule works. It also enabled you to see whether they had understood the rule or not.

▶ Workbook Activity 2 ◀

2. Divide the teachers into groups, and ask each group to look at one of the sets of examples in the Teacher's Workbook. Working together, they should:
   - decide what the examples show (i.e. what general rule they exemplify);
   - think of four or five other examples that follow the same rule, and write them down.

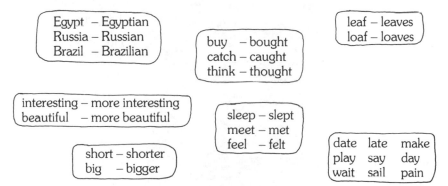

What do these examples show?
Can you think of more examples of the same type?
Write them down.

Egypt – Egyptian
Russia – Russian
Brazil – Brazilian

buy – bought
catch – caught
think – thought

leaf – leaves
loaf – loaves

interesting – more interesting
beautiful – more beautiful

sleep – slept
meet – met
feel – felt

short – shorter
big – bigger

date late make
play say day
wait sail pain

If necessary, discuss one set of examples together to make it clear what to do, e.g. leaf – leaves, loaf – loaves: examples of nouns ending in '-f' which change to '-ves' in the plural. Other examples: shelf – shelves, thief – thieves, knife – knives, half – halves, calf – calves.

3. Ask one teacher from each group to come out in turn and 'teach' their examples to the others. They should present the first one or two examples, but try to *elicit* the others. To make the activity more realistic, ask the other teachers to respond as their own students would.

During this activity, focus on the teachers' technique of eliciting. Pay attention to these points especially:

- The teacher should pause after asking each question, to give students time to think.
- The teacher should vary his or her questioning technique according to the difficulty of the question, letting good students answer difficult questions and directing easier questions at weaker students. In this way the whole class will be involved.
- The teacher should try to elicit 'onto the blackboard', building up a set of examples as students respond.

GETTING STUDENTS TO IMAGINE

▶ **Workbook Activity 3** ◀

1. Divide the teachers into pairs. Ask them to look at picture A in the Teacher's Workbook and to answer the questions on both sides of the picture. When they have finished, discuss the answers together.

A. Look at the picture and answer the questions.

Where is this woman standing?

What is she wearing?

What is she doing?

What is she holding in her hand?

What time of day is it?

Why is she standing here? What has happened?

How does she feel? Why?

What is she thinking? Write some of her thoughts in a few words.

Imagine this is a scene from a film. What will happen next?

How are the questions on the left of the picture different from those on the right?

2. Now talk about the *questions*; discuss the difference between the questions on the left of the picture and those on the right. Establish these points:
   – The questions on the left are about things that are quite *clear* in the picture. Each question either has a single correct answer or a small range of possible answers, e.g. She's standing by the sea / on a jetty; She's looking/gazing/staring out to sea, etc.
   The purpose of questions like these would be to elicit key vocabulary or structures, or to establish a situation or topic – they are the same kind of questions as those introduced in Activity 1.
   – The questions on the right require quite a different kind of answer. They require students to *interpret* what is in the picture (e.g. why the woman is standing there) or to *imagine* things beyond the picture itself (e.g. what will happen next). There are no single 'right' answers to these questions but a wide range of possible answers: students are encouraged to express their own ideas and feelings. The main purpose of questions like these is to involve the class in discussion and to stimulate freer use of language.
   Emphasise that both kinds of questions are important in a language class, but textbooks often include only questions of the first type. So teachers should take every opportunity to add questions of the second type which encourage students to give a more imaginative, personal response. Questions of this kind can of course be asked not only about pictures, but also about texts and dialogues, and are particularly useful in the study of literary texts.

3. Divide the teachers into pairs again, and ask them to look at picture B in the Teacher's Workbook.

> B. Think of three interesting questions to ask about the picture below. The questions should encourage students to *interpret* the picture or to *imagine* something. Write your questions down.

Ask teachers to write three questions about the picture which they could ask a class. The questions should either:

    – require students to interpret or explain the picture in some way (e.g. 'How long do you think they have been waiting?' 'Why are they looking unhappy?'), or:

    – require students to imagine something about the picture (e.g. 'What is each person thinking?' 'Write one word to describe the character of each person').

Encourage teachers to think of interesting and original questions.

4. When most pairs have finished, ask teachers to read out some of their questions. If you like, ask teachers to 'try out' their questions, with other teachers giving suitable answers.

5. Finally, discuss part C of the activity.

      C. Think of similar questions to ask about the pictures in Activity 1.

Possible questions:
Picture A: What country do you think this is? Why?
            What will these people do when they arrive home?
Picture B: What country do you think this is? Why?
            Choose one of the women. Imagine as much as you can about her. (What's her name? Is she married? What is her home like? What does she eat? etc.)
            Suddenly, the women are interrupted. Imagine what happens.

LESSON PREPARATION

► **Workbook Activity 4** ◄

Either organise the activity during the training session, with teachers working in pairs or groups, or let teachers prepare in their own time after the session.

FURTHER READING

J. Heaton (1981) *Using English in the Classroom* (Chapter 4: Questions and questioning techniques), Longman. A simple guide to using English for various purposes in class. Deals with questioning techniques and language needed to ask questions.

J. Sinclair and D. Brasil (1982) *Teacher Talk* (Part one), Oxford University Press. A more abstract description of the language used in the classroom. Discusses different ways in which teachers elicit responses from students.

Teaching material which is designed for eliciting from pictures:
A. Maley, A. Duff and F. Grellet (1980) *The Mind's Eye*, Cambridge University Press.
D. Byrne and A. Wright (1974) *What do you think?*, Longman.

15   Reading activities

Aims of this unit
- To show the importance of making students want to read a text.
- To show ways of increasing students' motivation in intensive reading.
- To show ways of helping students to understand the main information contained in a text.

This unit is concerned with techniques for helping students to read and understand texts. It deals with pre-reading activities, the use of comprehension questions, and simple reading tasks. It is not concerned with the use of texts as a basis for language practice; this is dealt with in Unit 5: Using a reading text. This unit includes groupwork techniques for answering questions on a text; groupwork is dealt with more generally in Unit 12: Pairwork and groupwork. The last part of this unit shows how questions can be used to elicit a personal response from students; this idea is developed more fully in Unit 14: Eliciting. Some of the techniques introduced in this unit (e.g. pre-reading, the use of 'tasks') are similar to those in Unit 17: Listening activities.

PRE-READING ACTIVITIES

Wanting to read

1. To establish the importance of pre-reading activities in class, begin by talking about reading in general. Make these points:
    - In real life, we do not normally read because we *have* to but because we *want* to. We usually have a purpose in reading: there is something we want to find out, some information we want to check or clarify, some opinion we want to match against our own, etc. We also have a purpose in reading when we read stories for pleasure: we want to find out how the story develops, 'what happens next'.
    - We do not usually begin reading with a completely empty mind – we have some *idea* of what we are going to read about. We will usually have certain *questions* in our mind (things we want to know), and we may also be able to make a number of *predictions* or *guesses* (things we expect to find out about).

2. To illustrate these points, give examples of different texts. Discuss with the teachers what questions they might have in mind as they start reading, and what guesses they might make about the text. The following examples show how headlines, chapter headings or book titles often make us think about the text before we begin to read.

Example one

A newspaper article, with the headline 'Plane crashes in desert'.
(The article will probably give details of the crash, explain how it happened, what caused it, etc. Questions the reader might have in mind: Which desert? Where? Any survivors? How did it happen? Whose fault? Which airline? Perhaps – Was anyone I know involved?)

Example two

A chapter in a popular science book called *Mosquitoes*.
(The chapter may tell us what mosquitoes look like, what their life cycle is, and perhaps how they spread malaria and how people are trying to control them. We might want to know: Why do only some mosquitoes carry malaria? How do they spread the disease? What chance is there of controlling it? etc.)

Example three

A romantic story called 'The quiet stranger'. The first line is 'The first time Vanessa met Jonathan, she did not notice anything unusual about him'.
(We would probably wonder: Who is Vanessa? Is Jonathan the quiet stranger? Why is he quiet? Where did they meet? What will she notice about him? Will she fall in love with him?)

Questions and guesses like these make us *want* to read (because we want to know the answers), and they also *help* us to read (because we are looking for particular information as we read and we can partly predict what we will find in the text).

3. Point out that in English classes the situation is often very different. Usually students read a text not because they want to, but because the teacher tells them to, or simply because it is there – it is the next activity in the textbook. So to help them to read, it is important to give the students some reason for reading and to give them information they want to find the answer to. This can be done in two ways:
   – By giving a few questions for students to think about as they read, and discussing the answers afterwards. (These are called 'guiding

questions' or 'signpost questions', and are introduced in Unit 5: Using a reading text.)
– By organising an activity before students read the text, which arouses their interest in the topic and makes them want to read. Activities of this kind are called 'pre-reading activities' or 'pre-reading tasks'.

Pre-reading activities

▶ Workbook Activity 1 ◀

1. Look at the picture of the earthquake in the Teacher's Workbook. Briefly discuss what seems to have happened and where it might be. Then divide the teachers into groups, and give each group a different pre-reading activity to do (A, B or C). Make it clear that they should do the activity *without* looking at the text.

Work in groups. Do *one* of these activities *before* you read the text.

A.

> You are going to read a text about the earthquake in the picture.
> What would you like to know about the earthquake? Write down at least *five* questions, which you hope the text will answer.

B.

> You are going to read a text about the earthquake in the picture.
> Try to *imagine* what the text will tell you about:
>   buildings
>   boats
>   people
>   hills around the city
>   trains
>   the land and the sea

C.

> You are going to read a text about the earthquake in the picture.
> Here are some words and phrases from the text. Can you guess how they are used in the text?
>   the sea-bed   the Richter scale   a huge wave
>   tremors   massive shocks   having a bath
>   Tokyo and Yokohama

2. Still sitting in groups, ask teachers to read the text and discuss it. (Teachers who did pre-reading Activity A should discuss the answers to their questions; teachers who did pre-reading Activities B or C should compare the text with their predictions.)

Now read the text.

> At two minutes to noon on 1 September 1923, the great clock in Tokyo stopped. Tokyo Bay shook as if a huge rug had been pulled from under it. Towering above the bay, the 4,000 metre Mount Fuji stood above a deep trench in the sea. It was from this trench that the earthquake came, at a magnitude of 8.3 on the Richter scale.
>   The sea drew back for a few moments. Then, a huge wave

swept over the city. Boats were carried inland, and buildings and people were dragged out to sea. The tremors dislodged part of a hillside, which gave way, brushing trains, stations and bodies into the water below. Large sections of the sea-bed sank 400 metres; the land rose by 250 metres in some places and sank in others. Three massive shocks wrecked the cities of Tokyo and Yokohama and, during the next six hours, there were 171 aftershocks.

The casualties were enormous, but there were also some lucky survivors. The most remarkable was a woman who was having a bath in her room at the Tokyo Grand Hotel. As the hotel collapsed, she and her bath gracefully descended to the street, leaving both her and the bathwater intact.

(from *Earthquakes and Volcanoes*: S. Steel)

3. Ask a teacher from each group to report briefly on their pre-reading activity. Discuss how successful each activity was in making teachers want to read the text.

   Make it clear that the activities are alternatives, and the teacher would only use one of them in class; they are presented together here to show a range of possibilities.

   If you like, mention other possible types of pre-reading activity, e.g.:
   - Students are given sentences which refer to the text, and they guess whether they are true or false.
   - Students are given a summary of the text with gaps; they try to guess what words should go in the gaps.
   - Students are given the topic of the text; they write a list of things they know and things they do not know about the topic.
   - If the text puts forward an opinion, students discuss the topic beforehand and give their own point of view.

4. Look at some of the texts in the textbook teachers are using, or in an appropriate textbook. Ask teachers to suggest possible pre-reading activities that could be used with them.

READING THE TEXT

Using questions on a text

► Workbook Activity 2 ◄

1. Look at the questions in the Teacher's Workbook, which refer to the text in Activity 1. Quickly work through them.

Here are some of the questions which followed the text.

1. What time did the earthquake start?
   What time did it finish?

2. Did it start: a) in the mountains?
   b) in the sea?
   c) in the city?

3. Beside each sentence, write T(=true), F(=false) or DK(=we don't know from the text).
   a) Parts of the sea became deeper.
   b) A hillside slid down onto the city.
   c) Most people died by drowning.
   d) The Grand Hotel survived the earthquake.
   e) The woman in the bath survived the earthquake.

Point out that there are two main aims in asking questions on a text:
- To *check comprehension* – to show the teacher (and the students themselves) how well the students have understood the text, and what needs to be more fully explained.
- To *help the students read* the text. If the questions are good ones, they should focus students' attention on the main points and lead them to think about the meaning of the text.

To achieve these aims, the teacher must make sure that the whole class is *involved* in answering the questions and that students know *why* answers are right or wrong; the questions should not be used simply to 'test' the students, but to lead them towards an understanding of the text.

2. Consider the three approaches to using questions described in the Teacher's Workbook, and discuss how well each approach involves the class and encourages students to think.

⟫⟶

Three teachers used the questions in different ways.

Teacher A:

> My students sat in groups
> to answer the questions.
> Then we went through
> the answers together.

Teacher B:

> I asked my students to write
> the answers to the questions.
> Then we went through the
> answers together.

Teacher C:

> I asked the questions round
> the class, and got different
> students to answer.

Which approach do you think is the most effective? Why?

Try to bring out these points:
– Getting students to work in groups and getting them to write the answers (teachers A and B) are both good ways of involving the whole class. When the teacher goes through the answers afterwards, all the students are likely to be interested in the answers and to want to discuss them.
– Of these two techniques (A and B), groupwork encourages more discussion, and so makes students think more carefully about the meaning of the text; it also gives a chance for good students to help those who are weaker. However, getting students to write the answers is easier to organise and control, and so may be more suitable for a large class. (Students should of course only be asked to write *short* answers – the aim is to check comprehension, not to practise writing.)
– Answering questions orally round the class (teacher C) is a very common technique, but not usually a very successful one for large classes. As only one student answers each question, most of the class

do not need to pay attention, and it is difficult for the teacher to see whether students have really understood the text.

Completing a table

▶ **Workbook Activity 3** ◀

1. Good questions should help the students to read by leading them towards the main ideas of the text. But answering questions is not the only way of doing this; we can also give students a *task* to do as they are reading: for example, they might read a text and label a diagram; read and choose a picture that fits the meaning of the text; read sentences which are not in the correct order and rearrange them; read and draw a picture, etc. One of the simplest kinds of reading task is for students to read a text and note down the main information in the form of a table or chart; this helps students to organise the information in a text in a clear and logical way. (This kind of task is sometimes called 'information transfer'.)

2. Give a demonstration to show how a 'table completion' task can be used as part of a reading activity.
   i)   As a pre-reading activity, write on the board: 'General examination'. Discuss briefly what happens when a doctor gives you a general examination; if you like, ask teachers if they have ever had one, and what happened.
   ii) Ask the teachers to read the text in the Teacher's Workbook and complete the table (either in pairs or working individually). If necessary, show them what to do by completing the first two lines together, using the blackboard.

≫→

Read the text and complete the table below.

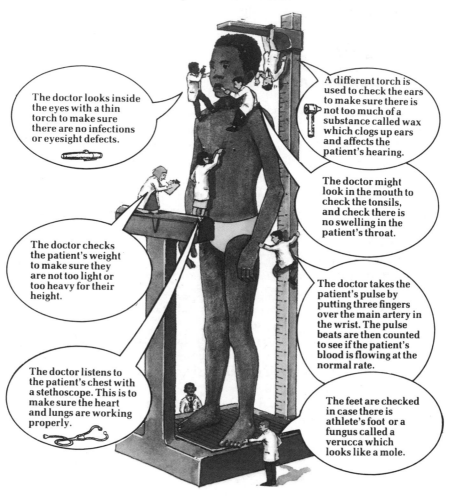

(from *The Young Scientist Book of Medicine:* P. Beasant)

iii) Go through the answers together, getting teachers to tell you what they wrote and building up a completed table on the blackboard:

THE DOCTOR

examines:		uses:	wants to know:
a)	eyes	torch	i) any infections? ii) eyesight OK?
b)	weight	(scales)	too light / too heavy?
c)	chest	stethoscope	Are heart and lungs working?
d)	ear	torch	too much wax?
e)	mouth	–	throat swollen?
f)	wrist/pulse	fingers (+ watch)	Is blood flowing normally?
g)	feet	–	athlete's foot? verucca?

As you go through the answers, ask detailed questions to check that the teachers have understood the text completely, e.g.:
Why does the doctor use a torch?
What's an eyesight defect? It means you can't see . . .?
What's *your* weight?
etc.

3. After your demonstration, discuss the activity. Make these points:
   - The main purpose of completing the table is to help *focus* students' attention on the main points of the text, and make it easier for them to organise the information in their minds.
   - Completing the table does not *replace* asking questions. Questions are still necessary to check detailed comprehension, as students could fill the table in without fully understanding the text. Trying to complete the table should make the students more interested in answering the questions and finding out the meaning of unfamiliar words.

   Point out that this type of task can be used with most texts which give factual information, and also with many texts which tell a story. It is easy for the teacher to prepare and organise, and requires no special aids or materials except the blackboard and the students' own exercise books.

4. Look at some of the texts in the textbooks the teachers are using, or in an appropriate textbook. Discuss which texts might be suitable for activities like the one you demonstrated. If you like, ask teachers to choose a suitable text and design a 'table completion' task for it.

Eliciting a personal response

▶ **Workbook Activity 4** ◀

1. Divide the teachers into groups. Ask them to read the text in the Teacher's Workbook and to work through the two sets of questions.

Work in groups. Read this text and answer the questions.

> When you are invited to a meal in Thailand, the words of the invitation literally mean 'come and eat rice'. Indeed, nearly all Thai dishes are eaten with rice, which grows there very easily as the climate is warm and there is plenty of rain.
>
> The food is always served in neatly cut up pieces, so there is no need to use knives and forks but, instead, special spoons and forks are used. The Thais used to eat with their hands and there are still some people who eat this way. There is a particular way of doing it. First they wash their right hand in a bowl of water – they only eat with their right hand. They are careful not to let the food touch the palm of their hand. After the meal, the hand is again carefully washed.
>
> The meal is usually made up of several different dishes, all of which are spicy. They are served in bowls which everyone shares, though each person has their own bowl of rice. As Thailand has a long coastline, it is not surprising that fish and shellfish play an important part in Thai cooking.

(from *What the World Eats*: T. and J. Watson)

A. 1. Why is rice a common food in Thailand?
2. Why is fish a common food?
3. Why are knives not needed to eat food?
4. Here are some statements about the traditional way of eating in Thailand. Which are *true*, and which are *false*?
    a) You should wash both hands before eating in Thailand.
    b) You should eat with the fingers of the right hand.
    c) You should wash your right hand after eating.

B. 1. Write two lists:
   - Things that are *the same* in Thailand as in your own country.
   - Things that are *different* in Thailand from your own country.
2. Imagine you are eating with a Thai family. What would you find *most* unusual. Why?
3. Do you think you would enjoy Thai food? Why? / Why not?

Compare the questions in A and those in B. What is the difference between them?

2. Quickly go through the answers. Then discuss how the questions in group A are different from those in group B. Establish that:
   i) The questions in group A are straightforward comprehension questions, focussing on the text itself. The questions in group B all go *beyond* the text; they require students to *respond* to the text and to contribute something personal that comes from their own experience or expresses their own feelings.
   ii) The questions in group B show three possible ways of eliciting a personal response from students:
       - By asking students to match what they read against their *own experience*.
       - By asking students to *imagine* themselves in a situation related to the text but beyond their own experience.
       - By asking students to express *feelings* or *opinions*.

   Now talk about the value of asking questions of this kind as part of a reading activity. Make these points:
   - Because they are talking about themselves, students usually want to answer questions like these; so it will also make them more interested in reading the text.
   - An important part of reading in real life is comparing what we read with our own experience; for example, it is interesting to read about another country because we can compare it with our own, or we can imagine ourselves being there. So questions in class which ask the student to give a personal response are natural questions to ask about a text.
   - Although personal questions go beyond the text, they also focus students' attention on the text itself and make them read it carefully.

3. Look at some of the texts in the teachers' own textbook or an appropriate textbook. Ask teachers to suggest questions they might ask which would require a personal response from the students.
   Emphasise that such questions would not replace 'normal' comprehension questions, but be used in addition to them. To make reading a

text interesting, it is important to include a *variety* of different activities: activities before reading the text, and questions and tasks of different kinds after reading the text.

LESSON PREPARATION

► Workbook Activity 5 ◄

Either organise the preparation during the training session, with teachers working together in pairs or groups, or let teachers prepare in their own time after the session.

Note: How the preparation is done will depend on the textbook that teachers are using. If the textbook contains interesting activities and questions, the main focus of the preparation should be on *organising* the activities (e.g. using group or pairwork). If the textbook contains only a few 'set' questions on the text, teachers will need to design their *own* activities.

FURTHER READING

C. Nuttall (1982) *Teaching Reading Skills in a Foreign Language*, Heinemann. A comprehensive account of reading skills: discusses the theory behind reading, examines individual reading skills, and gives practical ideas for classroom teaching.

E. Williams (1984) *Reading in the Language Classroom*, Macmillan. A shorter practical guide to developing reading skills: discusses different approaches to reading and contains examples of texts and activities.

F. Grellet (1981) *Developing Reading Skills*, Cambridge University Press. A sourcebook of ideas and activities for teachers who are able to develop their own reading materials.

Background text: Learning a language

This text compares different views of how languages are learnt. It provides a general background to all the units in the course, but is particularly relevant to the following units:
- Unit 6: Practising structures
- Unit 16: Correcting errors
- Unit 19: Using English in class

The text can be read by teachers in their own time, and used as a basis for discussion in the training session.

This text gives a very brief summary of some features of second language acquisition. The following books deal with the subject in depth:

W. Littlewood (1984) *Foreign and Second Language Learning*, Cambridge University Press.

R. Ellis (1985) *Understanding Second Language Acquisition*, Oxford University Press.

We cannot easily evaluate teaching methods without some idea of how students learn. Exactly how we learn our own or a second language is still not completely certain, but we do know in general terms what is involved in the process of language learning. In this text we shall look briefly at three different kinds of learning, and consider their importance in learning a language: *learning by heart*, *forming habits*, and *acquiring rules*.

Learning by heart

A traditional approach to learning is learning by heart, and many people still attempt to learn languages by learning set sentences, dialogues, and texts by heart. Learning by heart is likely to be most useful in learning things which are fixed and limited, and it is often found to be a useful way of mastering certain fixed items in a language, such as numerals or irregular past tense forms. The problem with learning by heart as a strategy for learning the whole of a language is that language is not something which is limited and finite; using a language involves understanding and producing an infinite variety of sentences. For example, we could easily learn the following dialogue by heart:

– Do you have any children?
– Yes, a boy and two girls.
We could then say that we have 'learnt' a small sample of English. But
this in itself would be of little use to us; for to speak English we may
need to make any one of hundreds of questions with 'Do you . . .?', and
to use the word 'children' in hundreds of quite different sentences.
Learning set sentences by heart may enable us to give a few fixed
responses, but it is not likely to prepare us for this great variety of
language that we need to understand and use. It seems clear that
language is not something that we can 'learn' in the same way that we
might learn a poem or a set of instructions; it is not a body of
knowledge but a set of skills, so 'learning a language' must mean
learning to use those skills.

Forming habits

Another view of how language is learnt is to see it as developing a set of
'habits' which we learn by imitation and which gradually become
automatic; in this view, language is seen as similar to more mechanical
activities such as eating or swimming. Central to this view is the belief
that children learn their first language by imitating their parents and by
reinforcement on the part of the parents (the parents 'reward' correct
sentences by responding positively to them). This view of language
learning is associated with the behaviourist school of psychology and is
reflected in the audio-lingual approach to language teaching, which
was popular in the 1950s and 1960s. Applied to learning a second
language, it emphasises the importance of repetition and drilling; and
as language is thought to be learnt by repeating correct sentences, it is
considered important for students to avoid making errors.

Two main arguments have been put forward against this view of
language learning. The first argument is concerned with the creative
nature of language, which we illustrated in the preceding section; in
using language we are continually required to produce completely new
sentences which we may never have used or even heard before, and it
is difficult to see how we could do this if learning depended entirely on
imitation and reinforcement. The second argument is based on
research into the way children learn their first language. Research has
suggested that children do not learn their first language only, or even
mainly, by imitation; they frequently produce sentences which they
could never have heard from adults, and so must have developed
independently. A simple example of this is children's use of plural
nouns: when English-speaking children first begin to use plurals, they
often say phrases such as 'two mans', 'three sheeps'. It is clear that they
have not learnt to produce these by imitation; rather it appears that they
have acquired a *rule* of the language, which at this stage they are
applying to all plural nouns.

Acquiring rules

This suggests a third view of the language learning process, which sees language as a system of rules. Learning a language involves being exposed to samples of language that we can understand; from this we can acquire the rules of the language and apply them to make an unlimited number of original sentences. During the process of learning either our first language or a second language, the rules we apply will often be incomplete or slightly different from the actual rules of the language, and this will lead to errors. In this view, therefore, errors are a natural part of the acquisition process and need not be completely avoided.

It is important to clarify what we mean by 'acquiring the rules' of a language. It means being able to *apply* the rules (in other words, to understand and use the language correctly); it does not necessarily mean knowing how to *explain* the rules (in other words, to talk about the language). All native speakers of English 'know' the difference between the present perfect and past tenses, in the sense that they use them correctly, but very few would be able to explain the difference; by contrast, some learners of English can explain the difference between the two tenses (they 'know' the rule) but they cannot use the tenses correctly. It is, of course, applying the rules that is important in language learning; and in the case of our first language this is an entirely subconscious process. It may be that in learning a second language too the best way to acquire rules is subconsciously, by reading and listening to language we understand and by attempting to communicate in the language, rather than by consciously 'learning grammar'.

We have considered three views of the learning process, learning by heart, forming habits by drilling and repetition, and acquiring rules naturally through attempts to communicate. All these are valid views of the ways in which language skills can be developed although the third is the most powerful. Habit formation undoubtedly has a role to play but if our aim is to develop the skill to communicate in unpredicted circumstances then we have to provide our learners with the opportunity to acquire the underlying rules of the language themselves.

Discussion

Following the ideas in this text, what conclusions might you come to about:
1. students' errors
2. repetition drills
3. explaining grammar rules
4. using English in class

16 Correcting errors

Aims of this unit
- To make teachers more aware of the significance of learners' errors.
- To help teachers develop positive strategies of error correction.
- To show teachers a range of techniques for correcting oral and written errors.

This unit sets out to help teachers develop sensitivity in correcting errors; it encourages them to develop a positive attitude towards their students' errors, and suggests ways of correcting errors that will help, rather than hinder, the learning process.

This unit is concerned with lexical and grammatical errors in both spoken and written language, but not with problems of handwriting or pronunciation. These are dealt with in Unit 11: Teaching handwriting and Unit 10: Teaching pronunciation.

[*Note:* For Activity 5 of this unit, teachers will need examples of their own students' errors or of typical learners they know. These can be either written errors or spoken errors which teachers have noted down. They will of course need to be told about this well in advance of the training session.]

INTRODUCTION

▶ Workbook Activity 1 ◀

1. Ask teachers to read and comment on the three approaches to error correction in the Teacher's Workbook.

   Here are three teachers' approaches to correcting errors.

   Teacher A:

   > I never let my students make mistakes. If they say anything wrong, I stop them and make them say it correctly. I don't want them to learn bad English from each other.

186

Teacher B:

> I correct students sometimes, but not all the time. If we're practising one particular language point, then I insist that they say it correctly. But if we're doing a freer activity then I try not to correct too much. If I do correct students, I try to do it in an encouraging way.

Teacher C:

> I try to correct errors as little as possible. I want my students to express themselves in English without worrying too much about making mistakes. Sometimes I notice points that everyone gets wrong, and deal with them later – but I never interrupt students to correct them.

Think of yourself as a *learner*. Which teacher would you prefer? Why?

2. Use teachers' comments as a basis for a discussion of the significance of students' errors and the importance of correcting them. Establish these points:
   - Teachers are often afraid of their students making errors. They feel (like teacher A) that students might 'learn their mistakes', and so they must make sure that everything they say is correct. This idea derives from views of language learning which were popular in the 1950s and 1960s; it was believed that language was learned by repetition of correct forms until they became automatic, and so repeating incorrect forms would be harmful.
   - It is now widely agreed that language is not learnt in this way; rather it is a system of rules that the learner has to acquire, and that 'trying out' language and making errors are a natural and unavoidable part of this process. (This is not a surprising idea – it may be helpful to refer to other complex skills in which errors are accepted as a natural part of the learning process, e.g. mastering chess, learning to cook, learning a musical instrument.)
   - Students' errors are a very useful way of showing what they have and have not learnt. So instead of seeing errors negatively, as a sign of failure (by the student or the teacher), we can see them *positively* as an indication of what we still need to teach. Obviously, if we try

to prevent students from making errors we can never find out what they do not know.

– Most teachers would agree (like teacher B in the Workbook activity) that we need to correct some errors, to help students learn the correct forms of the language. (Most students would also expect this – there is a danger in teacher C's class that students might feel that they were 'not being taught properly'.) But this does not mean that we have to correct students *all* the time – if we do, it might make them unwilling or unable to say anything at all.

3. Now discuss *when* it is important to correct students' errors. Make the general point that it depends on the kind of activity we are doing and the aim of the activity: whether we mainly want students to produce *accurate* language or whether we want them to express themselves freely and develop *fluency*. To make this clear, give two examples and comment on each.

Example one

You have just presented a number of verbs with irregular past tense forms. Now you are practising them using a simple picture story.
(The aim of this activity is to check that students can use the verbs correctly. You have to correct any major errors, especially those involving the verbs you have taught, or the activity will lose its point.)

Example two

There is some vacant land near your school. You are discussing with your students (in English) what should be done with it. You want them to give interesting ideas.
(In this activity, you want students to use English freely to talk about real life. You want them to express their ideas as fluently as possible; so you should be careful *not* to correct too much or you will interrupt the activity. It would be best either to correct only the most serious errors, and to do so quickly and quietly, or to remember the commonest errors and deal with them afterwards.)

CORRECTING SPOKEN ERRORS

Strategies for correcting errors

1. Discuss different possible ways of correcting errors. Begin by demonstrating an imaginary exchange between a teacher and a

student. Either act this out as a dialogue with a colleague, or read out both parts yourself. Explain that the teacher is practising daily routine, using the present simple tense:

T: Paul – what do you do in the morning?
S: I . . . am . . . get up . . . at half past six.
T: Hmm, that's not right, is it? I *get* up – not 'I am get up'. I *get* up. Antoine – what about you? . . .

Ask teachers to comment on this technique. Establish that:
– The teacher was very discouraging, although the student tried to give a good answer.
– The teacher did not give the student a chance to say the sentence correctly.
– Although the teacher asked a real question, he or she showed no interest in the student's answer.

Now discuss what else the teacher could have done. Try to elicit ideas from the teachers, and then give a short demonstration of each technique, if possible using a colleague as a 'student'.
– The teacher could correct the student in a more *positive* way, and give him a chance to say the sentence correctly, e.g.:

T: Well, all right, but – I *get up*. Again.
S: I get up at half past six.
T: Good.

– The teacher could help the student to *correct himself*, by showing where the error was in the sentence, e.g.:

T: Yes, OK, nearly. What should it be? I g . . .
S: I get up at half past six.
T: That's right – good.

This is a good technique if you think the student really knows the correct form, and so can correct his or her own mistake.
– The teacher could pass the question to *another student*, and then come back to the first student again, e.g.:

T: Well, nearly. Anyone else? What do you do in the morning? Yes – Pierre?
S2: I get up at seven o'clock.
T: Yes, that's it. I *get up*. Now, Paul – again.
S1: I get up at half past six.
T: Yes. Well done.

This technique helps to involve the rest of the class, but it should be used with care; it is important not to make the first student feel 'victimised'.

Summarise your discussion by emphasising these basic principles of positive error correction:
– As far as possible, encourage the students, focussing on what they have got right, not on what they have got wrong.
– Praise students for correct answers, and even for partly correct answers; in this way, they will feel they are making progress.
– Avoid humiliating students or making them feel that making a mistake is 'bad'.
– Correct errors quickly; if too much time is spent over correcting errors, it gives them too much importance and holds up the lesson.

▶ Workbook Activity 2 ◀

2. Point out that there is no single 'best' technique for correcting errors. The most important thing is for the teacher to be flexible and to be aware of the effect on each individual learner of correcting errors. So a good teacher will use different strategies according to the kind of error, the ability and personality of the student, and the general atmosphere of the class.

   Divide the teachers into pairs. Ask them to look at the examples of students' responses in the Teacher's Workbook and to decide what strategy they would use to correct the error in each case. They should try to imagine exactly what they might say to the student.

> Dear Marco,
>   I was very glad to get your letter and to hear about all the things you are doing.
>   Thank you for sending the stamps. They are very beautiful and I have added them to my collection.
>   I am sending you a few photographs of my family. The tall girl with the dark hair is my elder sister, and the shorter one is my cousin. I

Here is part of a letter, written by a student called Carlos to his pen-friend Marco.

You read this text with the class in an earlier lesson. Now you are asking questions to review the main words and structures.

You ask the question: 'What does Carlos do?'
What would you do if:
a) A student answers: 'Carlos collects the stamps'.
b) A student answers: 'He collects'.
c) A student cannot answer at all.
d) One of the *weakest* students answers: 'He collecting stamps'.

e) One of the *best* students answers: 'He collecting stamps'.

f) A student answers: 'He writes a letter'.

When most pairs have finished, discuss their answers together. There are of course no single 'correct' answers, but try to lead teachers towards positive and encouraging strategies.

Possible strategies:

a) Accept the answer – it is nearly correct. Or help the student to correct himself or herself (e.g. by saying 'Just "stamps". He collects . . .').

b) Indicate by a gesture that the sentence is incomplete. Or say: 'Yes, he collects. But he collects what?' Ask another student if necessary.

c) Ask another student, then perhaps give the first student a chance later. Or give the answer and let the student repeat it.

d) Accept the answer, and praise the student, but then say the correct form yourself, e.g. 'Yes, good – he collects stamps'.

e) Help the student to correct himself or herself: 'Well, nearly – What does he do? He . . .', or ask another student.

f) Accept the answer, giving the correct tense yourself. Then perhaps rephrase the question to make it clearer: 'Well yes, he has written a letter. But what does he do in his free time? What's his hobby?'

Helping students to correct themselves

▶ Workbook Activity 3 ◀

1. Point out that it is a good idea to give students a chance to correct their own errors, as long as this can be done easily and without holding up the class. We can often do this by using *gestures*, which indicate where the error is in the sentence and what kind of error it is.

Look at the examples in the pictures.

Discuss what the error is in each case, and what gestures the teacher is using to point the error out:

Example 1: Word order: 'you' and 'are' should be the other way round. The teacher is circling two fingers to show 'the other way round'.

Example 2: 'At' is missing. The teacher is 'counting out' the words on her fingers. An alternative would be to indicate 'insert a word', e.g. by pointing.
[*Note:* The use of gestures of course varies from one country to another. Discuss with the teachers what gestures *they* would find most appropriate.]

2. Divide the teachers into pairs. Ask them to look at the examples of spoken errors and decide what gestures they could use to indicate the error to the student.

> 1. Here are some sentences spoken by students. What is the error in each one?
> What *gestures* could you use to help the students correct the errors themselves?

> 2. Work in pairs. Act out each 'dialogue' between the teacher and the student.

3. Discuss together what gestures might be used, and if necessary demonstrate possible gestures yourself. Then ask them to practise short exchanges in pairs:
   i)   One teacher pretends to be a student, and says one of the sentences.
   ii) The other teacher uses gestures to show what the error is.
   iii) The first teacher gives the correct form.

CORRECTING WRITTEN WORK

Introduction

1. Correcting written work is very time-consuming for the teacher, and often seems to have very little effect on students' progress. So, especially with large classes and at lower levels, it is a good idea to give writing tasks which:
   - are easy and limited, so that students will not make too many mistakes;

– can easily be corrected in class.

Ask teachers to suggest different kinds of controlled writing activity which can be easily corrected, and make suggestions yourself, e.g. (at elementary – intermediate level) copying sentences in the correct order; matching halves of sentences; gap-filling; writing sentences following oral practice.

Note: Examples of these and other writing exercises can be found in Unit 11: Teaching handwriting, Unit 13: Writing activities and Unit 21: Using worksheets.

2. Now suggest a basic procedure for correcting simple written work in class:
   i) The teacher writes the correct answers on the board, or gets students to come out and write them. If spelling is not important, he or she can go through the answers orally.
   ii) As the teacher gives the answers, students correct their own work and the teacher moves around the class to supervise what they are doing; or students can exchange books and correct each other's work.
   iii) When the teacher notices errors made by a number of students, he or she can draw attention to these for the benefit of the whole class.

Techniques for correcting written work

1. With more advanced classes it is more important for the teacher to correct students' work individually, and even with lower level classes this will sometimes be necessary. As with oral work, the teacher's corrections should have a positive effect on the student's work rather than a discouraging one.

   Ask teachers to imagine an exercise in which students write sentences about what they and other people enjoy doing. Write this example of a student's sentence on the board:

   my bruther injoys to play football.

   Discuss what corrections the teacher should make. Try to bring out these points:
   – The student has made many mistakes, but the sentence is not as bad as it looks – the student has managed to write something that makes sense. Most of the mistakes are very minor ones.
   – The purpose of the exercise was to practise 'enjoy + -ing', so this part needs to be corrected, and the '-s' ending is also important; the

teacher can correct both these errors together by writing 'enjoys playing' above the line.
- It might be better to ignore the spelling mistakes; correcting them will distract attention from the main point. The teacher could make a note of them and include them in a later lesson.

▶ **Workbook Activity 4** ◀

2. Ask teachers to look at the example of corrected written work in the Teacher's Workbook, and discuss the way the teacher has corrected it.

Here is some written work, corrected by a teacher.

Machiko

> I think the most important sense is hearing.
> If I lose the ability of hearing, I also can't speak. ~~TO HEAR~~ ~~cannot speak either.~~
> To lose hearing means to lose two important functions of human).
>
> Deaf-and-dumb people cannot hear the noise even if the accident happens in their back. This is the most important problem for them. For example, suppose that they ride a bike in the busy street. We, normal people feel the danger by the noise which is made by cars and lorries. As a result of hearing the noise, we can avoid them and drive safely. Deaf-and-dumb people always expose their to danger. ... are always exposed to danger.

(marginal notes: problem; Lorry / lorries)

1. How could the teacher's corrections be made:
   - clearer?
   - less discouraging?
   - more useful to the student?

Point out that the effect of so many corrections would probably be to discourage the student – they make it appear that she has written almost nothing correctly. Discuss ways of correcting the student's work more positively and effectively. Get ideas from the teachers and make these suggestions yourself:
- The teacher could correct only the errors that seem most important, or only errors of a certain kind (e.g. items that were taught recently, or just problems with verbs).
- The teacher could reduce the amount of underlining and write corrections in the margin; this would make the page look less heavily corrected.

– The teacher could simply indicate where the student has made important errors, and ask her to try to correct them herself. This would encourage the student to look again at what she has written and think about possible errors:

> Deaf - and - dumb people cannot hear <u>the</u> noise
> even if <u>the</u> accident happens <u>in their back</u>.

[*Note:* For more advanced classes, some teachers develop systems of abbreviations which they regularly write in the margin to indicate different kinds of error, e.g. sp = spelling mistake, g = grammar mistake, WO = word order. This leaves the students to correct all their own mistakes, and gives good training in reading through and checking what they have written. Discuss this idea if it seems relevant and of interest to the teachers.]

3. Divide the teachers into pairs or small groups. Ask them to make their own corrections to the student's work, applying some of the ideas that were raised in the discussion.

> 2. Now correct the student's work yourself.
>
> > I think the most important sense is hearing.
> > If I lose the ability of hearing, I also can't speak.
> > To lose hearing means to lose two important function of human.
> > Deaf - and - dumb people cannot hear the noise even if the accident happens in their back. This is the most important ploblem for them. For example, suppose that they ride a bike in the busy street. We, normal people feel the dangerous by the noise which is made by cars and lorrys. As a result of hearing the noise, we can avoide them and drive safely. Deaf - and - dumb people always expose their to danger.

Common written errors

1. Written errors which students make consistently (or which many students make) can be very useful, because they show what the students have learnt and what areas might need to be taught again.
   Ask teachers to look again at the example on the board:

> my bruther injoye to play football.

Discuss what the teacher might need to 're-teach', assuming that many students in the class have made similar mistakes:
- The basic structure 'enjoy + -ing'. The teacher could give more practice of this form, using different examples.
- The use of a capital letter to start a sentence. It might be enough merely to remind students of this.
- Third person singular '-s' ending. Again, students probably 'know' this already, so they would just need reminding of it.

▶ **Workbook Activity 5** ◀

2. Divide the teachers into groups, and ask them to look at the examples of common students' errors which they have brought with them. (If teachers have not brought examples, they could remember errors that they have noticed, or you could build up a list of common errors on the board.)

Ask each group to choose five of the errors, and discuss them.

Work in groups.
Look at examples of common errors which your own students have made.
Choose *five* which you think are important, and discuss:
- What seems to be the cause of each error?
- Does it show something the students do not understand? Or is it something they understand but still get wrong?
- What should you do about it?

3. When most groups have finished, stop the activity. Ask one person from each group to report briefly on their discussion.

LESSON PREPARATION

▶ **Workbook Activity 6** ◀

Either organise the activity during the training session (as a continuation of the previous activity), or let teachers prepare in their own time after the session.

FURTHER READING

P. Hubbard (1983) *A Training Course of TEFL* (Chapter 4: Errors and mistakes), Oxford University Press. A detailed discussion of different types of error and their causes and of different approaches to error correction.

17   Listening activities

Aims of this unit
– To make teachers more aware of the importance of listening in learning English.
– To show teachers the advantages of focussed listening activities.
– To show teachers techniques for listening which they can use in their own classes.

This unit focusses on activities that are specifically designed for practice in listening, with or without a cassette recorder. If the teacher uses English as much as possible in class, students will also have opportunities to listen to English as part of other activities. Using English for 'chatting' to the class and for giving instructions and explanations is dealt with in Unit 19: Using English in class.

Part of this unit is concerned with techniques involved in using a text or dialogue for listening. Some of these techniques are also included in Unit 5: Using a reading text and Unit 15: Reading activities.

Preparation
For this unit you will need a cassette recorder.

INTRODUCTION

The importance of listening
Begin by establishing the importance of listening:
– We cannot develop speaking skills unless we also develop listening skills; to have a successful conversation, students must understand what is said to them. Later, the ability to understand spoken English may become very important (for listening to the radio, understanding foreign visitors, studying, etc.). To develop this ability, students need plenty of practice in listening to English spoken at normal speed.
– Listening to spoken English is an important way of *acquiring* the language – of 'picking up' structures and vocabulary. In a situation where learners are living in a country where English is the first language, they have plenty of 'exposure' to the language – they hear it all the time, and can acquire it more easily than learners who do not

hear English spoken around them. So we need to give these learners as much opportunity to listen to spoken English as possible.

Listening in real life

In real life, there are two ways in which we often listen:
- *'Casual' listening:* Sometimes we listen with no particular purpose in mind, and often without much concentration. Examples of this kind of listening are: listening to the radio while doing some housework; chatting to a friend. Usually we do not listen very closely, unless we hear something that particularly interests us, and afterwards we may not remember much of what we heard.
- *'Focussed' listening:* At other times we listen for a particular purpose, to find out information we need to know. Examples of this kind of listening are: listening to a piece of important news on the radio; listening to someone explaining how to operate a machine. In these situations, we listen much more closely; but we do not listen to everything we hear with equal concentration – we listen for the most important points or for particular information. Usually, we know beforehand what we are listening *for* (the things we want to know), and this *helps* us to listen.

Focussed listening

▶ **Workbook Activity 1** ◀

In class, we are usually concerned with the second kind of listening: we expect the students to listen closely and remember afterwards what they heard. But if we just ask the class to 'listen' and we ask questions afterwards, we are giving them a very difficult task. We can make it easier by telling them beforehand what to expect and what to listen for – this will help them to *focus* their listening.

Demonstrate two ways of doing this: by giving a simple *listening task* and by giving *guiding questions.*

》》》 ➤

Demonstration one

i)   Ask teachers to look at the table in the Teacher's Workbook.

> A. The trainer will talk to you about himself/herself.
>   Listen and write notes in the table.

Home town	
Brothers/sisters	
Children	
Interests	
Holidays	

Talk to them about yourself (or, if you prefer, someone else or an imaginary person). Include the information they need to complete the table, but add other details as well. As they listen, they should write brief notes in the table.

ii) Ask teachers to tell you the main points they noted down.

Demonstration two

i) Tell the teachers you will read them a text in which someone
    remembers things he did when he was a child. Explain that they
    should listen and try to find the answers to the questions in the
    Teacher's Workbook.

> B. You will hear a text about someone's childhood.
>   Listen and try to answer these questions.
>   1. Where did he stay?
>   2. What does he say about:
>   – the river?
>   – his bicycle?
>   – the fruit trees?

ii) Read this text aloud:

> I remember when I was a child we often went to stay with my
> grandfather – he had a farm in the country, and we used to stay
> there, and I had a wonderful time – there was so much for a child to
> do there. I remember there was a small river that ran past the farm,
> and I used to go swimming in it – I suppose the water must have
> been fairly clean. And another thing I remember was – I had a
> bicycle and I rode it round and round the fields, and along the river
> bank, too. And what else? Oh yes, climbing trees. There were quite
> a lot of fruit trees on the farm, peaches and apricots, mostly, and I
> used to climb these trees and pick the fruit for my grandfather. Of
> course sometimes I climbed them and picked the fruit when he
> wasn't looking as well, but I don't think he ever found out!
>
> (adapted from *Meanings into words* Intermediate: A. Doff, C. Jones and K.
> Mitchell)

iii) Go through the answers to the questions. If necessary, read the text a
     second time.

After your demonstrations, discuss the two techniques. Point out that the
table and the questions serve the same purpose: they *focus* the students'
attention by giving them something specific to listen for; they give them a
reason to listen and also *help* them to listen by leading them towards the
main points.

HELPING STUDENTS TO LISTEN

Using a dialogue for listening

► **Workbook Activity 2** ◄

1. Look at the dialogue in the Teacher's Workbook, and the teacher's description of her lesson.

> A teacher used this dialogue for listening. Below, she describes what she did and how well it worked.

Doctor: Now then, what seems to be the matter?
Peter: Well, I've got a sore throat. I've had it for three days now. It's really sore – it hurts when I try to swallow, and it's very painful if I try to eat anything hard, like bread or anything like that. And I feel a bit cold and shivery all the time.
Doctor: Open your mouth and let's have a look.

. . . .

Well, you've got a throat infection, but it's nothing serious. Here you are – take this to the chemist's and he'll give you some tablets to take. That should clear it up. If it isn't better in two or three days, come and see me again.

1. Which sentences are *true*, which are *false*?
   a) Peter has a sore throat.
   b) He feels hot.
   c) He can't eat bread.

> I told the class to close their books and listen, and I read the dialogue twice. Then I asked the questions. But they couldn't answer most of them. So I told them to open their books, and we read the dialogue together. Then they seemed to find it quite easy. They couldn't understand it from just listening – it was too difficult for them.

What could the teacher do to *help* the students to listen?

Point out that the teacher really only tested the class's comprehension by asking questions; when she found that they did not understand she moved to reading. Discuss what the teacher could do to help the students to listen and so improve their listening skills. Get the teachers to give their own ideas, and make these suggestions yourself:

– She could *introduce the topic* before getting the class to listen to the dialogue, e.g. by discussing what you say when you go to the doctor, what the doctor does, etc. This would help the students to *predict* what the dialogue would be about. If necessary, the teacher could also present new vocabulary at this point.

– She could give one or two 'guiding questions' before the listening stage, e.g.:

What's wrong with Peter's throat?

What does the doctor do?

This would help *focus students' attention* on the main points of the dialogue.

– She could divide the listening into *stages*, e.g.:

First listening: Students listen for main idea only, to answer the guiding questions.

Second listening: Students listen for details, e.g. How exactly does Peter feel? What things does he have to do?

For the second listening, the teacher could divide the dialogue into two sections, and check comprehension after each section. (This would be very important with a longer piece of listening.)

2. Summarise the points you have made by suggesting a possible procedure for using the dialogue, and demonstrate it if necessary:
   i) Introduce the topic.
   ii) Give guiding questions.
   iii) Read the dialogue. Students listen for the main idea and answer guiding questions.
   iv) Read the first part again, and ask questions to check detailed comprehension. Do the same with the second part.
   v) Students open their books. Read the dialogue while students follow.

[*Note:* If this procedure were followed, the questions in the book would be unnecessary, or could be used as written exercises for homework.]

Point out that, although you used a dialogue in your demonstration, exactly the same techniques could be applied when using a text for listening.

Using a cassette recorder

1. Discuss the advantages of using a cassette recorder for listening activities, and also some of the problems involved. Encourage teachers to talk about their own experiences of using the cassette recorder. Try to bring out these points:
   - The cassette recorder gives a chance for students to listen to a variety of voices apart from the teacher's, and it is a way of bringing native speakers' voices into the classroom. Students who have only heard English spoken by their teacher often have difficulty understanding other people.
   - Recorded material is useful for listening to dialogues, interviews, discussions, etc. where there is more than one person speaking. Otherwise the teacher has to act the part of more than one person.
   - Listening to a cassette recording is much more difficult than listening to the teacher. When we listen to someone 'face to face', there are many visual clues (e.g. gestures, lip movements) which help us to listen. When we listen to a cassette these clues are missing.
   - In a large class with bad acoustics, listening to a cassette may be very difficult indeed. Up to a point, trying to listen to something that is not clear can provide good listening practice, but if it is too difficult it will just be frustrating.

2. Point out that an important part of listening is being able to 'catch' words and phrases that we hear; students who have not had much chance to listen to English often fail to recognise words that they already know. The cassette recorder is very useful for giving practice in this, because the cassette can be stopped and a phrase played over and over again. This kind of listening practice is often called 'intensive listening'. Give a demonstration, using any piece of recorded material you have available:
   i) Introduce the listening, and give one or two guiding questions.
   ii) Play the cassette once without stopping, and discuss the guiding questions.
   iii) Play the cassette again. This time, focus on important points, pausing and asking what the person said each time. If teachers are unable to 'catch' the remark, rewind the cassette a little way and play it again.

   After your demonstration, discuss the technique. Emphasise that the aim is to focus on the most important remarks only, but *not* of course to go through the whole of a listening text phrase by phrase.

▶ **Workbook Activity 3** ◀

3. Ask teachers to look at the dialogue in Activity 2, and to follow the instructions in the Teacher's Workbook.

> Imagine you are using the dialogue in Activity 2 for intensive listening, using a cassette recorder.
> Which parts of the text would you focus the students' attention on? Underline them, and mark places where you would pause the recording.

When teachers have finished, discuss the dialogue together.

GETTING STUDENTS TO PREDICT

1. An important part of the skill of listening is being able to *predict* what the speaker is going to say next; as we saw earlier, we can help students to listen by giving them some idea of what they are going to listen to.

    When doing listening activities in class, we can also *ask* students to guess what they are going to hear next; this will help them develop listening skills, and is also a good way to keep the class actively involved in listening. This technique is especially useful for telling stories to the class; a natural part of listening to an interesting story is to wonder what will happen next.

    Demonstrate this by telling the teachers an imaginary story about yourself (or, even better, a real one). Stop frequently, and ask them to guess what you are going to say next. Try to get as many suggestions as possible each time, e.g.:

    A few nights ago, I was asleep at home as usual. At about three o'clock in the morning . . . (*What happened?*) . . . I was suddenly awakened by a noise . . . (*What noise?*) . . . of rushing water . . . (*What was it?*) It came from the bathroom, so I got up and went to investigate . . . (*What was it?*) I found to my dismay that the cold water pipe had burst and water was pouring all over the floor . . . (*So what did I do?*) So I got a bucket and put it underneath . . . (*What should I have done?*) Then I realised what I should have done. I went out into the hall and turned off the mains tap.

    After your demonstration, discuss the technique. Make these points:
    – Asking questions keeps the class involved, and is also a way of

checking that the students are following the story. (It is, of course, a technique used by story-tellers everywhere.)

– The same technique can be used with any kind of story – a story about yourself, a historical story, a folk tale, or a fable. Stories are one of the easiest ways for teachers to give listening practice if there are not enough listening activities in the textbook.

▶ Workbook Activity 4 ◀

2. Divide the teachers into pairs. Ask them to read the story in the Teacher's Workbook, and decide at which points they could stop and ask students to make predictions. When pairs have finished, ask them to practise telling the story to each other and pausing to ask questions.

> A. Work in pairs. Read this story.

> Once there was a boy called Ali, a poor fisherman's son. As he was going home one evening, he saw an old man lying by the side of the road, seriously ill. The boy was very kind, and he helped the old man to the nearest hospital. The old man thanked the boy and asked him for his name and address. The boy was ashamed to admit that his father was a poor fisherman, so he said, 'My name is Mustafa and my father is a teacher'. A few days later, the old man died in hospital, and left all his money to 'Mustafa, a local teacher's son who helped me in my hour of need'. Of course, because Ali had lied, he did not receive any of the old man's money.

> Mark *five* places in the story where you could stop and ask students to predict what will happen next. What question would you ask each time? Practise telling the story to your partner.

3. Ask teachers to think of another story of their own. (It can be any kind of story, real or imaginary.) Ask a few teachers to come out and tell their story, using the other teachers as a class.

> B. Think of a story of your own. Practise telling it, pausing every now and then to ask what will happen next.

LESSON PREPARATION

▶ Workbook Activity 5 ◀

Either organise the preparation during the training session, with teachers working together in pairs or groups, or let teachers prepare in their own time after the session.

FURTHER READING

G. Brown (1977) *Listening to Spoken English*, Longman. Examines the problems encountered in listening to conversational English and offers an approach to teaching listening skills.

G. Brown and G. Yule (1983) *Teaching the Spoken Language*, Cambridge University Press. Examines the nature of spoken language, and considers techniques for teaching spoken production and listening comprehension.

P. Ur (1984) *Teaching Listening Comprehension*, Cambridge University Press. Investigates the background to listening comprehension and gives practical suggestions for designing listening activities.

J. Morgan and M. Rinvolucri (1983) *Once Upon a Time*, Cambridge University Press. A resource book for teachers on story-telling in class.

18 Communicative activities

Aims of this unit
- To make teachers aware of some of the features of real communication.
- To show teachers simple ways of getting students to communicate with each other in the classroom.

This unit is concerned with simple communicative activities that teachers can use in their own classes: it deals with guessing games, 'information gap' exercises for pairwork, and activities in which students exchange personal information. Many activities of this kind require specially prepared material and are only suitable for small classes; this unit focusses on activities that can be used with large classes and without elaborate preparation.

    This unit is mainly concerned with controlled communicative activities. Freer communicative activities, such as discussion and role play, are included in other units – Unit 6: Practising structures, Unit 12: Pairwork and groupwork, Unit 14: Eliciting and Unit 20: Role play.

INTRODUCTION

This unit introduces techniques for getting students to communicate with each other in English. Begin by establishing some of the main features of real communication; discuss how people use language in real life, and compare this with the way language is often used in the classroom.

► **Workbook Activity 1** ◄

1. Ask teachers to look at the three short conversations in the Teacher's Workbook. Discuss:
   – in what situation each conversation might take place in real life;
   – why the person might be asking the question.

   A. Imagine you hear these conversations in real life. What might the situation be? Why is the person asking these questions?

There are of course many possible answers; encourage teachers to give as many ideas as they can, e.g.:
   – Father asking mother about daughter – he has just arrived home and she is not in the room, so he wonders where she is.
     A friend calling at Hana's house and asking her mother – she wants to go out with her.
   – Someone being interviewed for a job (e.g. as a secretary). The interviewer needs to know because the job involves typing.
   – Someone enquiring about a room which they want to rent, or someone booking a room in a hotel; they want to know if it is suitable.

From the discussion, establish these main points:
   – In all the conversations, the two people are *genuinely exchanging information*. There is something that one person does not know and wants to find out, and that is why he or she is asking a question. We can say that the person has a *'communicative need'*.
   – Although this is not the only reason why people communicate in real life, it is one of the main reasons; very often we talk in order to tell people things they do not know, or to find things out from other people.

2. Now ask teachers to look at the picture of the room in part B of the Workbook activity, and to imagine that it is being used for language practice in class.

B. Imagine students in a class are asking and answering questions about this picture. What might they say? Why are they asking these questions?

Discuss what questions students might ask and answer, e.g.:
    What kind of room is it? (*a bedroom*)
    Is there a cupboard in the room? (*Yes, there is*)
    How many chairs are there? (*two*)
    Where's the desk? (*by the window*)
    etc.
Compare this activity with the conversations in part A, and establish these points:
— In part B, the students are asking and answering questions, but they are *not* genuinely exchanging information. They are not asking the questions in order to find out anything they need to know (for example, they do not really want to know how many chairs there are, because they can *see* that there are two). So they do not have any 'communicative need'.
— The students are using similar language to the people in the 'real life' conversation, but the purpose of the questions is quite different – it is simply to *practise language*.
Although activities like this provide useful language practice, they are often not very interesting, because there is no real purpose in asking the questions, nor any need to listen to the answers. The activity would become more interesting if we could create a *reason* for asking the questions. We can do this by hiding the information, either from all the students or from some students, so that there is something they need to

find out. This is sometimes called an *'information gap'* – one person has information which another does not have, so there is a need to communicate. In this unit, you will deal with three simple kinds of 'information gap' activity: *guessing games, information gap exercises for pairwork*, and activities in which students exchange *personal information*.

GUESSING GAMES

1. Demonstrate a guessing game using a picture. Use the picture below, or any other fairly simple picture which shows people engaged in some activity (it could be a picture from a magazine or a drawing).

i)   Tell the teachers that you have a picture (but do not show it to them). In the picture there are a man, a woman and a train. They must find out exactly what the picture looks like by asking questions. You can only answer 'Yes' or 'No' – but you can help them by giving hints (e.g. 'You still don't know where the train is').
ii) When they have a clear idea of the picture, they should try to draw it.
iii) Finally, show them the picture.
After your demonstration, discuss the activity, and compare it with the way the picture was used in Activity 1:
– Hiding the picture gives students a genuine reason to ask questions: there is information they need to find out. They also have to listen carefully to the answers, so that they can draw the picture.
– Although the activity as a whole is controlled by the teacher, the students are mainly asking questions that *they* want to ask, not ones the teacher tells them to ask.

▶ **Workbook Activity 2** ◀

2. Read through the three examples of guessing games in the Teacher's Workbook, explaining anything that is not clear. Comment briefly on

each one, and discuss what other language could be practised using the same technique. Point out that they could all be used either as fairly free activities (perhaps for general revision of vocabulary), or as an interesting way to give quite controlled structure practice. Although they are called 'games', they provide intensive language practice, especially in asking questions – so they should not just be regarded as an 'extra' activity. (If you like, demonstrate the three guessing games, using your own flashcards and sentences on paper.)

A. *Guess the picture*

The teacher has a set of flashcards with simple pictures (e.g. clothes, food, places, actions). He or she chooses one card, but does *not* show it to the class. They must guess what it is by asking questions, e.g.:

T: Guess how I went to X.
Ss: Did you go by car?
　　Did you go by bus?
　　Did you walk?

B. *Guess the sentence*

The teacher writes a sentence on a piece of paper or card. He or she does not show the sentence, but writes the basic structure on the board, e.g.:
I went (somewhere) to (do something).
Students must guess the exact sentence by asking questions, e.g.:
　　Did you go to the park?
　　Did you go to school?
　　Did you go to the stadium?
　　Did you play football?

C. *Mime*

The teacher calls a student to the front and secretly gives her a sentence written on a piece of paper, which describes a simple activity. The student mimes the activity. The other students try to guess the situation.

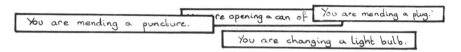

3. Discuss different ways of *organising* guessing games. Ask teachers to look at the pictures in the Teacher's Workbook, and discuss the two techniques.

> Here are two ways of organising guessing games in class. Which do you think is better? Why?

Make these points:
- In any guessing game, it is a good idea for the teacher to stand aside and let students take over the activity (as shown in both pictures).
- The technique shown in the left-hand picture (one student at the front, the others guessing) gives more students a chance to ask questions, but in a large class it might be difficult to involve all the students. The technique shown in the right-hand picture (two students at the front, one guessing and the rest of the class responding in chorus) is more highly organised and keeps the whole class involved, although most students do not have to say very much – so it might be a useful technique for a large class.
- Guessing games can also be organised with students working in small groups. The teacher gives a picture or a sentence to one student in each group, and the others in the group try to guess it. The pictures or sentences can be circulated from one group to the next, so it is not necessary to produce very many copies.

4. Divide the teachers into either three or six groups. Ask each group to look at one of the three types of guessing games, and make up a similar game of their own (using the same technique, but different examples).

5. Ask one teacher from each group to come out in turn and play the game, using the other teachers as a class.

6. If there is time, tell teachers briefly about other guessing games, and ask them to describe any they know themselves. Some games which are widely used in English language classes:
   - *Famous people:* One student pretends to be a famous person (alive or dead) who is known to the others. They try to guess who the person is, by asking questions, e.g.:

     Are you alive or dead? (*alive*)
     Are you English? (*yes*)
     Are you a writer? (*no*)
     etc.
   - *What's my line?:* One student chooses a job, and mimes a typical activity which it involves. The others try to guess the job by asking questions either about the activity or the job, e.g.:

     Were you mending something?
     Were you digging?
     Do you work outside?
     etc.
   - *What and where?:* The teacher sends two students out of the room. The other students hide an object. The two students come back and guess what the object is and where it is hidden, by asking questions, e.g.:

     Is it made of wood?
     Is it a pencil?
     Is it on this side of the room?
     Is it high or low?
     etc.

EXCHANGING INFORMATION

'Information gap' exercises

Many communicative activities are designed to be done by students working in pairs. To create a need to communicate, the two students in each pair are given *different* information. The activity can then work in various ways:
- One student has some information, and the other student has to find it out by asking questions.
- One student has some information and tells it to the other student.
- Both students have different information, and they tell each other.

▶ **Workbook Activity 3** ◀

1. Look at the examples of information gap exercises in the Teacher's Workbook, and explain how each one works.

> Here are some exercises for pairwork. In each pair, the two students are given different information.

> A.

STUDENT X	STUDENT Y
<table><tr><td>This evening</td><td></td></tr><tr><td>Tomorrow morning</td><td></td></tr><tr><td>Tomorrow afternoon</td><td></td></tr><tr><td>Tomorrow evening</td><td></td></tr></table>	Tonight Kim is going to stay at home, because he wants to write a letter to a friend. Tomorrow morning he has classes as usual at college; but he has the afternoon free, so he's going to help his father repair the roof on their house. In the evening he's been invited out to a party.

Procedure: Students sit in pairs. In each pair, Student X has an empty grid, and Student Y has the text, which he or she does not show to Student X. Student X completes the grid by asking questions, e.g.: What's he going to do tomorrow afternoon?

⟫→

B.

STUDENT X	STUDENT Y

STUDENT X

<u>Shopping list</u>

2 packets tea
1 kilo sugar
1 can orange juice
2 kilos rice
1 kilo beans
1 kilo oranges

STUDENT Y

YOU SELL:

tea   – 50p a packet
sugar   – 30p a kilo
rice   – 20p a kilo
orange juice – 25p a can

Procedure: Students sit in pairs. In each pair, Student X is a customer, and has a shopping list. Student Y is a shop assistant, and has a list of items in the shop and their prices. They do not look at each other's list. Student X tries to 'buy' the things on his or her list, e.g.:

A: Have you got any tea?
B: Yes, I have.
A: How much does it cost?
B: 50p a packet.

C. Find ten important differences.

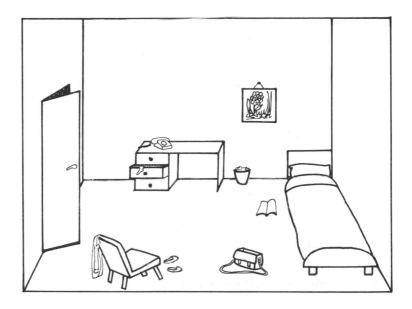

Procedure: The two students in each pair have pictures which are identical except for ten important differences. They do not look at each other's pictures, but try to find the differences by describing their picture, e.g. 'In my picture there's a boy lying in bed'. When they find a difference, they mark it on the picture.

[*Note:* If possible, *demonstrate* at least one of these exercises instead of just describing them. If you do this, you will need to copy the exercise onto two separate sheets of paper before the session, and make enough copies for every pair of teachers.]

2. Discuss the advantages and problems of using activities like these in class.
   Advantages: They provide intensive and interesting language practice. Although the exercises are quite controlled and use simple language, the students are really exchanging information and using language communicatively.
   Problems: They can easily be done in a small class (up to 20 students). In a large class there are the following problems:
   - *Preparation:* for a class of 40, the teacher would have to make 20 copies of each half of the exercise.
   - *Organisation:* the teacher would have to distribute 40 pieces of paper, make sure students in each pair get different parts of the exercise, and stop students looking at each other's information.

Discuss ways of adapting the activities for use in a large class. Get suggestions from the teachers, and give these ideas yourself:
- *Exercise A:* The students could copy the grid from the blackboard, then sit in groups. One student in each group could be given the text, and all the others ask questions. So for a class of 40, the teacher would only need to make about ten copies of the text.
- *Exercise B:* This could be done without any preparation by the teacher. Students could make their own lists, either of what they want to buy, or of what they have in the shop. (This could be done for homework before the lesson.)
- *Exercise C:* Copies of the picture would have to be produced beforehand. The class could be divided into two teams: team x has one picture (two or three students sharing), team y has the other. Students from each team take it in turns to say something about their picture.

Exchanging personal information

▶ Workbook Activity 4 ◀

1. One of the easiest and most interesting forms of communicative activity in the classroom is for students to tell each other about their own lives, interests, experiences, etc. When students talk about themselves, there is a natural 'information gap', because everybody has something slightly different to say.

   Demonstrate a simple activity in which students exchange information about their daily routine:
   i) Ask teachers to look at the grid in the Teacher's Workbook. Establish what questions they could ask about each topic, e.g.:
   When do you get up?
   When do you have breakfast? / What do you have for breakfast?
   When do you go to school? / How do you go to school?
   etc.

   1. Work in pairs. Ask your partner questions about his or her daily routine.

Get up?	
Breakfast?	

School?	
Lunch?	
Evening?	
Go out?	

2. Think of another activity like this, using a grid. Choose a topic that students would find interesting.

ii) Divide the teachers into pairs. They should take it in turns to ask questions and make brief notes in the grid. (They should make notes about their partner's routine, not their own.)

iii) When most pairs have finished, stop the activity. Ask a few teachers to tell you what their partner does (e.g. 'She gets up at seven o'clock, then she has some tea . . .').

2. After your demonstration, discuss the activity. Make these points:
   - Students are genuinely communicating – finding out things from each other that they did not know already, and which they need to know in order to complete the grid. Completing the grid is an essential part of the activity, because it makes the students *listen* to their partner's answers.
   - The activity gives intensive practice of time expressions and questions and answers using the present simple tense.

3. Divide the teachers into groups. Ask them to design a similar activity, using a grid. Suggest suitable topics, e.g.:
   What people like and dislike.
   What people are good/bad at doing.
   What makes people scared.
   Experiences (things people have and haven't done).
   Predictions (e.g. what people think will happen in the next ten years).
   Opinions (e.g. about well-known people).
   They should write the grid on a piece of paper.

⋙→

4. Ask one or two teachers to demonstrate their activity using the other teachers as a class. They should follow this procedure:
   i)   The teacher writes the grid on the board. The 'students' copy it.
   ii) 'Students' ask and answer questions in pairs, and complete the grid.
   iii) The teacher asks one or two 'students' what they found out about their partner.

LESSON PREPARATION

▶ **Workbook Activity 5** ◀

Either organise the preparation during the training session, with teachers working together in pairs or groups, or let teachers prepare in their own time after the session. Make sure that teachers can easily find enough paper for pair or group activities and that they can make enough copies for their class.

FURTHER READING

K. Johnson and K. Morrow (eds) (1981) *Communication in the Classroom*, Longman. A series of papers outlining the communicative approach to language teaching and its applications.

W. Littlewood (1981) *Communicative Language Teaching*, Cambridge University Press. An introduction to the principles of communicative language teaching, with practical examples.

J. Harmer (1983) *The Practice of English Language Teaching* (Chapter 8: Communicative activities), Longman. A description of various kinds of communicative activity, with examples of exercises.

19 Using English in class

Aims of this unit
- To show teachers the value of using English in class.
- To make teachers more aware of the different occasions when they could speak to their students in English.
- To give teachers a range of English expressions which they could use in their own classes.

This unit shows some of the opportunities for using simple English in the course of a lesson. It is mainly intended for teachers whose own language is not English and who teach classes of students who share a common language other than English.

This unit is concerned with the use of language rather than with teaching techniques. However, it includes a number of techniques and activities which are dealt with more fully in other units.

Preparation
For Activity 3 you will need a list of classroom expressions in the teachers' own language for them to translate into English. Details are given later in this unit.

INTRODUCTION

▶ Workbook Activity 1 ◀

1. Divide the teachers into pairs or groups and ask them to complete the table in the Teacher's Workbook. The purpose of this activity is to start teachers thinking about their own teaching and about opportunities for using English in class.

Think of your own lessons. In the activities below, do you normally use:
– mainly English?
– mainly the students' own language? ('L₁')
– a mixture of the two?

	English	L₁	Both
Introducing the lesson			
Checking attendance			
Organising where students sit			
Presenting new language			
Introducing a text			
Asking questions on a text			
Correcting errors			
Setting homework			

Briefly discuss with the teachers what answers they gave; but do not go into detail at this point about particular activities. Point out that there are two main ways in which English can be used in class:
– It can be used in teaching the lesson itself: giving examples, introducing a text, asking questions, etc.
– It can be used for activities which 'surround' the lesson, but which are not actually part of the teaching: checking attendance, telling students where to sit, 'chatting' to students, controlling the class.

2. Discuss the value of using English in class. Establish these points:
   – If the teacher uses English most of the time, it will give students practice in *listening* and *responding* to spoken English. This will help them 'pick up' words and expressions beyond the language of the textbook.
   – In the lesson itself, the language used is often unnatural and artificial. But the situations that occur in the classroom (e.g. a student arriving late, someone forgetting a book) give an opportunity for *real*, natural English to be used.
   – If the teacher uses English to say *real* things to the class, it will give the students the feeling that English is a real language which is used for *communication*, and not just a language that belongs to the textbook.

Emphasise that, although there are advantages in using English in class, teachers should not feel that they *must* use English all the time. Obviously, there are many occasions when it can be useful to use the students' own language. How much the teacher uses English will depend on the level of the class and the teacher's own language ability.

'SOCIAL' LANGUAGE

Instead of going straight to the textbook at the beginning of a lesson, the teacher can spend a few minutes 'chatting' to the class about topics of interest. After the very earliest stages, this can be done in English.

1. Give a few short demonstrations to show how this might be done. (Use the examples below as a guide, but of course talk about things the teachers have done themselves. Try to keep to simple language that teachers might use in their own classes.)

    – The teacher can talk and ask questions, but get the students to give only short responses, e.g.:

      T: Did you all enjoy the holiday?
      Ss: Yes.
      T: Did you? Yes, I enjoyed it, too. I went on a picnic with my family. Did you go on a picnic? Anyone?
      S: Yes.
      T: Who did you go with?
          (*and so on*)

      [*Note:* This would be a good technique for a large class or with low level students.]

    – The teacher can prompt individual students to talk more about things they have done, e.g.:

      T: What did you do? Did you go out?
      S: Yes, I went to a party.
      T: A party? That's nice. A birthday party?
      S: Yes, my friend's birthday.
      T: OK, tell us . . . what happened? What did you do at the party?
          (*and so on*)

    – The teacher can get students to talk and ask questions, e.g.:

      T: Right. Wang Xiao-Wen went to a party. Ask her some questions about it. What do you want to know? Yes?
      S1: What did you eat?
      S2: Was it a good party?   ⟫→

S3: Were there many people there?
(*and so on*)

[*Note:* In a large class it may be necessary to 'organise' the conversation more, so that the whole class is involved, e.g. T: Now everybody think of *one* question to ask Wang Xiao-Wen.]

After your demonstrations, discuss the purpose of 'chatting' in English in this way. Establish these points:

– It creates an opportunity for *real* language practice, and creates an 'English language' atmosphere in the class.
– Even more important, it establishes *contact* with the class, and helps students to feel *relaxed* and ready to learn. If we have a business appointment or meet a friend, we begin by chatting to establish a friendly atmosphere; it is just as important to do this when we meet a class of students.

▶ **Workbook Activity 2** ◀

2. Ask teachers to look at the topics in the Teacher's Workbook. Discuss what questions the teacher might ask about each one. Encourage teachers to think of 'follow-up' questions which would get the students to talk more and involve more of the class, e.g.:

What did you do yesterday? Did anyone go out? Where did you go? Who watched television? What did you watch? Did you like it? What was the film about? Tell the others about it.

Here are some possible topics for 'chatting' to the class at the beginning or end of a lesson.

1. What questions could you ask about each topic to encourage the students to talk?
2. Work in groups. Take it in turns to be 'teacher' – the rest of the group are your students. Choose one of the topics and 'chat' to your students.

3. Divide the teachers into groups. In each group, teachers take it in turns to be 'teacher' – the rest of the group are students. The 'teacher' chooses one of the topics (or a topic of his or her own) and practises 'chatting' to the class. To make the activity more realistic, the 'students' should respond in a similar way to students in their own class.

[*Note:* The 'teacher' should show genuine interest in students' answers, and should *not* pay too much attention to mistakes – the aim is to create a good atmosphere in the class!]

'ORGANISING' LANGUAGE

1. Teachers have to say many things simply to *organise* the lesson – starting or stopping an activity, getting students to do or not to do things, etc. Much of this language consists of simple commands and instructions, which are repeated lesson after lesson; so if the teacher says them in English students will quickly learn what they mean.
   Elicit from the teachers a range of simple classroom commands in English which could be used even with elementary students. If you like, build up a list on the board, e.g.:

Stand up (please).	Open/Close your books.
Sit down (please).	Stop talking.
Look! Look at me.	Come here, please.
Listen!	Come to the front.
Repeat!	Be quiet, please.
Again!	

   ▶ **Workbook Activity 3** ◀

2. Give each teacher a list with these organising expressions *translated into their own language*:
   a) Who would like to clean the blackboard?
   b) Could you close the window, please?
   c) Don't call out the answer. Wait till I ask you.
   d) Now, pay attention, everybody.
   e) Now practise the dialogue in pairs.
   f) (Kus), come and stand at the front.
   g) Read the text silently.
   h) When you have finished, raise your hand.
   i) Now listen. I'm going to read the text to you.
   j) Do exercise 6 for homework, please.
   k) Open your books at page 53.

Working alone or in pairs, ask teachers to write the equivalent English expressions in the Teacher's Workbook.

> A. Look at the list of expressions the trainer will give you. Write a simple English equivalent for each one.

3. Go through the answers together. There are of course several similar expressions in each case; accept any that convey the right meaning, e.g.:
   a) Would anyone like to clean the blackboard?
      Who will clean the blackboard?
      Would someone clean the blackboard, please?
      etc.
   Discuss what *gestures* might be useful in helping students to understand the expressions.

4. Divide the teachers into groups, and ask them to look at part B of the Activity. Give each group one or two of the situations to look at, and ask them to discuss what a teacher might need to say in English for each one.

> B. Work in groups. What could you say in English in these situations?
>   a) You are checking attendance.
>   b) You are about to begin a new lesson in the book.
>   c) The class have done some homework.
>   – You are going through the answers together.
>   – You want the students to correct each other's work.
>   – You want to know how many had the correct answer.
>   d) A student is not paying attention.
>   e) The bell rings for the end of the lesson.

Discuss the answers together.
Possible answers:
a) Who's absent today? Is anyone absent? Where's X today? Where were you yesterday, (Machiko)?
b) Today we're going to begin Lesson 5. Turn to Lesson 5 in your books. Today we're going to practise . . . In this lesson, we're going to read about . . .
c) – What's the answer to number 1? What about the next one? Has anyone got a different answer? Is that correct?
   – Everybody, change books. Give your book to the person next to you.
   – Who had the correct answer? Who got it right?
d) (Nadia), what are you doing? Stop talking at the back! (Mona), are you listening?

e) That's all for today. That's the end of the lesson. It's time to stop now. Please finish the exercise for homework. Goodbye, everyone.

EXPLANATIONS

Giving simple explanations

1. Most of the language we need for organising the class consists of simple expressions which can be used again and again – this provides an easy opportunity to use English. However, teachers do not only need to give simple commands and instructions to the class. Often they need to use more complex language, for example when explaining a new word or a grammar point, or explaining how an activity works. If the teacher can give these explanations in English it will provide very useful listening practice for the class; but of course the explanations must be as *simple* and *clear* as possible, so that the students understand.

Show how this can be done by giving two short demonstrations.

Demonstration one

i) Explain how to mend a bicycle tyre. Read out the explanation below, speaking in such a way that teachers will not easily understand (use no gestures or drawings, and speak quickly without repeating anything):

If you have a flat tyre on your bicycle, the first thing you need to do is to find out whereabouts the puncture is. So you turn the bicycle upside down and remove the inner tube with a pair of tyre levers. Then you take a bucket of water, pump up the inner tube slightly, and dip it into the water. You should see small bubbles coming out from the puncture. You can then mark the spot where the puncture is by making a small cross with a piece of chalk, after first drying the inner tube.

ii) After the demonstration, ask teachers how well they understood. They will probably only have a very general idea of what you were saying.

Demonstration two

i) Explain the process again, but this time doing everything possible to help the teachers understand. Use simple, short sentences; use gestures to show each stage of the process; use simple blackboard drawings (e.g. a bucket, a cross); give difficult words in the teachers' own language (e.g. puncture, inner tube, tyre lever):

227

You have a bicycle, but the tyre is flat (*gesture with hands, making a 'hissing' noise*) . . . you have a puncture . . . a puncture (*give translation*). So . . . you must mend it. But first you need to know: Where is the puncture? Where's the hole? So, what do you do? First turn the bicycle upside down (*gesture, or draw on the board*) . . . (*and so on*).

ii) After the demonstration, ask teachers how well they understood. If you have been successful, they should have understood everything. Discuss the techniques you used to make the explanation easier to understand.

▶ Workbook Activity 4 ◀

2. Divide the teachers into groups. Ask each group to practise giving *one* of the explanations in the Teacher's Workbook. In their group, they should 'rehearse' it until they can give it in the simplest way possible.

> Give one of these explanations as *simply* as you can in English. Imagine you are talking to people who speak very little English. Use gestures, drawings, and your own language to help!
> a) Explain how to make a cake.
> b) Explain how a mousetrap works.
> c) Explain how to bandage a wound.
> d) Explain everything you know about volcanoes.

3. Ask one teacher from each group to move to another group, and give the explanation he or she has prepared. The others should pretend to understand very little English and insist on the teacher using very simple language.

English or your own language?

▶ Workbook Activity 5 ◀

Giving explanations in English is worthwhile if it can be done successfully and without too much difficulty. However, there are many occasions when it is best to use the students' own language – either because the language needed is too complex, or because it is easier, quicker and more convenient.

Ask teachers to look at the examples in the Teacher's Workbook, and comment on each one. Encourage them to give their own opinions. (The comments after each example are of course only suggestions.)

1. You want to teach these words.
   How would you explain their meaning:
   - using English only?
   - using English and your own language?

   | skiing |
   | government |
   | liver |

Comments:

An explanation in English could be very confusing, especially if the concept is unfamiliar to students as well as the word. It would be better to give examples in English, and then to give a translation of the word.

2. You want to teach these structures.
   How would you explain the difference:
   - using English only?
   - using English and your own language?

   | How many | eggs oranges | are there? |

   | How much | bread meat | is there? |

Comments:

- It is possible to make the difference clear using simple English (e.g. 'I can count eggs – one egg, two eggs, three eggs . . .'), but it could be misunderstood (e.g. we can count loaves of bread, we can count money).
- By using the students' own language, we can give a clearer and fuller explanation, and refer to equivalent expressions in their language.
- It is best not to rely only on explanations in either language; it is more important to give plenty of examples and a chance for students to practise.

3. You are organising a role play. You want students to act out a conversation based on this situation. How would you explain the situation:
   - using English only?
   - using English and your own language?

   One student left his/her bag on a bus, containing some money, a book, and a towel. He/she goes to the lost property office.

   A second student is the person at the lost property office. He/she asks the student to describe the bag.

Comments:

- An advantage of using the students' own language is that the situation can be given more quickly and easily, leaving more time for practice.
- An advantage of using English is that it provides useful listening practice, and helps students by giving them some of the words they need (e.g. travel, leave, contain, towel).

– It is probably best to give the situation in clear, simple English, but repeating some parts in the students' own language (e.g. lost property office) to make the meaning clear.

LESSON PREPARATION

▶ **Workbook Activity 6** ◀

Either organise the preparation during the training session, with teachers working together in pairs or groups, or let teachers prepare in their own time after the session.

FURTHER READING

J. Willis (1981) *Teaching English Through English*, Longman. Shows how English can be used in a wide range of teaching situations, and contains many examples of useful language.
J. Heaton (1981) *Using English in the Classroom*, Longman. A simple guide to language used in the classroom, with exercises.

20 Role play

Aims of this unit

- To establish what role play is and why it is important.
- To show how to organise controlled role play based on a dialogue or text.
- To show how to organise free role play activities.

This unit focusses on role play techniques that can be used with large classes, and shows how role play can be based on topics and situations in the textbook. It builds on ideas for organising oral practice which were introduced in earlier units, especially: Unit 6: Practising structures, Unit 12: Pairwork and groupwork, and Unit 18: Communicative activities.

INTRODUCTION

► Workbook Activity 1 ◄

1. Ask the teachers to look at the examples of role play activities in the Teacher's Workbook. If necessary, quickly demonstrate the three activities: either act them out yourself with a colleague, or choose good teachers to do them.

   Look at these examples of role play activities.

   a)
   > One student imagines he/she is a farmer. Other students ask him/her questions about his/her daily routine.

   b)
   > A group of students imagine they are friends planning a holiday together. They try to decide where to go and what to do.

   ⫸→

c)

> One student has lost a bag. He/she is at the police station reporting it to the police. The other student is the police officer, and asks for details.

Which activity would be the easiest for your students to do? Which would be the most difficult? Why?

What other roles and situations would be suitable for role play activities in your own class?

Use the examples to establish what is meant by 'role play'. Try to bring out these key points:

i) Role play is a way of bringing situations from real life into the classroom. When we do role play, we ask students to *imagine*. They may imagine:
   – a *role:* in other words, they pretend to be a different person (e.g. a farmer);
   – a *situation:* in other words, they pretend to be doing something different (e.g. planning a holiday);
   – both a role and a situation (e.g. a police officer asking about a lost bag).

ii) In role play, students *improvise*. The situation is fixed, but they make up the exact words to say as they go along. (So reading a dialogue aloud is *not* the same as role play.)

2. Discuss the activities. Ask teachers to suggest:
   – which activity would be the easiest for their students to do and which would be the most difficult;
   – what other roles and situations would be suitable for role play activities in their own classes.

Point out that the situations we use for role play should as far as possible be within the experience of the students. In general, the more familiar a role or situation is, the easier it will be.

Suitable roles for school classes would be:
   – People familiar to students from everyday life, e.g. parents, brothers, sisters, teachers, shopkeepers, police officers.
   – Characters from the textbook, and from other books or from television.

Suitable situations:
   – Situations which students see or take part in in everyday life, e.g. shopping, holidays, using local transport, asking the way to places.
   – 'Fantasy' situations from stories they read, or from the textbook.

IMPROVISING DIALOGUES

▶ Workbook Activity 2 ◀

1. Point out that role play can often be based on a dialogue or text from the textbook. Used in this way, role play gives students a chance to use the language they have practised in a more creative way.

    Ask teachers to look at the dialogue in the Teacher's Workbook. Read through the dialogue, and ask teachers to imagine that they have already presented and practised it.

> 1. What role play activities could be based on this dialogue?

> Angela: Good morning. I want to send a letter to Singapore.
> Clerk: Yes – do you want to send it air mail or ordinary mail?
> Angela: I think I'll send it air mail. I want it to get there quickly. How much does it cost?
> Clerk: To Singapore? That will be 30 pence, please.
> Angela: (*gives the clerk 50 pence*) Here you are.
> Clerk: Here's your stamp, and here's 20 pence change.
> Angela: Thank you. Where's the post box?
> Clerk: You want the air mail box. It's over there, by the door.

(adapted from *Living English* Book 2: A. G. Abdalla et al.)

> 2. Plan a similar role play based on a dialogue or text in your textbook.

2. Demonstrate a role play activity based on the dialogue.

   i)   Write these prompts on the board to guide the role play:
      where?
      air mail / ordinary mail?
      how much?
      post box?
      thanks

     Talk as you write, to show what the prompts mean, e.g.:
     Look – you should talk about these things.
     First of all, say where you want to send the letter – to France, to Japan, to the next town?
     Then – how do you want to send it? By air mail or by ordinary mail?

Next – ask how much it costs.

Then ask about the post box. Where's the post box?

And at the end, of course you must thank the clerk – so say 'Thank you'.

ii) If necessary, go through the prompts one by one, and get teachers to give sentences or questions for each one.

iii) Call two teachers to the front: one is Angela, the other is the post office clerk. They should *improvise* a conversation, using the prompts to help them. Point out that:

– The conversation should be *similar* to the one in the textbook, but not exactly the same. They should think of new places, prices, etc., and the form of the questions and answers can be slightly different.

– The conversation can be *shorter* than the presentation dialogue. It should just cover the main points indicated by the prompts.

The conversation might sound something like this:

Angela: Good morning. I want to send a letter to England.
Clerk: Yes. Do you want to send it by air mail?
Angela: Yes, please. How much does it cost?
Clerk: 50 cents.
Angela: Give me a stamp, please. Where is the post box?
Clerk: Over there, on the left.
Angela: Thank you.

iv) Call out a few other pairs of teachers in turn, and ask them to have other conversations based on the prompts. If you like, 'guide' the conversations by giving an instruction each time, e.g.:

You want to send a large parcel.

You are sending a letter to Japan.

Your brother works in Saudi Arabia.

After your demonstration, discuss the technique with the teachers, and talk about other ways of organising the activity. Point out that, in your demonstration, only two people were talking at any one time; to involve more of the class, the activity could be done as pairwork. There are two ways of organising this:

– We could ask one or two 'good' pairs of students to improvise a conversation in front of the class, and then divide the class into pairs to have similar conversations.

– We could ask students to practise the role play privately in pairs first, and then ask one or two students to perform in front of the class.

3. Divide the teachers into groups. Ask each group to look at lessons in

their textbook and choose a suitable dialogue or text for a role play activity like the one you demonstrated.

[*Note:* If a text is chosen, it should have at least two characters so that it is possible to improvise a conversation based on it.]

Working together, they should plan a role play activity. Ask them to consider:

– what short conversations could be developed, based on the dialogue or text;
– what roles the students could take;
– what prompts could be written on the board to guide the role play.

4. When all the groups have finished, ask each group to 'try out' their role play, using the other teachers as a class. To make the activity more realistic, ask the other teachers to limit their English to the level of their students.

INTERVIEWS BASED ON A TEXT

▶ Workbook Activity 3 ◀

1. Ask the teachers to look at the texts in the Teacher's Workbook.

What role play activities could be based on these texts?

A.

If you met 15-year-old Jane Cole in the street, you might not notice anything special about her. But she is no ordinary schoolgirl, because as well as studying hard for her exams, she's training to take part in the European table tennis championship this summer. Jane will be one of the youngest contestants, but those who know her stamina and determination are confident that she will do well. Jane's main problem at the moment is finding time for both table tennis and schoolwork. For the last month, she's been get-

B.

Edward caught the express train early in the morning. He was going to the next town to visit his relations. He had got up very early, and he felt tired, so he soon fell asleep. About an hour later, he woke up suddenly in the middle of a dream. In his dream, he was in a crowded tunnel. People were pushing him from all directions, and pulling at his clothes. As he woke up, he realised that it wasn't only a dream – somebody was really pulling at his coat pocket. He opened his eyes just in time to catch sight of a man slipping out

ting up at six every day and doing an hour's table tennis practice before school; and then fitting in another hour in the afternoon.

of the compartment. His hand went to his pocket – his wallet was missing! He jumped up and ran into the corridor. But the man had vanished.

Ask the teachers to imagine that students have read these texts and are familiar with the language in them. Discuss what role play activities could be based on each text. Suggest the idea of improvising an *interview*, with one student playing the part of a character in the text.

Give demonstrations using each text, to show two slightly different ways of organising a role play interview.

Demonstration one

i) Read through the first text, and then ask one teacher to come to the front and take the role of Jane.
ii) The other teachers ask her questions about her training, free time, etc.
    [*Note:* They should ask not only questions which have answers in the text (e.g. What time do you get up?) but also questions which go beyond the text (e.g. Do you think you will win the championship? Why do you like table tennis?). The teacher acting the part of Jane does not have to answer using the exact words of the text.]
    If necessary, prompt questions by suggesting topics, e.g.:
        Ask her about her training.
        What about the evenings?
        Ask her about her friends.

Demonstration two

i) Read through the second text. This time ask teachers to think of three questions they would like to ask Edward, and to write them down (they can do this working alone or in pairs).
ii) Ask one teacher to come to the front and take the role of Edward. The other teachers ask him questions.

After your demonstrations, discuss the activity. Make these points:
– Role play interviews are a way of bringing a text to life and making it seem real to the students, as well as giving language practice.
– They are simple to organise, and can easily be done in a large class.
– The activity is more likely to be successful in a large class if all the students have a chance to *prepare* questions (as in your second demonstration).

2. Divide the teachers into groups. Ask them to choose a text from their textbook that would be suitable for a role play interview. They should decide:
   – what role the 'student at the front' would take;
   – what questions they might expect the other students to ask.

3. When groups have finished, ask one teacher from each group to describe their activity. If you like, ask each group to 'try out' their activity, using the other teachers as a class.

FREE ROLE PLAY

Organising free role play

Explain that so far in this unit you have been concerned with fairly controlled role play, based on dialogues and texts in the textbook. You will now consider freer kinds of role play, using situations which go beyond the textbook.

1. Ask teachers to look again at the third example in Activity 1.

C.
> One student has lost a bag.
> He/she is at the police station
> reporting it to the police.
> The other student is the
> police officer, and asks for details.

Point out that, if this role play is not based on a text or a dialogue in the textbook, the students themselves have to decide what language to use and how the conversation should develop. So in order to use an activity like this in class, careful *preparation* would be necessary.

Discuss with the teachers how to prepare for a role play like this in class. As far as possible, get them to give their own ideas and suggestions. Try to bring out these ideas:
i) The teacher could prepare with the *whole class*, by.
   – discussing what the speakers might say (e.g. the police officer would ask the student how he/she lost the bag);
   – writing prompts on the board to guide the role play, and any key vocabulary.
ii) The teacher could divide the class into *pairs*, and:
   – let them discuss together what they might say;
   – let them all 'try out' the role play privately, before calling on one or two pairs to act it out in front of the class.

2. Now demonstrate the role play, following the ideas you have discussed.
   i)   Tell the class the situation.
   ii) Elicit from the class some of the questions the police officer might ask (e.g. when, where and how he/she lost the bag; what it looks like; what it contains).
        Build up a list of prompts on the board, e.g.:
        When? Where? How?
        Describe it – colour
                      big/small
                      leather/plastic/cloth
        Contents
   iii) Divide the class into pairs to practise the conversation. One person in each pair should take the role of the person who has lost the bag, the other should be the police officer.
   iv) Ask one or two pairs to come to the front in turn and improvise the conversation.

3. Point out that it is also possible to ask students to prepare a role play for *homework*, to be performed later in class. Outline one way of organising this:
   i)   Students divide into pairs or small groups, choosing their own partners. The teacher gives four or five different role play situations. Each group chooses one of them.
   ii) In their own time (outside the class), each group prepares their role play. They can ask the teacher for help, but the teacher should not give them ready-made dialogues to learn.
   iii) The teacher arranges a time for each group to perform their role play. This can be spread over several weeks, with just five minutes of a lesson being used for two or three groups' role plays.

Situations for free role play

▶ Workbook Activity 4 ◀

1. Point out that, for free role play activities in their own classes, it is a good idea to choose situations which are not exactly the same as those in the textbook, but which are based on the same general *topics*. These topics will be familiar to the students, and they will be able to draw on language they have already learnt.
   Look at the list of topics in the Teacher's Workbook and discuss them.

1. Which of these topics are covered in the textbook you use?
   What other topics does the textbook cover?

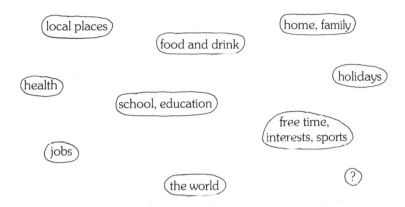

2. Point out that suitable *situations* for a role play can be drawn from these topic areas. Ask teachers to look at the examples in the second part of the Workbook activity, and if necessary give others yourself.

> 2. Choose *three* of the topics. For each one, think of suitable situations for free role play. Examples:
>
> Topic: School, education.
> Situation: You meet some foreign visitors to your country. They are interested in your school. Answer their questions about it.
>
> Topic: Health.
> Situation: A visitor to your town is ill. Find out what is the matter with him/her. Tell him/her where to find a doctor.

Then divide the teachers into groups. Ask them to think of suitable situations for free role play based on the topics, and to write them down.

3. When they have finished, ask each group to read out their situations. Encourage teachers to make notes of good ideas so that they can try them out in their own classes. If there is time, try out some of the ideas.

Conclusion

To finish the session, discuss the value of role play as a class activity. Try to bring out these points:
- Role play increases motivation. Always talking about real life can become very dull, and the chance to imagine different situations adds

interest to a lesson. (Refer to the 'interview' role plays you demonstrated. Talking about a sportsman's or sportswoman's work may be more interesting than talking about your own.)

– Role play gives a chance to use language in new contexts and for new topics. (Refer to the free role plays you demonstrated. Reporting a lost bag gives a chance to practise vocabulary of size, shape, colour, clothing, etc., and also to use the past tense in a natural context.)

– Children and even teenagers and adults often imagine themselves in different situations and roles when they play games. So by using role play in class, we are building on something that students naturally enjoy.

– Because they are 'acting out' a situation, role play encourages students to use natural expressions and intonation, as well as gestures.

LESSON PREPARATION

► **Workbook Activity 5** ◄

Either organise the preparation during the training session, with teachers working together in pairs or groups, or let teachers prepare in their own time after the session.

FURTHER READING

W. Littlewood (1981) *Communicative Language Teaching*, Cambridge University Press. Describes the principles behind role play and gives examples from published textbooks.

A. Maley and A. Duff (1982 2nd edition) *Drama Techniques in Language Learning*, Cambridge University Press. A sourcebook of ideas for role play, mime, and dramatisation.

K. Jones (1982) *Simulations in Language Teaching*, Cambridge University Press. Describes the principles behind using simulations and gives practical advice on preparation, monitoring and follow-up.

G. Porter Ladousse (1987) *Role Play*, Oxford University Press. A sourcebook of ideas for role play.

Background text: Preparing for communication

This text outlines differences between controlled practice and real communication, and suggests ways in which classroom teaching can lead from one to the other. It provides a background to all the units concerned with communicative techniques used in developing productive skills, especially:
- Unit 12: Pairwork and groupwork
- Unit 18: Communicative activities
- Unit 19: Using English in class
- Unit 20: Role play

The text can be read by teachers in their own time, and used as a basis for discussion in the training session.

The ideas presented in this text summarise the main methodological principles associated with 'communicative' language teaching. A full account of these principles can be found in the following books:

W. Littlewood (1981) *Communicative Language Teaching*, Cambridge University Press.

K. Johnson and K. Morrow (eds) (1981) *Communication in the Classroom*, Longman.

Our aim in practising oral English is to develop students' ability to communicate freely and spontaneously in English. To achieve this aim, we need to ask the following questions: What is real communication like? How is it different from the kind of controlled practice that usually takes place in language classes? How can we bring features of real communication into language practice?

Consider the two examples below. Conversation A shows a controlled exercise practising the structure 'should'; conversation B shows how the same structure might be used in real communication.

A. T: I feel tired.
   S: You should have a rest.
   T: I feel ill.
   S: You should see a doctor.
   T: I feel hungry.
   S: You should have a sandwich.

B. – I'd like to try and study in Britain for a few months. What do you think I should do?
   – Well, first of all you should go and see the British Council. They'll give you a list of

language schools in Britain where you could go and study, and they'll also tell you if there are any ways of getting a grant or a scholarship. And then you could try . . .

As well as being at a more advanced level, there are several ways in which the language in B is different from that in A:

1. In B, the friend giving advice uses not just the single structure 'should', but a whole range of structures ('will', 'if', 'could', 'ways of . . .-ing'), expressing a variety of different functions (giving advice, making predictions, discussing possibilities). In order to communicate, he or she needs to know how to combine different structures together in context.

2. In B, the language is unpredictable. The friend uses the structure 'should', but he or she could have replied in many other ways: by using a different structure (e.g. 'If I were you . . .') or by giving a different response altogether (e.g. 'I've no idea' or 'What's the matter? Don't you like it here?'). To continue the conversation, the two speakers have to pay attention and respond to what the other person is saying. In A, the language is almost completely predictable; the responses are more or less fixed, and there is no chance for a conversation to develop.

3. In B, the speakers are using language for a purpose; there are things the first speaker does not know, and that is why he or she is asking the friend's advice. Although of course the speakers need to use structures correctly, their attention is focussed on conveying a message, on *what* they are talking about, not on the language they are using. In A, the only reason for using language is to practise 'should' – the teacher is not really seeking advice or even pretending to. The practice is 'meaningful' in the sense that students must be aware of the meaning of what they are saying; but their attention is mainly focussed on 'getting the structure right', not on the message they are conveying. They do not even have the option of expressing the same message in a different way, e.g. 'Why not have a rest?'

4. The two friends in B are probably talking directly to each other in private; at most, there might be one or two other people listening to the conversation or taking part in it. It is private, face-to-face interaction; the two speakers react to each other and their personalities affect the way the conversation develops. In A, the 'conversation' is a public, formalised interaction, dominated by the teacher and with the whole class listening. There is nothing personal about the responses; they will be the same whichever student makes them.

This comparison highlights a considerable gap between traditional structural practice and the way we communicate in real life. This does not mean that traditional structural practice is therefore a waste of time; on the contrary, it is a very useful way of practising the structure 'should'. But it does suggest that this kind of practice *alone* will not prepare students very well for real communication in English. This might be achieved by giving practice which is controlled but which also includes some of the features of real communication. The analysis above suggests some ways in which this could be done:

- By giving practice involving more than just single sentences, so that students have a chance to use combinations of different functions and structures.
- By encouraging students to give a variety of responses, rather than insisting on one 'set' answer; by encouraging students to give personal responses; and by doing practice which naturally leads to unpredictable, creative language.
- By giving students a purpose for using language (e.g. through discussion, games, problem-solving, information gap activities); and by paying attention to what students are saying, not only to whether they are using language correctly.
- By organising activities in pairs and small groups, to give students the opportunity to use language in private, face-to-face interaction.

These activities will complement other more structure-based practice and should involve your students in real communication.

Discussion

Look at these examples of exercises and class activities:

Unit 1 Activity 4	Unit 18 Activities 2, 3 and 4
Unit 6 Activities 2 and 4	Unit 19 Activity 2
Unit 12 Activity 1	Unit 20 Activities 2, 3 and 4
Unit 14 Activity 3	

Do they include any of the features of real communication mentioned in the text? Which features?

21 Using worksheets

Aims of this unit
- To show teachers what worksheets (or workcards) are and how they can be used.
- To show teachers how to produce exercises on worksheets for their own classes.
- To encourage teachers to build up a stock of worksheets in their school which can be shared by other teachers.

Worksheets can be a great help to the teacher in organising oral activities in pairs and small groups, and also for simple reading and writing tasks. This unit aims to make teachers more familiar with the idea of worksheets, and to show how they can be produced without undue effort and expense.

This unit assumes that teachers are familiar with the basic principles and techniques of pairwork; these are dealt with in Unit 12: Pairwork and groupwork.

Preparation
For the demonstration under 'Worksheets for oral practice', you will need to make copies of the demonstration sheet. You should make enough copies so that there is one between every two teachers on the course.

In this unit, teachers practise making their own worksheets. For these activities you will need to provide:
- A good supply of typing or duplicating paper.
- Black felt-tip pens (one between every three teachers).

INTRODUCTION

1. Introduce the basic idea of *worksheets*. Explain that they are exercises written or typed on sheets of paper, which are given out to the class and then collected at the end of the lesson so that they can be used again. The exercises can be stuck onto or written directly on pieces of card so that they last longer and can be stored more easily; in that case they are usually called *workcards*. Worksheets and workcards can be used for oral practice in pairs or groups, or for reading and writing practice, with students working in pairs or on their own.

   Talk about the reasons why worksheets can be useful, concentrating on those that are most relevant to the teachers' own classes:
   - The textbook may not give enough practice, so teachers may feel it useful to add exercises of their own.
   - The exercises in the textbook may not be very interesting or may be unsuitable for the class, so teachers may wish to adapt them to make them suit the needs of the class better.
   - Teachers may need to create special exercises because they want to organise the class in a particular way. For example, they may want students to spend some time working alone at their own speed, and this will be easier to organise if students are given individual worksheets.
   - In some classes, there may not be enough textbooks for all the students, or the teacher may have the only copy; in this case worksheets will be the main material used by the class.
   - The teacher may use worksheets simply for variety, to make a change from the textbook and to give the students something different to look at.

   ▶ **Workbook Activity 1** ◀

2. Emphasise that teachers should regard the textbook as a useful tool to help them in their teaching, but not as something that has to be followed slavishly. If necessary, they should not be afraid to supplement the textbook, by *adding* exercises they think could be useful or by *adapting* exercises to suit the needs of their class.

   Ask teachers to look at the table in Activity 1A and discuss where there is most opportunity for adding exercises or adapting existing exercises. Either conduct this as a discussion with all the teachers together, or let teachers work alone or in pairs for a few minutes, and then discuss their conclusions afterwards.

   ⟫→

A. Think about your textbook. Does it provide enough of each activity below? Tick *Yes* or *No*.

	Yes	No
Controlled oral practice		
Free oral practice		
Reading		
Writing		
Grammar exercises		
Vocabulary development		

Now think about each activity again. Are the exercises in the textbook good enough? How interesting are they? How well do they suit the students' needs? Could they be improved in any way?

3. Divide the teachers into pairs. Ask them to look at the flow chart in part B of Activity 1, and to say either how they have supplemented the textbook or why they have never done so.

[*Note:* The purpose of this discussion is to start teachers thinking about possible ways of adding to the textbook and to prepare them for the idea of making their own worksheets.]

B.

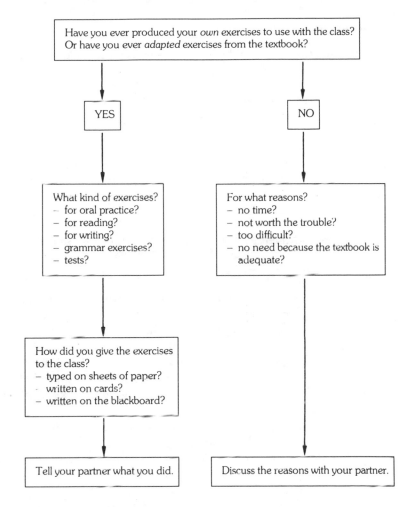

Have you *ever* produced your *own* exercises to use with the class?
Or have you *ever adapted* exercises from the textbook?

YES — NO

What kind of exercises?
- for oral practice?
- for reading?
- for writing?
- grammar exercises?
- tests?

For what reasons?
- no time?
- not worth the trouble?
- too difficult?
- no need because the textbook is adequate?

How did you give the exercises to the class?
- typed on sheets of paper?
- written on cards?
- written on the blackboard?

Tell your partner what you did.

Discuss the reasons with your partner.

4. Conduct a brief discussion with all the teachers together. First ask any teachers who have used their own exercises in class to tell you what they did. Then discuss some of the problems that teachers feel would prevent them from producing their own material. Do not go into too much detail about this now – you will discuss ways of producing worksheets later in the unit.

WORKSHEETS FOR ORAL PRACTICE

Demonstration

1. Give a demonstration of how a worksheet can be used for oral practice in pairs.

Demonstration sheet

What's your favourite...

... colour ?
... song ?
... sport ?
... book ?

... radio or T.V. programme ?
... topic of conversation ?
... way of relaxing ?

ASK YOUR PARTNER THESE QUESTIONS. WRITE HIS/HER ANSWERS ON A PIECE OF PAPER.

i) Divide the class into pairs or groups of three. Give each pair a copy of the demonstration sheet, which gives an example of a worksheet exercise. Quickly ask the first two questions round the class to get a range of answers.

ii) Teachers take it in turns to ask their partner the questions, and note down the answers on a separate sheet of paper. When most pairs have finished, stop the activity, and take back all the worksheets.

iii) As a round-up to the activity, ask different teachers what they found out from their partner.

[*Note:* This activity is designed to work at the teachers' own language level. A simpler version of the activity could be done in exactly the same way in teachers' own classes. Try to make your demonstration as realistic as possible, so that it shows clearly how to use a worksheet in class. Make sure you:

– distribute copies of the worksheet quickly and efficiently;
– do not allow anyone to write on the worksheet;
– collect all the worksheets at the end of the activity (explain that you would keep them to use again).]

2. After your demonstration, discuss the advantages of using a worksheet for this activity, rather than just writing prompts on the blackboard. Bring out these points:

– Using a worksheet encourages students to work in pairs; their attention is focussed on the *activity*, not on the teacher or the rest of the class. If the information were on the blackboard, the students would keep having to turn round to look at it.

- Using a worksheet *saves time* in the lesson – the teacher does not have to spend time writing or drawing on the blackboard. Although it takes time to produce the worksheet, it can then be used again in different classes and by different teachers.
- Giving out a worksheet makes a *change of activity*. It gives the students something new to look at, which they have not seen before.

Point out that to be used successfully for oral practice, a worksheet must:
- Provide enough practice. The activity should continue for at least a few minutes, or it is not worthwhile.
- Practise language which is already fairly well known. So worksheets are most useful as an extension to the practice in the textbook, or for review.
- Have very simple instructions, if necessary in the students' own language. Students must be able to do the activity without having to ask the teacher for help.

Examples of oral exercises

▶ **Workbook Activity 2** ◀

Ask teachers to look at the example exercises in the Teacher's Workbook. They are at different levels and would of course be used quite separately with different classes; for use in class they would be written out larger and on separate sheets of paper or on cards.

Work in pairs. Try out each exercise. *After each one,* discuss the questions below.

A.

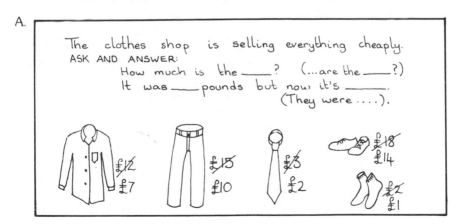

B.

Ask and answer. What's he/she doing? What are they doing?
He's ——ing. She's ——ing. They're ——ing.

C.

Find groups of three. Say how they are similar.
<u>Example</u>: Lions, tigers and giraffes are all African
animals.

lion	Malaysia	tiger	maize	hotel
milk	screwdriver	lemonade	cinema	Pakistan
wheat	snake	frog	hammer	tea
giraffe	Japan	hospital	rice	lizard
saw				

1. What structures or vocabulary does this exercise practise?
2. What level of students is it suitable for?
3. How much time would it take?
4. What preparation would you need to do beforehand?

1. Divide the teachers into pairs. Ask them to try out each exercise to see how it works and then discuss the questions.

2. When teachers have finished, discuss the exercises together. Ask teachers how suitable the exercises would be for their own classes, and what changes they would need to make.
   Possible answers to the discussion questions:
   A. Practises questions with 'How much?', prices, vocabulary for clothes. Elementary level. *Preparation:* Identify the articles of clothing, and ask one or two questions round the class.
   B. Practises present continuous tense (sentences and questions) with 'action' verbs. Elementary level. *Preparation:* Whole exercise could be done round the class, with pairwork as the final stage.
   C. Practises 'category' words, e.g. building, tool, reptile, crop, and the

structure 'They are all ...', and leads to freer discussion. Intermediate–advanced level (but could be used at a lower level with simpler items). *Preparation:* Could be attempted in pairs first, then discussed with the whole class.

Making worksheets for oral practice

1. Divide the teachers into pairs or small groups, and give each group several sheets of paper and a black felt-tip pen. Ask them to look at lessons in the textbook that they have taught recently or which they will teach soon, or at lessons in a suitable textbook, and to find places where it would be useful to *add* or *adapt* an exercise. The exercises should either:
   – give further oral practice of a language point; or
   – review language which has been taught earlier.
   Working together, each group should make two or three worksheets, each comprising one oral exercise. Go from group to group, giving help and advice. When teachers finish a worksheet, look at it and discuss it with them, and suggest possible improvements.
   Points to watch for:
   – The worksheets should be clear, simple and attractive to look at.
   – Instructions should either be in very simple English, or in the students' own language.
   – Each worksheet should provide at least a few minutes' activity.

2. When they have finished, collect the worksheets together. If there is time, let groups 'try out' each others' worksheet exercises, and discuss how successful they were.
   If possible, have photocopies made of the best worksheets for teachers to take away with them.

WORKSHEETS FOR READING AND WRITING

Examples of reading and writing exercises

► Workbook Activity 3 ◄

1. Give time for teachers to read through the exercises in the Teacher's Workbook. Make it clear that they are at different levels and would be written on separate worksheets for use in class. Discuss what level each exercise would be used at and what skills it develops.

Work through each exercise orally. After each one, discuss the questions below.

1. What level is the exercise?
2. What skills does it develop?
3. How clear are the instructions? Should they be in the students' own language?

A.

Match the two halves, (a) and (b).	
(a)	(b)
A pilot	designs machines
A nurse	takes care of books
An engineer	flies aeroplanes
A farmer	looks after sick people
A librarian	grows crops

B.

Copy the words in the correct order.

headlight   radiator
bumper   bonnet
tyre
windscreen
steering wheel

1._ _ _ _ _ _ _ _ 5._ _ _ _ _ _ _
2._ _ _ _ _ _ _ _ 6._ _ _ _ _ _ _
3._ _ _ _ _ _ _ _ 7._ _ _ _ _ _ _
4._ _ _ _ _ _ _

C.

Write these words in alphabetical order:

green   great   gave

grapefruit   good

greatest   give

given   glove

D.

Copy the text, and add the missing words.

Your friend has fallen over and cut his/her knee. This is
what you should do: First, ... your hands with soap and
water. Then, ... at the cut and remove any .... that
you can see there. Then .... the cut with a little water –
but be careful, because it might .... ! After that, take
a clean cloth and .... the cut carefully. Finally, tie a
.... over the cut, to stop it getting dirty again.

    dirt   wash   dry
    look   clean bandage
    hurt

---

2. Now talk about how the worksheets could be used in class:
   - The simplest way to use them is to make enough copies of each worksheet for every student (or for every pair of students). All the students do the activity *at the same time*, working individually or in pairs. After the activity, the teacher goes through the answers or students exchange books and check each other's work.
   - Another way is to build up a set of *different* worksheets, with several copies of each (they can also be written on cards so that they last longer). Different students can then use different worksheets in the same lesson. This means that fewer copies have to be made, and it allows students to work at their own level and their own speed – good students can be given more difficult tasks, or can finish several tasks in one lesson. The teacher can correct a student's work when he or she finishes a task.
   - However the worksheets are used, students should always write on a separate sheet of paper, not on the worksheet itself; one of the main advantages of worksheets is that they can be collected at the end of the lesson and used again.
   - Because students are working alone without much supervision by the teacher, it is important that worksheet exercises should be *simple* and fairly *controlled*, so that students do not make many mistakes. The instructions should be clear and easy to understand, and if necessary should be in the student's own language.

Making worksheets for reading and writing

1. Divide the teachers into pairs or small groups, and give each group several sheets of paper and a felt-tip pen. Ask them to look again at lessons in the textbook which they have taught recently or will teach soon, or at lessons in a suitable textbook. This time they should think of exercises which would practise reading and writing.

Point out to teachers that they do not have to invent their own original texts; they can create interesting exercises by using the texts and examples in the textbook. Suggest some ideas, e.g.:

- Reproducing part of a text from the book, but with gaps for students to fill.
- Giving part of a text but with some factual mistakes; students have to write the correct version.
- Giving a text with the sentences in the wrong order.

For other ideas, ask teachers to look at the exercises in Unit 9 Activity 3, Unit 11 Activity 4, and Unit 13 Activity 1.

Working together, each group should make one or two worksheets. Go from group to group giving help and advice.

2. When teachers have finished, collect the worksheets together. If there is time, let groups try out each other's worksheets and comment on them. If possible, make photocopies of the best worksheets for teachers to take away with them.

Building up a set of worksheets

It is most useful if teachers can build up a set of worksheets, so that they can be used regularly as an alternative or addition to the textbook. Discuss how this can be done; get as many suggestions from teachers as you can, and help them' see how they might overcome difficulties. Give these ideas yourself:

Materials

- The simplest way to make a worksheet is to write it on a piece of paper (a full sheet or half sheet of typing paper), using a black pen so that it can be photocopied – or of course to type it. This is a good method if you want to make many copies of one worksheet to give out to the whole class (e.g. for oral practice).
- If you want to build up a set of different activities, with a few copies of each (e.g. for reading and writing practice), it is better to make *workcards* by writing or sticking exercises on pieces of card – these will last longer.
- Another method is to fold a piece of card to make a 'booklet', and write the exercise on the inside:

- Paper worksheets can be protected by polythene bags (these can often be bought very cheaply). The exercise is written on one half of a sheet of typing paper, the paper folded in half and put in a polythene bag, and the opening of the bag stapled together:

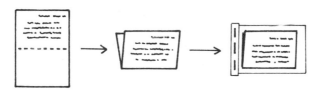

Storage

- If the worksheets are single sheets of paper, they can be stored in labelled envelopes or in folders; if they are on card, they can be stored in boxes.
- Each worksheet can be given a reference number so that it can be found easily: a reference to a unit in the textbook (e.g. I/12/1 = Book I Unit 12, Worksheet 1); letters A, B, C to indicate level; or a letter to indicate type of activity (e.g. O = oral practice).

Sharing the work

Producing large numbers of worksheets is very time-consuming, and would be too much work for one teacher. There are many ways of sharing the work so that it becomes quite easy and also allows the worksheets to be used in more classes:

- Teachers in one school can share the work of producing worksheets, and build up a set which they can all use.
- Neighbouring schools can meet to exchange copies of worksheets (this could be organised by inspectors or supervisors).
- Training sessions can be devoted to producing and trying out worksheets, with paper and copying facilities provided.

LESSON PREPARATION

▶ Workbook Activity 4 ◀

By the end of the training session, teachers should have a selection of exercises to use for worksheets in their own classes. Make sure that they can find paper for worksheets and that they can make enough copies for their class. Teachers can do their final preparation for the lesson in their own time after the session.

FURTHER READING

A. Harrison (1983) *A Language Testing Handbook*, Macmillan. Some of the ideas in this book can be applied to the design of challenging worksheets.

Very little has been published in this area. Practical ideas often appear in the journals, however, especially *Practical English Teaching* (Mary Glasgow) and *Modern English Teacher* (Modern English Publications).

22   Classroom tests

Aims of this unit
- To show teachers the value of giving regular tests in class, and to show the importance of testing particular skills.
- To familiarise teachers with different types of test, and enable them to judge their effectiveness.
- To show teachers how to design a range of simple classroom tests.

Teachers often regard testing as a matter for 'experts' outside the class, and not something that they can be involved in themselves. This unit sets out to show the importance to teachers of being aware of different testing techniques, and shows how tests can be used informally in the class to give useful information to both the teacher and the students.

Testing techniques are often similar to teaching techniques, but with a different purpose. Some of the ideas presented in this unit for testing also appear in other units as teaching ideas, especially in Unit 5: Using a reading text, Unit 13: Writing activities, Unit 15: Reading activities and Unit 17: Listening activities.

INTRODUCTION

The value of testing

As they progress through the various stages of learning English, students are usually given formal tests and examinations from time to time (at the end of a year, before starting a new course, etc.). But in addition to these formal kinds of test, the teacher can also give regular informal tests to measure the students' progress.

Begin by discussing why it is important to give regular tests to the class. Establish these points:
- They tell the *teacher* what the students can and cannot do, and therefore how successful the teaching has been; and they show what areas need to be taught in the future.
- They tell the *students* how well they are progressing, and where they need to focus their attention as learners. Regular tests also encourage students to take their learning seriously, and give them a series of definite goals to aim towards.

What should we test?

Students are often given a general 'grade' which shows their ability in English. (This may be expressed in various ways, e.g. 'C +' or '$\frac{6}{10}$' or 'tenth in the class' or 'above average'.) This does not really tell either the teacher or the students very much unless they know exactly what the grade is based on. It is not very useful to talk in general about 'ability in English': one student may be very good at listening but bad at writing; another student may speak fluently but make many grammar mistakes, and so on. So, in order to comment on a student's progress, we need to test particular skills and abilities.

▶ Workbook Activity 1 ◀

1. Ask teachers to look at the list of categories under 'language' and 'skills' in the Teacher's Workbook:

    We can test **language** (to find out what students have *learnt*):
    – grammar
    – vocabulary
    – spelling
    – pronunciation

    We can test **skills** (to find out what students can *do*):
    – listening
    – reading
    – speaking
    – writing

    Which of these are the most *important* for your students? Which are the *easiest* to test?

    Discuss which areas are the most important for the teachers' own classes. Obviously, there is no 'correct' answer: it depends on the type of class, what the students expect to do in the future, the examination system, etc. Get teachers to give their own ideas, and try to bring out these points:
    i)   Tests often focus on grammar and vocabulary; but if we expect students to develop the ability to understand and use English, it is important to test *skills* as well as knowledge of the language.
    ii) Most people would regard all the skills as useful in some way:
         – listening, for understanding spoken English on radio and television;
         – reading, for study purposes (books, journals, etc.), and for understanding written instructions in English;
         – speaking, for social contact with foreigners;

– writing, probably only for study purposes.

iii) In deciding what is important, we should not only consider students' future needs; for example, most school students may never need to write English after they leave school, but it is still important because it helps in *learning* the language.

iv) The receptive skills – listening and reading – are especially important because they will enable students to continue learning the language on their own.

2. Ask teachers to look at the five questions, and to match them with the categories in the list.

> Imagine you are testing students to find out these things:
> 1. Can they follow street directions?
> 2. Can they form the past simple tense correctly?
> 3. Can they write a few sentences about their family?
> 4. Do they know common words for rooms and furniture?
> 5. Can they understand a simple description of their town?
> Which main area would each test focus on?
> Think of five questions like these about your own students.

Answers:
1. Listening (and vocabulary)   2. Grammar   3. Writing (and grammar, vocabulary)   4. Vocabulary   5. Reading or listening (and vocabulary)

3. Ask teachers to think of specific skills and abilities which they could test in their own students. Ask them to think of a few questions like those in the Teacher's Workbook activity.

TESTING RECEPTIVE SKILLS

Make these general points about testing the 'receptive' skills of reading and listening:
– If the aim is to test reading or listening skills, students should not be asked to *write* too much; otherwise the test will be unfair to students whose comprehension is good but who are bad at writing.
– The questions should test comprehension of the main 'message' of the text, so they should focus on main points rather than on individual details.
– The students should not be able to guess the correct answer without understanding the text.

– The questions should be reasonably easy for the teacher to set and mark; this is particularly important in a large class.

Reading comprehension tests

▶ **Workbook Activity 2** ◀

1. Ask teachers to read the text in the Teacher's Workbook and then answer the questions.
(Make it clear that these are only examples of *question types*, so several questions focus on the same points in the text. In a real test, each point would of course be covered by only one question.)

Read this text, and answer the questions.

The dagona tree, which is common in the dry regions of Africa, has an unusual appearance. The fully-grown dagona is about twenty feet tall and has a thin trunk, about nine inches across. The trunk is bare for most of its height and the spiky branches, which have many small leaves, stand out from the top of the trunk, giving the tree the appearance of a large brush stuck in the ground.

The dagona tree has many uses. In October it produces large, round fruit with yellow flesh inside which can be eaten raw or made into a refreshing drink. The flesh can also be dried and made into flour. The outer skin of the fruit can be used for making glue; first it is dried, then the skin is pounded and mixed with water to make the glue. The bark of the tree is made up of fibres of great strength which are used to make ropes. And the spiky branches can be hollowed out and used as musical pipes.

(fictional description based on a text from *Reading for a purpose* Book 1: N. J. H. Grant and S. O. Unoh)

A. *True or false?*
   Look at the following statements. Write T for true, F for false, and DK (don't know) if you can't tell from the text.

   a) The dagona tree grows in Africa.
   b) The dagona is common in rain forests.
   c) The dagona produces fruit twice a year.
   d) The flesh of the fruit can be used as a medicine.

B. *Multiple choice*
Choose the correct answer.

The dagona tree is: a) common in parts of Africa
b) found in sandy regions
c) common throughout the world
d) unusual in dry regions of the world

The tree looks like a brush because the branches:
a) are long and thin
b) are stuck in the ground
c) have many small leaves
d) grow out from the top of the trunk

C. *Open-ended questions*
Give short answers to these questions.

What does the fruit look like?
The fruit has four uses. What are they?
Why is the bark good for making ropes?

D. *Information transfer*
Complete this table.

Part of tree	Use
a) flesh of fruit	food, drink, flour
b) skin of fruit	
c)	
d)	

What are the good and bad points of each type of question?

2. Discuss the four question types. Ask teachers to comment on the good and bad points of each.
   A. *True or False?:* It is easy for the teacher to think of good questions which cover the main points of the text. The questions only test comprehension (no writing involved), and are easy to mark. The

main problem with true/false questions in tests is that students can guess the answer; if the choice is between 'true' and 'false' only, they have a 50% chance of being right each time! The chances of guessing are reduced by giving three choices: 'true', 'false', and 'don't know'.

B. *Multiple choice:* These are widely used in formal tests because they are easy to mark, test only comprehension, and (if they are well designed) there is only a small chance of guessing the right answer. But it is difficult to write good multiple choice questions – often they are either too easy or confusingly difficult, or focus on minor details of the text. If you like, give a few examples of bad multiple choice questions, and discuss what is wrong with them, e.g.;

> Ropes are made from: a) the bark of the tree.
> b) the trunk of the tree.
> c) fibres of great strength.
> d) skin mixed with water.

Both (a) and (c) are correct, and (d) is too obviously wrong.

C. *Open-ended questions:* They are easy for the teacher to write, but may be difficult to mark. (For example, 'Why is the bark good for making ropes?' could be answered: 'It is strong', 'It contains strong fibres', 'It has long fibres', etc. Other answers might seem 'half-right', e.g. 'Fibres'.)

D. *Information transfer:* Instead of answering a question, the student has to record information from the text in a different form, e.g. by completing a table, labelling a picture, drawing a diagram. This is often a good way of testing comprehension of the main points of a text, although it may not show whether the student has understood the text completely.

Emphasise that none of these question types is 'better' or 'worse' than the others for testing; each kind has good and bad points, and is useful in its own way. For an informal test, it is usually best to use a *mixture* of different types of question, each focussing on different parts of the text.

3. As a possible extension to this activity, choose a text from the textbook (or another text at the same level), and ask teachers to make up a series of questions to test reading comprehension, using any of the types you have discussed.

Listening comprehension tests

Point out that the same kinds of questions can be used to test listening comprehension as for reading comprehension. Ask teachers to look again at the text and questions in Workbook Activity 2, and imagine that the

text is read out by the teacher as a *listening test*. Discuss what differences there should be in the questions. Try to bring out these points:
– Obviously, they should be simpler, and there should not be too many. In reading, the students can keep referring back to the text, but in listening they have to retain what they hear in their minds. The text itself should also be fairly short.
– In listening, we can test students' ability to recognise words and phrases which would present no problem in reading. So we could include questions which can be answered directly from the text, e.g.:
    The leaves are made into flour. True / False / We don't know?
    Which part of the tree is used for ropes?
– If the main aim is to test the listening skill, we should avoid giving students too much to write; so open-ended questions should have very short (one or two word) answers.

TESTING GRAMMAR AND WRITING

1. Make these points about testing grammar and writing:
    – It is very easy to test grammar – there are definite answers, marking is easy, etc. Because of this it is very common for 'writing' tests to focus on grammar.
    – If tests only focus on grammar, they will not show us how well students can write in English to express meaning. If we want to encourage students to develop writing skills, then it is important to give tests in which students have to express meaning in written sentences, not merely write correct grammatical forms.

    ▶ **Workbook Activity 3** ◀

2. Divide the teachers into pairs. Ask them to look at the examples of written tests in the Teacher's Workbook and quickly work through them so that they can see what they involve.

    Look at these tests.
    Which ones mainly test *grammar?*
    Which ones mainly test *writing skills?*
    Number them from 1 to 5 according to how much they focus on grammar or writing (1 = grammar, 5 = writing).

A.
| Give the past tense forms of these verbs: |
| meet   go   come   see   hear   take |

B.

> What did you do before
> you came here today?
>
> Write *three* sentences.

C.

> Write these notes as full sentences. Put the
> verbs into the correct form.
>
> I/spend/last week/try/find/job.
> I/buy/newspaper/look/advertisements.
> I/see/interesting/job/shoe factory.
> I/go/interview/but/not/get/job.

D.

> Fill in the gaps with suitable verbs.
>
> Yesterday John .... lunch in a restaurant. Then he
> .... his friend Peter and they .... to a football
> match together. When they arrived, they .... thirsty,
> so they .... some lemonade.

E.

> Fill the gaps with a suitable word or phrase.
>
> 1. I feel so tired! I .... at five o'clock this
>   morning.
> 2. There used to be a cinema in the town, but it
>   .... last month.
> 3. When I was a boy, we .... a large house by
>   the sea.

Discuss which tests mainly focus on grammar and which focus on
writing.

A possible order:
1. A – It tests forms of the verb out of context.
2. D – The student has to choose the verbs that fit the context and
   then write them in the correct tense.
3. C – The student has to change the form of verbs and also add
   words.
4. E – The student has to supply complete phrases that fit the
   context.
5. B – This is a completely free sentence writing test.

Marking free writing tests

1. The most natural kind of writing test is one which simply requires the student to write freely in English, like Test B in Workbook Activity 3. However, tests of this kind have two disadvantages:
   - Because students are free to write what they like, they are likely to make many mistakes of different kinds. So the test will tell us very little about what they can and cannot do, or how much progress they have made.
   - Because there is no single correct answer, free writing tests are difficult to mark precisely and marking takes a long time.

   ▶ **Workbook Activity 4** ◀

2. Ask teachers to look at the examples of students' writing in the Teacher's Workbook, and to try to give each a mark.

   Here are two students' answers to Test B in the last activity. Work in pairs. Give each answer a mark out of ten.

thes mooreeng, I have beakfes and I get up a 7.30 Am
I have go to studeng only 5 menuts and after I have gore
to the shool.

This morning I got up AT six o'clock. and I had
to readed per one hour in my room.
AT HALf PasT six I had to weut in The park.
after I have come at the school on foot
It was raining.
Now I'm going to lunch

Discuss different ways of marking them, and bring out these points:
   - We could count all the mistakes the student has made, and subtract, say, half a mark for each mistake. This is called *'negative marking'*.

— We could give, say, three marks for each sentence. If a student has written the sentence more or less correctly, they are given three marks; if they have made some mistakes but the sentence can be easily understood, they are given two marks; if the sentence is very hard to understand, they are given one mark. This is called *'positive marking'*.

Discuss the two approaches. Point out that positive marking gives more emphasis to the content and meaning the student is trying to express; by giving a positive mark, we reward students for what they *can* do rather than 'punish' them for what they cannot do; obviously, this will have a better effect on their attitude to learning.

ORAL TESTS

1. If we want to encourage students to speak, we should give oral tests from time to time; otherwise, students will always regard speaking as less 'serious' than the other skills. Obviously, it is very difficult to test speaking, especially with large classes. Whereas with listening, reading and writing students can all be tested at the same time, with speaking each student (or pair of students) must be tested in turn.

There are two main ways of testing students' speaking ability: by continuous assessment throughout the year, and by giving short oral tests to each student.

Continuous assessment

The teacher can either give a mark for general willingness and ability to speak in all the lessons, or else note down marks for certain oral activities done in class (e.g. role play). This system will of course only be successful if the teacher *tells* the students that they are being given marks for speaking.

Short oral tests

Explain how this can be organised even with quite a large class:
— The teacher gives the whole class a set of general topics to prepare a few weeks before the test (e.g. talk about your family, talk about a sport you enjoy).
— Over two or three lessons (while the class is doing a reading or writing activity, or a test), the teacher calls each student out in turn and quietly tests them on one of the topics. Each test lasts 30–60 seconds. The students do not, of course, know which topic they will be asked to speak about.

– Teachers can give a mark immediately. To help them do this, they can use a 'marking grid'. Show an example of this on the board:

	1	2	3	4	5
CONTENT					
FLUENCY					

Give some examples of marks:
– Students who speak easily with good pronunciation, and who have plenty to say, could be given 10 (the maximum mark: 5 + 5).
– Students who can make themselves understood but have some pronunciation problems, and who produce two or three sentences, might be given 7 (3 + 4).

▶ **Workbook Activity 5** ◀

2. Ask teachers to look at the topics for oral tests in the Teacher's Workbook, and discuss which would be suitable for their own classes.

> Imagine you are giving short oral tests to your students (one minute each).
> Which of these topics would be suitable?
>
> a) Talk about yourself and your family.
> b) Ask the teacher some questions.
> c) Describe your village/town.
> d) Talk about a friend.
> e) Talk about your school.
> f) Talk about transport in your region.
>
> Think of five other topics that you could use, and write them down.

3. Divide the teachers into pairs. Ask them to think of five other topics which they could use for oral tests, and to write them in the space provided in the Teacher's Workbook. When they have finished, ask teachers to tell you what topics they thought of.

4. As a possible extension to this activity, you could demonstrate giving oral tests, using the topics the teachers have suggested, while they are starting their lesson preparation. Call teachers out in turn while the others are working; they should behave as 'students', using the kind of language that their own students would use.

LESSON PREPARATION

▶ **Workbook Activity 6** ◀

Either organise the preparation during the training session, with teachers working together in pairs or groups, or let teachers prepare in their own time after the session.

FURTHER READING

J. Heaton (1987, 2nd edition) *Writing English Language Tests*, Longman. Deals with the principles of testing, and examines ways of testing the four skills.

A. Mathews et al. (1985) *At the Chalkface* (Section C: Achievement Testing), Edward Arnold. A practical guide to different kinds of achievement test.

P. Hubbard et al. (1983) *A Training Course for TEFL* (Chapter 9: Testing), Oxford University Press. A detailed discussion of tests and question types.

A. Harrison (1983) *A Language Testing Handbook*, Macmillan. Looks at various techniques for assessing students' performance.

23 Planning a week's teaching

Aims of this unit
- To encourage teachers to think of long-term aims in their teaching, and to plan their lessons as part of a continuing course.
- To show the importance of using a variety of different activities and techniques to motivate students and help them learn.
- To review techniques that were introduced in earlier units.

This unit refers to many of the activities and teaching techniques introduced in earlier units, and shows how they can be integrated into a general lesson plan. In doing this, it acts as a review of the course as a whole. It also further develops ideas about lesson planning which were introduced in Unit 8: Planning a lesson.

Preparation
Before using this unit, ask teachers to look through the lessons in the textbook which they will teach in the coming week (or any series of five or six lessons that they might soon be teaching), and familiarise themselves with them.

INTRODUCTION

The easiest way to teach is to plan one day at a time, to follow the teacher's notes closely, and to use just a few techniques again and again in every lesson. This approach to teaching has two drawbacks:
- It will produce lessons which are well-prepared and run smoothly, but which lack variety. As a result, both the teacher and the students are likely to lose interest.
- Different students learn in different ways: some students learn best by listening, some by repetition, some by actively speaking, some by learning grammar, and so on. If the teacher always uses the same techniques, some students may not have the chance to learn in the way that suits them.

In order to keep students interested in learning English it is important to include a variety of activities and techniques in the lesson, and to vary lessons so that there is something different every day. To do this successfully, teachers need to plan not just the next day's lesson, but think of their teaching over a longer period.

Ask teachers to look at a series of five or six lessons in a textbook which teachers might soon be teaching. Discuss:
– What is the general aim of the whole series of lessons?
– What are the main language areas which are taught in the lessons?
– How much variety is there in the lessons? (e.g. Is language always presented in the same way? Do reading texts always have the same kind of questions? Does each lesson contain the same kind of activities?)

LEARNING ACTIVITIES

It is not enough to introduce a range of different activities into lessons just for the sake of variety. The teacher needs to have a clear idea of:
– what *stage* of the lesson different activities are suitable for;
– what *skills* different activities develop;
– what the *learning value* of different activities is (What and how much do students learn from it? Is it worth doing often or only occasionally?);
– what *level* different activities are suitable for.

1. Make sure that teachers are aware of the main stages of a lesson. (These are dealt with in detail in Unit 8: Planning a lesson.) Build up a list on the board, and discuss briefly what happens at each stage:
    i) *Presentation:* The teacher presents new vocabulary and structures.
    ii) *Practice:* Students begin to use the language in a controlled way.
    iii) *Production:* Students use language more freely, combining new language with what they already know.
    iv) *Review:* Teacher reviews language learnt in previous lessons.
    v) *Reading:* Students read a text, and answer questions or do a 'task' (e.g. completing a table).
    vi) *Listening:* Students listen to the teacher or a cassette, and answer questions or do a task.

2. Now talk about the four skills: speaking, listening, reading and writing. Make these points:
    – At each stage of the lesson, activities usually focus on one skill more than the others. For example: in controlled practice the focus is either on speaking or on writing; during a reading activity, the main focus is on reading.
    – But there are opportunities to develop *all* the skills at any stage of the lesson. For example: in a reading activity, students can discuss the topic before reading the text, they can listen to the teacher's

questions, they can write answers or do a gap-filling exercise after reading the text. When reviewing language from an earlier lesson, the teacher can ask questions, get students to ask questions and make sentences, ask students to write on the board, and so on.
– To develop all the skills successfully, we need to include a variety of activities at each stage of the lesson.
Talk about each skill in turn. Ask teachers to suggest some of the activities that might help to develop each skill, e.g. for listening: listening to the teacher reading a text; listening to the teacher's questions; listening to the teacher giving examples of a new word; in pairwork, listening to what another student says; following the teacher's instructions, etc.

► **Workbook Activity 1** ◄

3. Divide the teachers into groups, and ask them to look at the list of learning activities in the Teacher's Workbook.

> Work in groups. Look at each of these activities in turn. Try to think about them from the *student's* point of view. Discuss:
> 1. For what *stage* of the lesson is the activity suitable?
> 2. How *valuable* is the activity? What do students learn from it?
> 3. Is the activity suited to one *level* (e.g. first year students) more than others?
> 4. How often do students do this activity in your class?

Learning activity (activities done in class)	Stage	Learning value A/B/C/D/E	Level	Your class?
Listening to a text				
Answering questions on a text				
Reading aloud				
Silent reading				
Repetition drills				
Substitution drills				
Question/answer practice (whole class)				

⟩⟩⟩→

Learning activity (activities done in class)	Stage	Learning value A/B/C/D/E	Level	Your class?
Oral practice in pairs				
Guessing games				
Copying words/ sentences				
Dictation				
Paragraph writing				
Role play				
Free discussion of a topic				
Correcting each other's written work				

Look at the list again. Which activities could you include in a series of lessons you might teach soon?

Read through the instructions and explain the scale from A to E under 'Learning value':
A = Very valuable – students learn a lot from this activity, and it is always a useful way to spend time in the lesson.
B = Valuable – a worthwhile activity.
C = Quite valuable – not the most useful kind of activity, but students learn something from it.
D = Not very valuable – students do not derive much benefit from this activity.
E = Not at all valuable – the students learn almost nothing from this activity and it wastes time in the lesson.
Emphasise that teachers should *discuss* each activity in their group, and try to agree on the answers. If you like, choose a 'secretary' in each group to note down the answers agreed by the whole group.

4. When one group has finished, stop the activity (it does not matter if not all groups discuss all the activities). Go through the list item by item, encouraging as much discussion as possible. Make it clear that there are no 'correct' answers; the purpose of the activity is to get teachers to

think about the range of different learning activities and the value of each one from the *student's point of view*.

TEACHING TECHNIQUES

In the last section, teachers saw that a variety of *learning activities* can be included at each stage of the lesson; and that some activities are of great value to the students and enable them to learn a lot, while others are much less worthwhile.

When planning lessons, it is not enough just to plan what activities to include. We must also plan how to organise these activities – in other words, what *teaching techniques* to use. The same activity can be done in quite different ways and with quite different results, according to what techniques the teacher uses.

► Workbook Activity 2 ◄

1. Ask teachers to look at the two 'lesson plans' in the Teacher's Workbook, which show how the same activity can be organised in different ways.

Here are two different ways of using a reading text.

Teacher A	Teacher B
1. Introduces the text with a short discussion of the topic.	1. Reads out a vocabulary list from the book. Students repeat in chorus.
2. Gives a guiding question. Reads the text. Students listen while reading, then answer the question.	2. Reads the text aloud sentence by sentence. Students repeat.
3. Presents new words, using examples in English.	3. Students read the text aloud round the class.
4. Asks a series of questions on the text. Students give short answers.	4. Asks questions from the book, and gives the answers. Students repeat in chorus.
5. Asks a few personal questions based on the text.	5. Asks the same questions again. Students answer round the class.

What are the main differences in the teachers' techniques?
What do you think the students would *learn* from each of these lessons?

Try to bring out these points:
– Both teachers present new vocabulary, read a text, and ask

questions based on it, but in quite different ways. Teacher A presents vocabulary in context, makes sure students understand the text, and gets students to talk about themselves. Teacher B simply gets students to learn the lesson by heart.

– Teacher A's students would have practice in guessing the meanings of words, reading in order to understand, listening to words used in context, listening and responding to questions, and talking about themselves in English. Teacher B's students would learn a few set sentences by heart, and know the set answers to a few questions – they would not develop any language learning *skills* from the lesson (except the rather useless skill of reading aloud).

[*Note:* Techniques for using reading texts are dealt with in detail in Unit 5: Using a reading text and Unit 15: Reading activities.]

2. If you like, consider other activities at different stages of the lesson, and discuss possible teaching techniques that could be used for them. Some suitable activities for discussion would be:
   – presenting new words;   – free discussion of a topic;
   – teaching grammar points;   – controlled writing.
   – practising a dialogue;

Teaching aids

► Workbook Activity 3 ◄

1. Divide the teachers into groups, and ask them to discuss each of the teaching aids listed in the Teacher's Workbook, using the questions given.

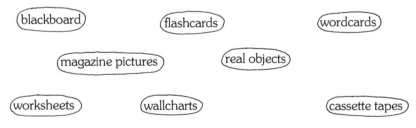

Which of these teaching aids have you used in your own class?
How useful are they? What activities can they be used for?
Which ones could you use in a series of lessons you might teach soon?

2. Discuss the items together. Then ask teachers to look at lessons they might teach in the textbook, and to suggest ways of using the teaching aids they have discussed.

[*Note:* These teaching aids are dealt with in detail in the following units: Unit 4: Using the blackboard, Unit 7: Using visual aids, Unit 9: Teaching basic reading, Unit 17: Listening activities, and Unit 21: Using worksheets.]

TYPES OF INTERACTION

► Workbook Activity 4 ◄

1. Point out that many different types of interaction are possible in the class: there are various ways in which the teacher can talk to students, students to the teacher, and students to each other.

    Look at the pictures in the Teacher's Workbook, which show different types of interaction, and ask teachers to identify them. If you like, build up a list on the board to show how we can use symbols to represent each type. (These symbols are often used in teacher's books, and may be useful for including in lesson plans.)

    T → C (teacher to class)
    T → S (teacher to individual students)
    S → T (student to teacher, e.g. student asks a question)
    S → S (student to student – 'public' pairwork)
    S→S, S→S, . . . (student to student – simultaneous pairwork)
    Then ask teachers to look at the activities listed, and to suggest types of interaction that would be suitable for each one.

What kind of interaction is shown in each picture?

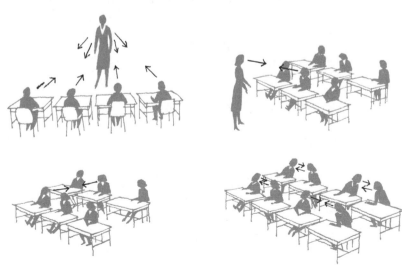

What kind of interaction would be suitable for each activity below?
drills
question/answer practice
answering questions on a text
role play
guessing games
correcting written exercises

Possible answers:
Drills: A mixture of teacher to class (chorus drilling), and teacher to individual students.
Question/answer practice: Teacher to student, then student to student (public pairs), then simultaneous pairwork.
Answering questions on a text: Teacher asking students in turn, or students working together in pairs and teacher going through answers afterwards.
Role play: Two students in front of the class, or students working in pairs.
Guessing games: Students asking the teacher questions, or asking one student at the front, or students working in pairs.
Correcting written exercises: Teacher with the whole class, or students working in pairs (correcting each other's work).

2. Ask teachers to look at the lessons they might teach in the textbook. Ask them to suggest ways of using some of the types of interaction that you have discussed. Point out that, just as teachers should try to use a variety of activities and techniques in their classes, so they should also try to use different kinds of interaction to suit different purposes.

[*Note:* Different types of interaction are dealt with in detail in Unit 2: Asking questions, Unit 12: Pairwork and groupwork, and Unit 18: Communicative activities.]

LESSON PREPARATION

► **Workbook Activity 5** ◄

Either organise the preparation during the training session, with teachers working together in pairs or groups, or let teachers prepare in their own time after the session.

FURTHER READING

P. Hubbard et al. (1983) *A Training Course for TEFL* (Chapter 5: Planning and preparation), Oxford University Press. A detailed analysis of the language content of a lesson; designed to help teachers evaluate and supplement the textbook.

J. Harmer (1983) *The Practice of English Language Teaching* (Chapter 11: Planning), Longman. A general description of the principles behind lesson planning.

24 Self-evaluation

Aims of this unit
- To make teachers more aware of the factors that affect learning, and of the learning that takes place in their own classes.
- To make teachers more aware of their own teaching, and to develop a concept of 'good teaching'.

One of the most important attributes of good teaching is self-awareness – the ability to reflect on one's own teaching and so gradually improve and develop one's skill as a teacher. This unit is concerned with developing this self-awareness; it encourages teachers to think critically about what happens in their own classes, and to be prepared to observe and comment on each other's teaching.

This unit is not concerned with particular teaching techniques, but brings together many of the ideas introduced in earlier units. In particular, it aims to reinforce the skills of self-awareness developed through the 'Self-evaluation sheets' accompanying each unit.

GOOD AND BAD TEACHING

Introduction

1. Begin by establishing what is meant by 'self-evaluation': that it is the ability of teachers to judge their own teaching honestly and to see clearly how much learning is taking place in the class.

2. Make these points:
   i) Self-evaluation is not something that can be *taught*. It can be gradually *developed* by teachers themselves as they become more aware of their own teaching and of all the different factors that affect learning.
   ii) In order to evaluate themselves, teachers must learn to *observe themselves*. Obviously, teachers cannot normally observe themselves directly, but there are ways in which they can observe themselves indirectly:
      - By careful planning before the lesson, followed by careful reflection after the lesson on what actually took place.

– By observing other teachers' lessons and comparing them with what happens in their own classes.

– By inviting other teachers to observe their classes, and discussing the lesson with them afterwards.

(This unit is mainly concerned with the first of these approaches, since it can be followed by any teacher without making special arrangements with colleagues.)

Good teaching

▶ **Workbook Activity 1** ◀

In evaluating themselves, teachers are striving towards better teaching; in order to do this, they must have some idea of what good teaching is. This does not, of course, mean that there is a single definition of 'good teaching' that can be applied to all teachers, but that teachers should develop their own personal concept of good teaching.

1. Ask teachers to turn to the person next to them. They should try to agree on *five* important characteristics of good teaching, and write them in the Teacher's Workbook in the form of simple descriptive sentences. Give a few examples so that teachers understand what to do, e.g.:

   Teacher arrives on time.
   Teacher controls the class.
   Teacher develops speaking skills.

   When teachers have written their five characteristics, they should choose the one they think is the *most* important.

   1. Work with a partner. Try to agree on *five* important characteristics of good teaching. Write them down.
   2. Now choose the one you think is *most* important.
   3. Evaluate yourself. How far are these five characteristics true of your own teaching?

2. Ask each pair in turn to read out the characteristic they have chosen. Write them in a list on the board, but without repeating identical or very similar points; you will probably finish with a list of between five and ten key characteristics which represent the teachers' view of good teaching. Discuss which are the most important characteristics of all – if you like, you could ask teachers to 'vote' on this by raising their hands.

3. Point out that it is features like these that inspectors or supervisors

look for when they observe a lesson and evaluate a teacher; but teachers can also use them to evaluate themselves and so improve their teaching. Ask teachers to evaluate themselves now. Ask them to look at the characteristics they have written in the Teacher's Workbook, and consider how far they are true of their own teaching.
[*Note:* This should be a private activity. If you like, let teachers talk about it in pairs, but do not try to make teachers 'confess' in public.]

Bad teaching

1. Repeat the activity, with teachers working in pairs. This time, ask teachers to agree on five characteristics of *bad* teaching, and to write them in the Teacher's Workbook. If necessary, you could again give a few examples to show what to do, e.g.:
   Teacher never smiles.
   Teacher doesn't check understanding.
   Students have to learn everything by heart.
   When they have finished, ask teachers to choose the characteristic they think is *most harmful*.

   1. With your partner, try to agree on *five* important characteristics of bad teaching. Write them down.
   2. Choose the one you think is *most* harmful.
   3. Evaluate yourself again. How far are these five characteristics true of your own teaching?

2. Ask each pair in turn to read out the characteristic they have chosen and build up a list on the board. Discuss which are the most harmful characteristics of all.

3. Point out that these are some of the features which teachers should try to *avoid* in their own teaching. Allow a minute or so for teachers to consider privately whether any of these features apply to themselves. Point out that their answers should not be simply 'Yes' or 'No', but that it is a question of *degree*. They should ask themselves, e.g. 'Do I smile enough?' 'Do I check understanding often enough?' 'Do I make students learn too much by heart?'

Observation categories

1. We should not think of teaching as something the teacher does in isolation (like 'swimming' or 'walking') – it is a three-way relationship between the *teacher*, the *materials* he or she is using, and the *students*. So when we talk about 'good teaching' we may be thinking of quite

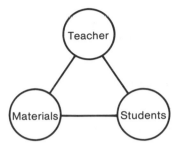

different things. For example, we might judge how well teachers 'teach the lesson' – how they present new words, how they write on the blackboard, whether they follow the lesson plan, etc. Or we might consider how well teachers manage the class – whether they involve all the students, how they ask questions, how much they correct students, etc. Or we might consider the teachers themselves – how well they speak English, whether they seem interested in the lesson, what their personality is like. Teachers can often be 'good' in some respects but not so good in others – for example, one teacher may give clear explanations but be unable to control the class; another teacher may keep the students amused but fail to teach them anything.

Because of this, when we observe a lesson it is useful to divide teaching into different *categories*, so that we can focus on different aspects of teaching. It is also useful to think of different categories when observing one's own teaching.

▶ Workbook Activity 2 ◀

2. Write these headings on the board:

    A. Teaching procedure
    B. Use of teaching aids
    C. Management of the class
    D. Teacher's personality
    E. Command of English

Ask teachers to imagine that they are observing a lesson taught by a colleague and trying to evaluate it. What might they look for within each category? Take each category in turn, and ask teachers to suggest possible questions they might ask, e.g.:
Teaching procedure:
Are the aims of the lesson clear?
Are the stages of the lesson clear?
How does the teacher present new language?
What kind of questions does the teacher ask?
(Obviously, there are many possible answers and the categories

overlap. The aim of this activity is to give a general idea of what each category involves. Do not go into too much detail at this point.)

3. Ask teachers to look at the questions in the Teacher's Workbook and think about the answers. Suggested categories are given below.

Look at the questions below.
– Which category does each question belong to? Write a letter beside the question.
– How important is each question? Write a number from 0 (= not important) to 5 (= very important).

	Category	How important?
1. Is the aim of the lesson clear?		
2. Does the teacher write clearly on the board?		
3. Do students participate actively in the lesson?		
4. Does the teacher do a variety of activities?		
5. Are the stages of the lesson clear?		
6. Does the teacher have clear pronunciation?		
7. Does the teacher smile often?		
8. Does the teacher use visuals appropriately?		
9. Does the teacher speak naturally?		
10. Does the teacher encourage students to ask questions?		
11. Does the teacher encourage real use of language?		
12. Does the teacher seem interested in the lesson?		

HELPING STUDENTS TO LEARN

Introduction

It is important not to forget the purpose of teaching, which is to enable students to *learn*; although the teacher's behaviour is important, we can only judge its success by how well the students succeed in learning. There are two important ways in which the teacher can improve the students' chances of learning successfully:
- By creating a productive working atmosphere in the classroom and a good relationship with the class.
- By being sensitive to the needs of individual students – recognising that students are different and have different needs and problems.

Classroom climate

▶ Workbook Activity 3 ◀

1. First establish what is meant by 'classroom climate': it is the general atmosphere that exists in the class, and the relationship between the teacher and the students. Point out that the classroom climate is strongly affected by the teachers' *attitude*, and also by their *behaviour* – how they correct mistakes, how they ask questions, how they maintain discipline, how much they use English, etc.

2. Divide the teachers into pairs or small groups. Ask them to look at the examples of teachers' behaviour in the Teacher's Workbook, and decide which would have a good effect on the classroom climate and which would have a bad effect. If you like, ask teachers to give a 'score' for each one, on a scale from −2 to +2, (−2 = very harmful, −1 = harmful, 0 = no effect, +1 = beneficial, +2 = very beneficial).

   Look at these statements. Each one describes a teacher's behaviour in class. Which of them would have a *good* effect on the classroom climate? Which would have a *bad* effect?
   a) The teacher corrects *every* error.
   b) The teacher hardly ever corrects errors.
   c) The teacher lets students know who is first, second, last, etc. in the class.
   d) The teacher praises students who answer correctly.
   e) The teacher criticises students who repeatedly make mistakes.
   f) The teacher punishes students who behave badly.
   g) The teacher usually chooses good students to answer.
   h) The teacher often chooses weaker students to answer.
   i) The teacher uses only English in the lesson.

    j) The teacher mostly uses English in the lesson.
    k) The teacher translates everything into the students' own language.

3. When most pairs have finished, go through the statements together. Ask teachers what scores they gave and briefly discuss each statement. Encourage teachers to consider which of the statements apply to their *own* teaching behaviour in class.
Obviously answers will vary according to the type of class, age of students, accepted customs in the school, etc.
Possible answers:
a)   Probably harmful – it is likely to discourage fluency. But it depends on how the teacher corrects the errors; it will be less harmful if the teacher corrects 'gently'.
b)   Probably also harmful, as the students may feel that they are not being helped enough.
c)   This depends on the recognised system in the school – students may expect it. But in general it is likely to discourage all the lower half of the class, and make language learning seem unnecessarily competitive.
d)   Will certainly have a good effect by encouraging students; but if the teacher praises too much it will have no effect at all.
e)   Will usually have a bad effect, by discouraging weaker students; it could be beneficial to criticise more confident students occasionally.
f)   Depends on the circumstances and type of class.
g)   Bad effect if good students are allowed to dominate the class and make weaker students feel neglected; the teacher should try to balance questions, asking easier ones to weaker students.
h)   Good effect, as long as weaker students are not made to feel victimised.
i), j) English has to be used in a mixed nationality class. But if all students share the same first language, it is unnecessary to use only English, and could be frustrating if students do not understand. A good solution would be to use mainly English, but the first language occasionally for difficult explanations and instructions.
k)   Very harmful, as it gives the class no feeling that English is a language that can be used to communicate, and gives them no chance to hear or use English naturally.

The students

1. Emphasise the importance for teachers of trying to see their students as *individuals*, not merely as a 'class'; only in this way can teachers begin

to adapt their teaching to suit particular students' needs. This is quite difficult to do, especially with large classes, and requires some effort on the part of the teacher. Discuss ways in which the teacher can find out more about individual students (e.g. getting them to talk and write about themselves as part of the lesson, thinking about what they can and cannot do and trying to explain why, discussing 'problem' students with other teachers, trying to spend time with students outside the class).

Point out that if the teacher does not know the students well, it is easy to misinterpret their behaviour. Give some examples:
- A student may seem to be 'slow' but in fact may simply be unable to read the blackboard or may have hearing difficulties.
- A student who does not appear to pay attention and works badly may in fact be finding the lesson too easy and would benefit from being given more difficult tasks.

Many problems of this kind can be solved by creating a relaxed atmosphere in the class and a closer relationship with the students.

▶ **Workbook Activity 4** ◀

2. Divide the teachers into pairs. Ask them to talk to their partner about individual students in their class, using the questions in the Teacher's Workbook as a guide.

> Think about *one* of the classes you have taught.
> Are there any students who:
> - find the lessons very easy?
> - have difficulty understanding the lessons?
> - are very quiet or unwilling to participate?
> - are difficult to control?
> - have difficulty seeing or hearing?
> - have problems with reading or writing their own language?
>
> Work with a partner. Tell your partner about them and discuss what you could do to help them and keep them involved in the class.

3. As a possible round-up to the activity, ask teachers to tell you what conclusions they came to, and any new ideas they had as a result of their discussion.

LESSON PREPARATION

▶ Workbook Activity 5 ◀

Either organise the preparation during the training session, with teachers working together in pairs or groups, or let teachers prepare in their own time after the session.

Observation

If possible, arrange for teachers to *observe each other's lessons*. This could be organised in the following way:

   i)   Before the lesson, the teacher shows the observer the lesson plan and explains briefly what he or she intends to do.

  ii) After the lesson, the teacher answers the questions in the 'Self-evaluation sheet' in the Teacher's Workbook. The observer answers the same questions, but with reference to the lesson he or she observed.

 iii) As soon as possible after the teachers have taught and observed their lessons, organise a follow-up session. The teacher and observer of each lesson sit together in pairs and compare their notes on the lesson. Afterwards, go through the questions on the 'Self-evaluation sheet' and discuss the lessons together.